RICHARD E. G[...] in Mbabane, Swaziland. His films include *Withnail and I*, *How to Get Ahead in Advertising*, *Henry and June*, *LA Story*, *Dracula*, *The Player*, *Jack and Sarah*, *Portrait of a Lady*, *Keep the Aspidistra Flying* and *Spice World: The Movie*. He lives in London with his family.

ALSO BY RICHARD E. GRANT

*With Nails*

# BY DESIGN

## A HOLLYWOOD NOVEL

## RICHARD E. GRANT

PICADOR

First published 1998 by Picador

This edition published 1999 by Picador
an imprint of Macmillan Publishers Ltd
25 Eccleston Place, London SW1W 9NF
Basingstoke and Oxford
Associated companies throughout the world
www.macmillan.co.uk

ISBN 0 330 36829 X

1 3 5 7 9 8 6 4 2

A CIP catalogue record for this book is available from
the British Library.

Typeset by SetSystems Ltd, Saffron Walden, Essex
Printed and bound in Great Britain by
Mackays of Chatham plc, Chatham, Kent

FOR JOAN AND OLIVIA

# CONTENTS

x

*Anyone who is anyone came from nowhere. Take my word for it. I know. And I was christened Vyvian. Believe me, this also helped. Built my resistance for what was out there when I scratched my way free of an adolescent frenzy of acne, fired by ambitions so astronautically grandiose as to be laughable.*

*Now if you think this is going to be about people you don't know, trust me. Cos they're in here; you're in here. Trust me. Other people do. So if you think you recognize someone, chances are you're dead right. OK?*

*OK. I worked out a long time ago that all you really need to get going is the one invitation. The right one, of course. But only one. This may take the passing of many moons, but you'll know in your very marrow the moment you've got that gold-trimmed, ivory-coloured card inviting you in.*

*I'd better tell you what I look like, as people have a tendency to comment. Tall. Around the two-metre mark. Pipe-cleaner thin. Teased as a teen, envied as an adult. Mid- ... Dark-haired and discreet. I know this is starting to sound like some sleazy singles a but that's not entirely inappropriate to our set-up. You are the or person who will know precisely what is going on in my head – privilege for which people have paid a good deal more than you he I like knowing that you have to 'hold' me. In your hands. I intimate. Which is how I like to operate, at my Concorde Ma best. People-wrangling – that's my trade.*

*The only other human who has got this close is Marga. But deaf and dumb. Or that's the way we decided to play it. In fac not deaf and definitely not dumb. But nobody knows that you. In case you're wondering whether I'm speaking to you*

1

# PART ONE

★

# OUT OF AFRICA

The invitation. That is *everything*. This is the journey I took to secure mine.

Nowhere. That's where I was dumped at birth. Drive-in cinema, single main street, bigots, two banks and boredom tattooed onto every psyche. Could've been the Midwest, the Outback, the Down Under, except it wasn't. It was an amalgam in a corner of Africa called Zweeghella. Not the Blixen idyll that every tourist still tries in vain to reach, but desolate and left behind like *The Last Picture Show* without Cybill Shepherd. A way of life achieved not by consensus, but rather by an appalling inertia induced by unremitting heat. No room given to any 'fancy notions'. Imagination locked tight behind closed doors, its sole escape route a lethargic adultery. Slow, because there was no pressure from anywhere ever to get up and go-go. Thoughts as plainly thunked down as the collective lager glasses demanding a fill-up at any of the numerous bars. But Heaven forfend you should dare to suggest leaving. 'Who do you think you *are*?' was the von Karajan-conducted chorale that greeted any such notions.

Marga and I compared notes on this phenomenon while sitting in the lower halves of the two fridges placed opposite each other in my mother's pantry. This was the coolest place in the house, and our regular rendezvous to investigate our dense friendship, based not so much on mutual attraction as a shared revulsion for everyone else and the country in which we sweltered. She was wearing a polka-dot bikini and a scarf around most of her face to conceal her acne; I was flicking my greasy fringe from side to side, curtaining the outbreak on my forehead.

'It's all right for you, you've got freckles.'

'Oh, yeah? You can wear make-up.'

'What are you two doing in there?' cross-droned my mother, which instantly turned our tetchy duet into a solo of resistance.

'Trying to cool down.'

Countered by, 'There's no need to adopt that tone with me, young man. You still haven't answered my question.'

'Getting cool.'

'Don't be daft. There's a pool in the garden and trees under which to cool off by the acre. Out. Now!'

'But we like it in here. It's dark.'

'Who's *we*?'

'Just Marga.'

'Open up immediately. What in God's name do you two think you are doing in there? Marga, answer me!'

Marga tried, only Marga generally spoke in a whisper and, under threat, clamped down to the decibel level of an insect's burp.

'This is a pantry, in a kitchen, not Rick's Café in—'

'*Casablanca*, yes, I know.'

'I'll thank you not to complete my sentences – what in the hell are you two doing in there?' The hysterical incline of her voice coincided with our emergence.

'Cooling off.'

Oh, if only you knew, Mater, what plans had been formulated and devised while freezing our bahookies off – why, you'd be ordering brass plaques to affix to those two refrigerators declaring, *This is where it all began.*

'What do the pair of you think you look like? Hmmmm?'

Our escape from the dark larder, looking like a couple of spazoid refugees in ill-fitting swimwear, was denied any foreshadowing of greatness. Compounded by her admonition: 'Get some sun. Might do both your complexions some good.' I could swear that Marga yelped. What was unmistakable, however, was the ferocity of ill-concealed hatred blistering up her eyes as she concurred: 'It's all so obvious. We have to get out.'

'Exactly. And you'll both feel a lot better for it. Why don't you wash your hair while you're about it?'

Scuffling away, I ventured a 'Hasn't a clue, has she?'

'*I heard that.*'

What precisely *was* it that fuelled us so ruthlessly to further our pitiless dissection of the jalopy brains we perceived to be forever ambling in our midst?

Indifference. Theirs, not ours. The invisible battle line. Their war cry, 'What the hell do you think is out there that isn't to be found right here?' Even to *ask* deserved nothing less than to be struck down by a fully articulated three-ton truck loaded up with pineapples.

Not that I am bitter or twisted, you understand. What I witnessed most was neglect. Of wives by husbands, children by parents, men by women, and roads by government. Care. What happened to it? 'Attention' meant something military. Care and attention. This *is* my Quixotic quest. My mantra. My money source.

Marga was, and is, my best friend. I need to tell you how and why. Known each other since tots and so close that we have often been mistaken for brother and sister. But our alliance really began when I went with her to her high school graduation ball when nobody else would.

Why not?

Acne.

She was attractive, tall, athletic, academic, A-ish all the way, except for the AK, as we called it. And I'm not talking just the average adolescent outbreak. This was lunar. A facial landscape as volcanically plugged by plukes and pustulations as you would not wish upon a fleet of cheeses. She grew her hair, pulled it forward and down to try and curtain herself off from view, and, this being the early seventies, her *Klute* look for the most part succeeded in that it deflected the outright stare of which she was radar-aware.

Marga's mother was called Wylma. Hers was a life so throttled of attention (on account of her husband's inveterate philandering) that she made it her business to pry and steer her ample self into the domestic sinew of every family she could lay her claws into. Always in an avalanche of 'good intentions', concealing a lethal undertow of accountable *you owe me*s. Wylma's way was to bake herself in. Quite literally. No sooner had someone breezed into town and set up house than she would wheel herself round, cake tin before her, dispensing bonhomie with the discretion of a bulldozer fleet. All capitulated. All remained in her debt. For how could anyone repay a lifetime's supply of fruit cakes and rum-soaked trifles? Her generosity was dolloped out with a fanatical precision sufficient to hearten a professional zealot. Just in case you were in any doubt, or marginally forgetful, she kept the personal details of her victims in a little black book, alongside the recipe of the particular confection she had concocted for each one. It was an invaluable lesson. Write *everything* down. From Wylma I also learned that 'taking an interest' is a social asset of inestimable value and, more often than not, folk are hugely delighted to talk at *length* about themselves, and then waft away with the impression that you are a 'very interesting person', when in fact all you have done is cup your ear to their ceaseless bleatings.

Like I said, care and attention.

Although on the scale of *actual* care and attention for her daughter, I'd venture twenty below zero. And I'd long been telling Marga that her mother's obsession with baking had buggered her skin.

Despite all this, Wylma's determination to be the mother of all mothers meant that she sat up nights at her sewing machine, furiously working out the *Vogue* pattern for Marga's ball gown, as she insisted on calling it, while dwelling non-stop on Marga's skin problems. But that was nothing new. She felt justified in talking about it ceaselessly. In public. In private. She would *sotto voce* to total strangers about it while Marga stood silently by, apologizing and then detailing just what a social impediment it was. 'What man will ever look at her?' As if her daughter had grown a four-foot hump out of her left shoulder. Always finished off with a brimful of tears and cowlike eyes, entreating all and sundry for sympathy. For *her*. Wylma. Mother of the wretched girl, in imminent denial of a son-in-law and grandchildren.

Made up, dressed and ready to go, Marga looked not unlike the hundred other girls off to their last big bash before becoming bona fide adults. Except that Wylma's effective public relations act on behalf of acne sufferers worldwide and her daughter in particular was such that people identified outbreaks on her that had yet to happen. To say that she was under some pressure to secure a date, well, I hope you appreciate the gravity of her request for me to do the honours.

And I was glad to oblige. I like a challenge. For the one weapon I am blessed with in my armoury for life is charm. A magazine of the stuff. I never left Marga's side and attended to her every need with all the devotion and single-mindedness of a murderer. Killing all doubts that looked our way. Dancing and canoodling, so that when she said, flat-voiced, 'Kiss me,' I never missed a beat, waiting for a slow song, which was slotted between every four fast ones. Cupped her face, centred us in the middle of the dance floor, beneath the art department's home-made mirror ball, and worked my tongue round hers with all the conviction I could muster. Now, you well know that in the very face of repulsion lies the vulnerable heart so needy that you are momentarily blinded, and mercifully lust kicks in and takes over.

Suddenly, hers was the only face I wanted to be welded to. Wet with. We kissed and kissed like the world was about to end. After which was the tacit understanding that that was that. Requiring no further developments. No promises. No nothings. A reconnoitre of the roomful of eyeballs riveted our way told all. Victory. Unequivocal. We left like Cinderellas at the stroke of, which we knew would have the precise effect of causing an avalanche of interest the following day. Which it did. The social sympathy-case was now the centre of attention for the first time outside of her mother's jurisdiction, as she shrugged off multiple *how many times did you* *do it?*s and *oh my God I can't believe it*s. And Marga would never forget it. Or forgive her mother.

'You are poisoning me!' hurtled from her throat at Wylma, who was waiting up in order to interrogate us about the night's activities.

'I beg your pardon?' stentoriously issued from her mater's bosomage.

Marga stood rigid. Shaking. Pointing.

'You! You you you you *you*!' Swivelled and stomped out. The blow struck at the heart of this baking Über-ma was of a force sufficient to rupture her emotional Richter scale. Staring at her fist, it took a full five minutes before she realized that her hand had squashed its own prized bake, triggering a rhinolike bray. 'MARGA!' A sound so brutal in its betrayal that in that instant Marga's mind was made up. And when it was, it was. She was waiting for Wylma as she wheeled into the bedroom. Face frontal. Punched her full out. Flattened. Turned, stepped over the gasping, shocked flesh below and walked. Never said a word to anyone. Except to me.

And that was that. Marga became a mute.

From then on, when we talked, we talked in secret. We pored over magazines, *Architectural Digest* for me, *Vogue* and *Harper's* for her. And we hatched a plan. Marga wanted to go where they knew how to do skin scrapes and grafts. I had always harboured notions of being obscenely rich and famous, and Hollywood, being the epicentre of such ideals, was our mutual destiny. However, as I couldn't act sufficiently unselfconsciously even to get into a school play, the prospect of being an actor was a no-no. But two talents I had honed were firstly the ability to get people telling me their innermost schemes and dreams, and secondly an unerring eye for advising people on what to wear. Trivial, you may well scoff, but oh how these talents have stood me in good stead, missiling my life into the sphere of the mega-talented and hysterically rich.

Then, one day:

'Vyvian, I think I've found us a way out of here.'

Marga pulled a crumpled bit of paper out of her pocket. I recognized it instantly as the cover of the *Architectural Digest* special issue featuring Hollywood homes. She smoothed out its creases and placed it on the ground. Then ceremoniously unfolded an advert for dermabrasion beside it. Looked at me and said, 'We can have this.'

'How?'

Marga had recently qualified as a masseuse, the perfect occupation for a mute, and one of her clients, it turned out, was the new American ambassador and his wife: Mr Randy Andy and Miss Goody Two-Shoes. 'Can't keep his hands off me. I shan't go into detail, but I'll just say that his "diplomatic pouch" has been "erupting" every time I give him a workout. So far I've pretended not to notice. Last week, he started feeling me up. I withdrew, then he grabbed my hand and forced me to grip his weenie and wank him off.

'This is where you come in. I want you to pay him a visit, mid-massage. Your cue will be a coughing noise from me. I'll give you my Instamatic and I want you to get pictures of him lying there with his hand over my hand, holding his thing.'

'But what happens if he just jumps up or covers his face?'

'Believe me, his eyes are scrunched so tightly shut when he is jerking away that nothing will distract him until you have knocked off a couple of snaps. When he realizes what's happening, I'll clamp my hand so tightly round his knob, he won't be able to move.'

'Then what?'

'You carry on snapping, and I'll do some talking. About us two witnesses against his one. About attempted sex with a minor. About sexual harassment and the reputation he preserves as diplomat, husband and father. About how all this can be settled by greasing up green cards for us to get into the USA.'

'Margs, we can never pull this off. He is all-powerful. You're talking like this is a film. Real life isn't like that. We'll both get into deep shite.'

'Don't be so pathetic. It's the oldest trick in the book. How do you think Mata Hari got started?'

'Margs, we're in Zweeghella in the middle of Africa. It just won't work.'

'So what ideas do you have to offer instead?'

I didn't.

I got the Instamatic.

Rehearsed my entrance.

She coughed.

I snapped.

He gasped.

She clamped.

We threatened.

He laughed.

She squeezed.

He yelled.

She held.

On.

Till his predicament predicated a proposition.

'Now will you please let it go?' he wheezed.

'Not until Vyvian has your signature on this piece of paper.'

She squeezed harder.

He signed.

As far as I know, Marga never spoke to her mother again, nor to her father for that matter, whose philanderous guilt came home to roost upon his conscience like so many buzzards. Forced to stew upon their inadequacies as parents, they mutually decided to throw money at her. Mainly into a special account. Guilt with a fixed interest rate. This nest egg proved invaluable.

We flew Luxavia to Luxembourg. Cheapest flight and full of first-timers from the Third World landing in the First. Leaving the intense heat of an African summer and breathing in the arctic gale of a European winter froze our blood over. With fear, trepidation and a lot of *what the fuck are we doing here?*s.

Followed the backpackers and boarded a bus for Belgium. Snow, which neither of us had ever seen before, swathed the landscape in a dull fluorescent light that was frankly eerie. Marga was silent. Stared. Scared.

We shuffled about the station in Brussels until we found the train bound for Ostend. Spent the journey trying to revive our frozen feet. Walked past restaurants full of warm people, all of whom seemed to be eating snails. Or pigs. Bought burgers from a van parked on the street corner instead, then loped back to our cheap hotel and into beds that sagged in the middle.

We had never seen so many white people before.

The alarm clock didn't go off and we had about three and a half minutes to dress and run, with suitcases, to catch the ferry to England. We seasicked our way across the Channel, then boarded a train and examined the tribe of unfriendly faces and patchwork parcelled-up countryside through the window. Victoria Station was a panic attack of people. All going very determinedly in all directions.

We felt and probably looked like a couple of refugee ramblers just in from a gruelling Himalayan walking expedition gone wrong. Overwhelmed, we lugged our bags and selves into a Pizzaland that featured bright orange everything and badly painted snowscapes. Our sophisticated palates had never actually tasted pizza before, though we had longed to, ever since seeing them in American movies. (Zweeghella got its first pizza parlour a decade later.)

We took the tube to Heathrow, checked in our luggage, dawdled through Duty Free for two hours, then boarded the flight for Los Angeles. It was a curious relief to be strapped in again. No decisions to be made. Yet.

I woke up an hour before we landed, feeling very Tom Thumbish, wondering what the hell I was doing, having flown halfway around the planet, about to disembark into my future. Doing what?

I hadn't a clue. Looked at the crumpled Hollywood homes page in my hand then out of the window at the endless expanse of houses stretching in all directions below.

Marga was dumb with the impending reality . . .

'Where are we supposed to go now?' we asked ourselves, standing like two stray Munchkins outside the terminal.

At the car hire, we joined the jet-lagged queue and signed up for a week's rental. Got into the wrong side and nosed out into the afternoon traffic armed with a map and a single idea: get to the ocean. Once there, we would be forced to stop.

By some miracle we got there and parked the car near Santa Monica Pier. Got out and stared at the sea, wondering how long it would take us to sail back to Africa.

'I'm thirsty' got us motoring towards a drugstore, where Marga picked up a copy of *LA Weekly*. We sat on a park bench, stranded between the roller skaters, and scoured the Personals.

'You're doing the talking. I'm going mute – for good. Except with you,' announced Marga, handing me a section of massage adverts she had torn out.

'Here's some change, there's a phone box.'

'What'll I say?'

'You'll know when someone answers.'

'But we don't even have a place to stay, let alone a contact phone number.'

'We'll sleep in the car.'

I heard myself describing Marga as a 'deaf and dumb but profoundly gifted masseuse, who learnt her skills from a Balinese master' to a succession of total strangers and answering machines. A few of them asked questions that sounded like they were in code. Which I later realized they were. So far, all of them were male. All of them after what Marga and I subsequently nicknamed 'the

Ambassador'. The first female voice was a surprise relief. Buoyantly friendly and transmitting from only a few blocks away.

'Come by right now, if you like. There's plenty of parking round the back. We're on the corner of Arizona Avenue and Sixth Street. We'd like to meet you both. Are you Australian?'

'No, British.'

'Great! My name's Vivian.'

'So's mine.'

'Look forward to meeting you.' God, she was chirpy. And God were we grateful. She sounded so enthusiastic and sincere. We felt instantly saved.

Marga said, 'See, it's easy.' Then insisted on going back to the drugstore to buy a pack of surgical masks so that she wouldn't have to reveal her entire face to a prospective employer.

Vivian was five foot and sported a poodle perm of furiously dyed blonde hair that reached down to her waist. Perky in every way. Tank top, bare midriff and Lycra shorts, white ankle socks and pristine trainers. Tanned. 'I luuuuve that you wear a mask. So impressive. So hygienic. Everyone masseusing should. You're Vivian, right?'

'Right, it's spelt with a *y*.'

Vivian was nodding throughout this sentence, giving me her undivided nuclear attention.

'Interesting. Very interesting. I never met a man called Vivian with a *y* before. How long have you been in California?'

'About one and a half hours.'

This stalled her.

'Are you kidding me?'

'No. We just got off the plane.'

'You're kidding me, right? How could you possibly be so suntanned? It's the middle of winter.'

My turn to stall.

'We've just come back from Africa. Marga was commissioned to massage the King of Zweeghella for a couple of weeks following a polo injury.'

17

'You don't say?'

I think it was the royal word that harpooned her interest. In no time she was saying what an honour it would be to have Marga on her books and in fact she might even have a possible appointment, pending a phone call.

We both slumped into the sofa and stared at each other, as Vivian chirruped away to someone called April.

'Marga is a gift, April. She's deaf and dumb, won't hear any of Syd's abuse, and she's just returned from massaging the African royal family in Africa.'

We both shifted focus back to the pint-sized proprietress, who was giving us the broadest smile and thumbs-up gesture.

'Just hold a moment and I'll ask – Vyvian, April wants to know if you can get over there in the next hour?'

'Nice!'

Vivian was nodding her approval back vigorously, which made her springy hair boing up and down. I heard her say, 'Sure thing . . . Not at all. Glad I could be of service. OK, bye.'

For a second I thought Marga was going to speak, but her intake of breath was counter-bombarded by a flurry of chat from Vivian.

'I take it you've heard of Syd Shirelle, song and dance legend of the silver screen? Well, he's really old now. And really crabby. He's been through every masseuse in this town and worn them out with his demands and abusive talk, but I reckon that what with Marga being deaf and all she wouldn't know either way. It might just be the perfect combination. His wife April is at her wits' end dealing with the old guy. She's fifty-seven years his junior and wife number four, so she is willing to try anyone and anything to keep him happy. Am I putting you off?'

She cocked her head to one side as if to soften this information, confirming the overall friendly puppy effect.

'No need to bother with your own table, towels and oils. April has a full supply of all the necessaries.'

She then perched on a stool and wrote down detailed instructions of how to get there and what code to punch in at the gates.

'Vyvian, I'm not gonna charge you any commission for this booking seeing as it's your first time and it might be Marga's one and only time with Syd. But if it works out between the two of them, we'll do it officially. OK?'

Again, my nodding head spoke for me.

'Give me a call in the morning, OK? Where are you gonna be staying?'

'The Beverly Hills Hotel,' skidded off my tongue.

We walked out to the car, got in and drove off waving at our new best friend and saviour in an advanced state of jet lag and shock. Once around the corner, I pulled over and dared a look at Marga. 'Jesus! – One night we're in Ostend. The next we are in Hollywood!'

'I thought she said it was in Bel Air?'

'Marga! It doesn't matter *where*. We are *here*!'

'Why have you pulled over? Let's get there, else I'm going to fall asleep.'

We followed Vivian's directions along Santa Monica Boulevard, north on the 405 freeway, in more traffic than we'd seen in our lives, and turned off onto Sunset Boulevard. Wound along and turned left up Delfern Drive.

'What's the big deal?' asked Marga with undiluted irritation.

'What's the big deal? What's the big deal? Marga, we have just landed in the middle of somewhere, from the middle of nowhere and we're about to meet Syd Shirelle in his fucking house! That's the big deal!'

She made no attempt to disguise her disdain.

'So? Vivian says this Syd is a pain in the ass?'

'Who cares? It's Syd Shirelle. D'you know how many films I've seen him in?'

'So long as he pays, I don't care how many he's done. He's just a man.'

I suddenly realized that we were dressed like a couple of travelling tinkers. 'We can't go in looking like this.'

'What did you have in mind? He's probably half blind. Who cares?'

'Oh, for fuck's sake Marga, give me a break. This could be our ticket.'

Parked the car and opened a suitcase. Retrieved the only suit I owned, which was black linen (and supposed to look crumpled, I convinced myself), a white T-shirt and a clean pair of socks. Marga reluctantly agreed to put on a black tracksuit and could not understand what I was fussing about.

'We are in a movie, Marga. It's like the first scene of our new life.'

The electric gates opened slowly, post my punching in the code. And we were *in*.

A Chinese butler greeted us at the door with a discreet bow, then ushered us into the living room, where he requested us to wait for Miss April.

I couldn't believe it: out of the bush and into Syd-Shirelle-land, all within the space of forty-eight hours?

No such thoughts seemed to be troubling Marga, who had her hand to her face, waving the air in front of her mask, indicating something 'off'. The house had a weird smell. The smell of someone very old. Not exactly a medical smell, nor anything as specific as cat shit, but a stale dried urine odour.

Mid-sniff, April legged in, reeking like a Duty Free counter, which for once was welcome relief. She was very tall, elegant, immaculately dressed and coiffed as if about to go out for the evening. Reached out and *How d'you do*d, didn't waste time with pleasantries, but led us along a dimly lit corridor to Syd's bedroom. Looking at least 102, he lay in the middle of a vast bed, eyes shut, like a shrivelled miniature of his screen self. An eyelid retracted backwards and he said, 'Who's the faggot?'

'Don't take any notice. He's slightly deaf. Sydney! This is – what did you say your name was again?'

20

'Marga.'

'Her name is Marga.'

Syd frowned and demanded, 'What?'

'MARGA.'

'There's no need to shout, I'm not *that* fucking deaf.'

Ling, the Chinese butler, obviously knew the ritual and quietly entered carrying a fold-out massage table which he erected beside the bed, then disappeared and returned with a pile of towels, massage oils and a pillow.

April leant over her husband and helped pull him up into a sitting position.

Without invitation, Marga went over and deftly picked Syd up and laid him down on the table. Sydney was so taken aback, he couldn't find words fast enough to resist or comply. April's face looked on the 'wow-ish' side, while my brain was still trying to compute the fact of my being in this inner sanctum at all.

Marga looked up at Ling, April and me and, with a meaningful nod, indicated that we were to leave. We all walked out of the bedroom in total silence.

'Your sister is quite extraordinary.' I was about to tell her we were not related, but didn't interrupt, and that's how this idea became 'fact'. 'Syd has never let anyone do what she's just done. Ever. Marga might just be the answer to my prayers.'

Ling offered me a drink and left April and me in the living room.

'Vivian never mentioned Marga before. But I guess she's been working in Africa, I think she said. With a royal family?'

'That's correct. We've in fact only just arrived in Los Angeles.'

'Where are you staying?'

'We're booked into the Beverly Hills Hotel.'

I expected her to burst out laughing at this blatant lie, but she didn't.

'I don't mean to be rude,' I continued, 'but I'm so jet-lagged, would you mind if I lay down for an hour till Marga is done?'

'Not at all. I'll get Ling to show you into the guest suite.'

I lay on the bed staring at the ceiling wondering how long it would be before we were deported.

★

When Ling woke me up and asked me to have a word with April, it took me a minute to realize where I actually was.

I was led back down the corridor to Syd's bedroom and to my fate.

Marga was folding up the towels and tidying away the bottles of oils. Syd was back in the bed, looking flushed and revived. April sat beside him, stroking and holding his hand.

'What's your name?' he barked.

'Vyvian,' I replied, upping the volume a little.

'Where are you from?'

'I'm English, sir.'

'So you *are* a faggot!'

April caught up and interjected with a 'Sydney!'

'Aw, shaddup, April, what would you know?'

April displayed a crockery of teeth in an embarrassed smile, lowered her voice and said, 'He doesn't mean it.'

'Yes I do!' snapped Shirelle. His hearing obviously intercepted what suited him. 'Your sister is a fucking miracle worker. I'm hiring her here and now. Night and day, I want her on call, d'you understand?'

My head was doing its automatic nodding act.

'This is what I've decided. You're gonna stay in the guest cottage in the garden, either till I fire her or I die. Whichever comes first. She is to be on an exclusive deal with me. My lawyer will see that you're properly remunerated. Only one house rule: you can't bring any of your boyfriends onto the property. You wanna fuck, you go elsewhere. D'you understand? Now get out and let me get to sleep. I'm exhausted.'

The four of us trooped out in silent, single file and it was only when we were well out of his hearing range that April turned and apologized profusely.

'I'm so, so sorry. It's just that he's spent his whole life cocooned from any reality and just assumes that he'll get what he wants, no matter how outrageous his demands.'

'I must admit, we've never been in this situation before.'

'Where did you stay when Marga was working for the African royal family?'

'Uh . . . in the palace actually, but that had been prearranged.'

'So you would possibly consider staying here, that is if you agree to take my husband on as a client? The cottage is very comfortable, and Ling can open it up for you if you are interested?'

If we were *interested*? I dared not look at Marga in case we both burst out laughing. So opted for a reprise of head nodding, to convey a show of serious consideration. My pause got April visibly panicked.

'It would be no problem for me to cancel your booking at the hotel. I can even pay the cancellation fee. I'm sorry to sound so desperate, but Syd has never taken to anyone like he has done to your sister, let alone offer accommodation. He has never, as far as I know, had any guests to stay, other than my mother, who only survived one visit. Please stay. Even if it's only for tonight.'

She was pleading. Begging.

I looked up and said, 'Well, this is not our usual *modus operandi*' – a little Latin goes a long way – 'but why not let's have a look at the cottage and let Marga be the judge? I'll know in a second whether she'll stay or not.'

April went off to get Ling. Marga and I stared at each other in utter wide-eyed disbelief. The adrenalin rush that zoomed up and down my entrails suppressed all signs of jet lag.

Our little party followed Ling out into the garden, past the pool, past the tennis court, towards a dark building in the distance. Crickets and cicadas, stars and cool night air. Like being in the middle of the countryside. We walked down a curving slope to a substantial house. All in darkness.

Ling fiddled with keys and torch, opened the door and flicked a switch. 'Cottage' indeed. Slightly musty smell, but nothing bad like the main house.

April put herself into 'tour' gear. We played our roles with as much conviction as we could muster, nodding and 'approving' as we appraised everything room by room.

'What do you think? D'you think it might work for you even just for a trial period?'

I heard my tongue articulate this proviso.

'April, it's all fine with me, but I'll only know for sure by whether Marga takes to her bedroom or not. If she lies down on the bed and closes her eyes, we're in with a chance, but if not, I'm afraid we're going to have to go and stay at the Beverly Hills Hotel and commute.'

April looked positively stricken.

Ling was adjusting the heat and air-conditioning thermostat already. I took Marga's hand and we followed April into the larger of the two bedrooms.

'This is where my mother stayed and she found it very comfortable.'

I led Marga to the bed to let her continue with the charade. But plonking herself down immediately and getting us fully ensconced was not what she had in mind. For a terrible moment, I honestly thought she might blow our whole cover by either talking or walking out, leaving me to stew and come up with some explanation.

She walked around the bed, prodding and testing it. Sitting down. Getting up. Then walked to the window and tried to open it. She took a dramatic deep breath, as if she was going to suffocate. April freaked and yelled for Ling, who came rushing in and was instructed to release the locks as quickly as possible.

Marga released her breath in a great whoosh once the window was opened. She then turned and completed her dumbshow by lying down on the bed and closing her eyes.

The three of us just stared at her. Marga's *coup de grâce*, though, was a slow burning smile that silked across her face.

24

April looked at me. I looked at her. Nodded affirmation and she squealed, 'Oh joy! So she'll stay?'

'Definitely.'

The poor soul was so relieved she flung her arms around me and gave me a hug of some intensity. Ling smiled too and let loose a couple of bows. 'I'll have Ling stock up the refrigerator in the morning. D'you think Marga could give Syd an early morning workout? Around nine?'

'Shouldn't be a problem.'

We were unpacked and installed before you'd have time to say San Fernando Valley.

★

If you can't believe this, neither could we. But it's all true. Exactly how it happened.

God, I loved my new life!

God, did they welcome us into theirs.

Especially April, who when we pitched up was clearly in the last throes of serious emotional neglect, living a life of near-total isolation tending to her old curmudgeon.

She was brimming with confession. Couldn't wait to give vent.

Syd was hardly 'welcoming' in any conventional sense, but who were we to argue when he had given us a home and living?

Marga dealt with him three times a day, giving him the massage of a lifetime. I kept out of his way, and was paid visits by April, who was always finding some excuse to drop by.

'I can't believe it. Your sister is a gift from God. Nobody has survived working on him this long.'

'But Marga's only been here for a week.'

'A week? That's a lifetime compared to the majority.'

'What did the others do wrong?'

'Nothing to do with them. All to do with Syd. They couldn't take the verbal abuse and constant harassment. I hope this doesn't sound unkind, but maybe it's because she's deaf?'

25

April lowered her volume for this supposition, as if she might be overheard.

'How long have you been married to him?'

She looked at the golfball-sized diamond on her finger and declared, 'Five years.'

My silent nodding prompted an outpouring.

'I *do* love him. Don't get me wrong. But I have never been so lonely in all my life. He won't let me go anywhere. Two years after we were married, he just took to his bed. No apparent reason. Just did. And that was that. This man who danced his whole life long. Bedridden. Nothing actually wrong with him. The doctors have all confirmed that. Every time I bring the subject of mobility up with him, he quotes the marriage vows at me. Wagging his finger and saying, "In *sickness* and in health, till *death* us do part." It's pretty creepy. But I think he enjoys doing it, because I always react really badly.'

The thought of which prompted a welling of tears.

'But surely you must get out of the house to go shopping?'

'No. He sends Ling.'

'When did you manage to buy all your beautiful clothes, then?'

She blushed.

'During the time my mother came to stay and from before, when Syd was still mobile. Only he hated my mother because she was younger than *him*. They got into a terrible argument one night and my mother accused him of being my jailer and he screamed back that we were just a pair of gold-diggers and that if she didn't get out of the house immediately he'd call the police.'

She dressed up every morning as if she was about to go out to some grand function, looking all the more incongruous against the luxurious but dilapidated surroundings. The house was time-warped in terms of design and furnishings circa 1946, and clearly needed a major overhaul.

'When last did Syd leave the house, then?'

'Oh, *he* goes out, every other night. Ling drives him around his old haunts and he just sits in the back of the car and rants and moans. I used to go along, but I can't stand it any more. He's an insomniac. My mother thinks it's because he's been so mean to people all his life. He's getting paid back for all his cruelty by not being able to sleep properly.'

'Haven't you got any friends?'

Her dam burst.

'They all gave up on me. He chased them all away. Every one.'

'Doesn't he have any?'

This stopped her crying, as she looked up in disbelief.

'Are you kidding me? We are talking about one of the most hated men in Hollywood. He has no friends.'

'So why do you stick it out, then?'

'I'd lose everything. *Everything.* I can't afford to do that. We have a prenuptial agreement. If I leave him, that's it. Zero. I swore I would never be poor again. And I won't. I'll stick it out even if he does live to see a hundred. I want a family of my own.'

I couldn't help asking why her hair was set in such a matronly style. April blinked twice and flustered, 'He likes it that way. He has a hairdresser come by once a week.'

'Why not just refuse?'

This thought rolled around her head like a hard-boiled sweet in search of escape.

'I couldn't.'

'Why not? If he's in bed all day, what's the worst he can do to you? Divorce you because you refuse to have your hair fixed like he wants it?'

Such revolutionary ideas were destabilizing her orientation.

'I don't think you really understand.'

'April, he is making the rules. You are complying. Allowing him to do so makes you his prisoner. You have everything going for you. You're young. You're beautiful. You're wasting your life.'

'I *do* love him, you know,' she assured us both. Unconvincingly.

'What do you do?' she asked, as if the thought had suddenly surprised itself like sherbet in her mouth.

27

I was totally unprepared. I couldn't nod my way out of this one.

'I'm an art historian and interior designer,' I lied.

'Oh, wow. I envy you that. I have no education. That's what Syd loved about me most. No threat, he said. Do you think you could redecorate our house?'

'Absolutely!'

'He wouldn't let you, but I'm going to ask him anyway.'

'How could he stop you?'

It was her turn to shake her head. She looked at her Cartier watch and bolted for the door.

'I almost forgot the time. Thanks, Vyvian. See you later.' And was off. High-heeling her way back to her self-imposed hell.

Marga returned, took off her surgical mask to wash her face, then lay down on the sofa.

'He never stops talking. I thought the massage would put him to sleep, but it has the reverse effect. Blames everyone for everything. That is if he isn't talking about sex. He's obsessed. I'm going to take a bath.'

'Can you believe our luck, Margs?'

'What luck?'

'This luck!'

'How else was it supposed to happen? I want my face fixed. We got a job. So what?'

'But this is Syd Shirelle, Margs, not just any old nobody.'

'He's worse. And you're star-struck. Excuse me.'

While she was in the bath, Ling phoned to say that he wasn't able to drive Syd that evening and would I be prepared to do chauffeur duty?

'But he hates me!'

'No problem. Hates everyone. You not alone. He give all directions. I leave keys on dining room table. Sayonara.'

April was waiting for me when I got to the main house and spoke in a near whisper.

'Whatever you do, please don't breathe a word about what I said today, OK?'

She was midway through giving car instructions when Syd barked behind me. I had never seen him walking in real life before, and he seemed to have enlarged since I first saw him crumpled up on his bed.

'C'mon, you faggot, what are we waiting for? Get the fucking car out!' Not exactly the song and dance you might expect from this old trouper. He walked without the aid of a stick, very upright, to the front door, and waited for me to drive the car out of the garage to come and pick him up.

Refused my help to get in and surprised me by sitting in the front seat of the 1962 Silver Cloud Rolls-Royce, which purred along in perfect condition. 'Turn left out of the gate and don't ask any questions.'

I wasn't about to.

'This car is the only British thing I've ever been able to stand. Except for David Niven. He made me laugh. And your sister. She's got an ass like two perfect cantaloupe melons. Of equal density. Turn left on Sunset.'

I did as I was told and he went quiet for a couple of minutes. Gathering himself. I kept thinking that his familiar voice was going to break out into a medley of his greatest hits, but his targets were totally non-melodic.

'Keep going till I tell you otherwise. You Brits are a nation of bullies. I can say that because I'm one myself. A bully, not a Brit. You never got over your loss of Empire. I never get over the fact that my career is over. I'm an old Prince who married the Showgirl. That's where my link with Olivier begins and ends. I met him once. All rolling eyes and fucking flattery and, "Oh, Sydney, you're the master" – like fuck. "And you're an old ham." He laughed like I was Syd fucking Caesar. But I meant it. And he knew it. You're all hypocrites: your fucking anti-fur brigade claiming this and that and the next moment they're all riding around the countryside chasing foxes dressed up like fucking doormen.

'I bought each of my four wives full-length mink coats out of the money I earned dancing my butt off all those years ago, so there is no way I'm gonna be trading 'em in for some animal rights conscience crap. I don't have one. Stay in the right lane.

'Marilyn was lucky. Didn't live long enough for people to smoke her out. So she was abused. So who fucking wasn't? So who fucking cares? Nobody forced her to take her clothes off. It took every power of persuasion to get her to keep them on. She was a dumb, stupid, manipulative non-talent who got where she got by wearing permanent knee pads and blow-jobbing her way upwards. The only person I felt sorry for was Tony Curtis who had to kiss those lips that had been wrapped around every Tom, Dick and Harry in this town. The only good thing she did was to give Larry a go for his money by making him wait an eternity before she ever turned up on the set. My first wife had an English butler who held his nose so high up in the air he thought his shit didn't smell. I kicked his lily-white ass right out the door. But you wanna know what *really* gets up my nose? I'll tell you. The way you Brits think you have a monopoly on irony, and use it to beat every upstanding American over the head at every turn. You carry on as if it was an exclusive plutonium supply. Well, listen up, Buddy-boy. *We* won the war. The lot. The whole fucking shebang. And now the world marches to an American tune. To which I say, if you're gonna take a dump, sit on the pot. And shit. When your dancing days are done, hang up your shoes. Tie up your tonsils. Go gracefully. Get out.

'Nobody tells you how to prepare for your old age. That's why I'm learning Japanese. Hardest fucking language on the planet and I'm gonna crack it before my triple-bypassed selfish old heart gives out.

'The big mistake everyone makes in this town is thinking they're gonna be the only ones who won't get old. But they all do. No matter how many nips and tucks they've had. I wear a piece. It's a fucking sight. I know that. But if I didn't, I'd look even worse than

30

I do. Difference between me and the majority of them is that I *know* I'm old.

'The fucking tragedy of it is, is that as wise and full of wisdom as I now am, it's all *too fucking late. It's all fucking backwards.*

'None of the women I grew up with in this business look anything like normal people. They have entered the no-longer-human ranks of the post-plastic-surgery era. It's frightening. I can't look them in the eye any more. Most of the old-timers get on the bandwagon of some crappy TV show, or attach themselves to charity events and appeals, and fucking Talkathons, doing anything to keep themselves noticed. It's *disgusting*.

'Take a right when you see the sign for Doheny.

'You get these old stars cogitating on screen and you know by the look of terror in their eyes that they can't remember a single fucking line of dialogue to save their lives. The only time anyone truly wishes you well is when you're terminally ill. You wouldn't believe the fucking skunks and raccoons who came out of the woodwork when I had my triple bypass. The obit columnists were poised to ink in my death dates. You could hear the distant whooping of some unknown just off the bus, hollering, "Make room for *ME*." I'm no different. Just more honest.'

I nosed the car south on Doheny and dared ask a question.

'What was Mae West like?'

'Improbable. Now shaddup.'

The car coasted downhill and we stopped at the lights.

'Turn left onto Santa Monica Boulevard. Why the fuck did you ask me about Mae?'

I was silent.

'I'm asking you a question, you fuck.'

'I'm choosing not to reply.'

His silence was a terror of splutters. I crossed the busy intersection, half expecting him to jam his thumb onto the ejector button. A couple of blocks further, he said, 'Mae was smart. Got out before she crashed. Unlike Louise Brooks. She *really* fucked up. Swanson

31

made a comeback at the age of fifty-three in *Sunset Boulevard*. Then never got a squeak of work after that role. Which proves my theory.'

'She was in *Airport '75*.'

'Shaddup. Doesn't count. She proved that you only really need to do one great role and that's it. It's your passport, your respect, your *you*-ness, and no one can take it away from you. Not even if you descend into TV or camp. Now go on towards Highland Avenue and keep a sharp lookout on the left. When you see a yellow neon sign saying PLEASURE CHEST, make a sharp left. I've got a list of the stuff I want you to get.'

Santa Monica Boulevard seemed never-ending. Syd was silent for the rest of the journey, anxious not to miss the sign.

'Turn.'

I did and parked in the busy lot. He passed me the list and slid down into his seat, so that his toupee was just visible above the window line. There were three bikers talking beside the door. The one with the toothpick and three teeth grunted, 'Nice auto, man,' gesturing to the gleaming Rolls.

I smiled like a schoolgirl, nodded and went inside. Up to the counter, where a Gargantua of pale flesh, trussed into a black gauze excuse of fabric, leant forward and asked, 'How can I help you?'

Frankly my main concern was for the glass-topped counter, supporting the weight of her ginormousness. Black lips, black hair, black nail polish and all things Gothic. I gingerly placed the list before her.

Keeping my eyes down, I realized that I was staring at a line-up of dildos and plastic penises in every colour and size. 'Batteries *not* included' proclaimed some. I dared a look left and saw all manner of leatherwear, zips, masks, chains and handcuffs. Tried a right and spied a technicolour rack of video titles, one of which read *Stuffed Little Holes*. Godzilla shouted out Syd's requested titles to someone called Buckie who was lurking unseen in a stockroom.

A dozen colourful cassettes featuring couplings of every variation were neatly stacked into a carrier bag.

'Oh, I almost forgot,' she said running a black fingernail down the list. 'You wanted a bottle of Wet. Large or small?'

'Large,' I answered in the smallest voice.

'I thought so,' she smiled, revealing a row of teeth embedded with diamonds. 'See you soon. Enjoy!'

★

This became a weekly ritual. I would drive him, and he would reminisce. As the months went by, he even stopped 'shadupping' me all over the place.

April stopped having her hair set in the Queen of England's Merino Ram look and shed years instantly.

Syd reluctantly agreed to let me overhaul 'one room. And one room *only*.'

I had the breakfast room painted top to bottom, ceiling and floor, in the closest approximation of Matisse blue that I could mix. A solid blue box of the most intense colour that when hit by the morning sun was dazzling. He was determined to hate it, but stood like a little boy in his dressing gown and slippers at the threshold when he arrived for breakfast. Looked. Shut his eyes. Then blinked them open, hard. Walked in and sat down, without saying a word.

April started to weep and went off to mop herself into order.

'He wants you to do another room!' was the command from on high. Approbation of the highest order without his actually having to say anything complimentary.

'What colour do you want to go for next, sir?'

He looked at me and oh so reluctantly said, 'You choose.'

And this process went on, room by room, till the whole house was transformed into a Mediterranean palette of colours.

★

Some august body invited Syd to be guest of honour at a Beverly Hilton 'tribute dinner', which provoked him to say, 'They must be worried I'm about to die. I've flown too many missions and been shot down by too much press to bother with any of that fucking baloney.'

Of course he went. Of course he got himself into the best shape he could. Of course he even did a trademark swivel-turn and tap routine and *of course* he thanked his 'peers' for all their 'love and support' throughout a lifetime in showbusiness. And of course people rose to their feet. And cried.

'For themselves,' he said, rewinding the event on video, and freeze-framing on various enemies in close-up. Pointing out whom he had fucked. And which smiling faces had fucked him over.

'How can you be a decent human being if you want to be famous? It's a paradox that can't be fixed. I should know. I wanted it so bad when I was young and now if someone even recognizes me from five hundred paces I wanna go over and punch 'em. It's why I've given up going out in the daytime. The last time I sat in a restaurant, it was nudge-nudge, fucking wink-wink throughout, with me pretending not to notice.

'Even when the civilians at the next table made a great show of taking snaps of each other, they turned at the last second to flash in my old face. Same thing happened with a video camera. They thought if they left it lying on its side I wouldn't notice. But they forgot that the little red light was flashing at me the whole time. So I was forced to move. But best of all was this old cunt who comes over and says, "Oh, Mr Shirelle, what an honour, what a treat. My mother is your biggest fan and she would just love to have your autograph. She's ninety-six." So I oblige and sign a Canada Dry coaster. I look over and see a woman in a wheelchair, staring down into her lap. Dressed to the nines and not knowing who or where she is. She is the size of an apple. Her daughter returns, shouting – "I GOT YOU SYD SHIRELLE'S AUTOGRAPH. HE'S AN ACTOR. DONE A LOT OF MOVIES. WE'LL RENT SOME" – because of course, her mother is deaf.

'The woman was so gaga that she just fell forward onto her plate. On my way out people stood and elbowed me in the ribs while telling me how much they loved my old movies and how their kids loved the TV reruns. I came home black and blue and swore that that was it.'

★

One evening, April, Marga, Ling and I were summoned to have dinner with Syd at the Palm Restaurant. Ling was thoroughly unprepared for this level of intimacy and did his best to excuse himself. But Syd was entertaining no refusals. I was instructed to drive, and the five of us piled into the Rolls and headed for – what?

A great but subdued fuss was made of Syd when he greeted staff he had known for the best part of his life. He ordered steaks and lobsters, despite the fact that both Marga and Ling were vegetarians. 'You're gonna eat food that says, "I know who I am and I know what I want."'

Marga and Ling stuck to the potatoes and salad.

'This is my last supper. I want Vyvian to design and coordinate my funeral arrangements. I've chosen the music. I've chosen the clips. Tomorrow I'm going to film the videotape of my last speech, which I want shown just before I get flamed.'

April burst into tears. I felt a little overwhelmed myself – quite apart from the bizarre honour of being offered funeral-designing duties, it was the first time he had ever called me by my name.

'When do you plan on dying, then?'

'Shaddup! I'll tell you. As soon as you're ready. That's when. And don't expect a golden handshake from me either, because there ain't one coming.'

★

And Syd was as good as his word. He shuffled off the mortal coil in his sleep, after a final massage from Marga, just as the arrangements were completed. The funeral home was decked out as a bottle-green Garden of Eden with wall-to-wall leaves interspersed with clusters of velvet-white gardenias, the perfume of which was overwhelming. The coffin was draped with black silk, scattered with white petals. Placed either side were two extra-large video screens.

His turnout was spectacular. No one wanted to miss that photo opportunity, nor the chance to share their most cherished memories of the life and times of their 'dear, dear friend and colleague, Syd Shirelle'. And a sprinkling of younger stars paid their respects, including Java Hall, Georgia Sepulveda, Ted Moby and many more.

Once the eulogy was delivered by veteran director Mort Buchinsky, and various *remember when*s were discharged, the lights dimmed, the candles flickered and the video playback began.

There was an audible gasp when Syd's voice familiar'd forth.

'I know none of you liked me. So you don't have to pretend. I'm locked inside here now, so I'm afraid I won't be able to hear your sincere denials. Relax. I know and you know that we're all just a bunch of hucksters and fakers, hustlers and sons of bitches. Most of you are so old now you can't even finish off your old stories any more. It's called anecdotage. Shaddup for once and let it all go!

(This prompted people to laugh.)

'What else is there to do? You're mostly too old to fuck. Too old to work. So all you've got left is to fuck everyone else over by trashing 'em behind their backs. You old hellraisers now just look like hell. You old beauties look like fucking mummies. Old age? I don't recommend it.

(Even bigger laugh.)

'*This* is the Viper room. See if you can spot the Python, Puffadder, Boa Constrictor, Anaconda and Mamba among yourselves? This is the inner cabal. Here all our secrets are known. Who fucked who. Who belongs to who. Whose hair is dyed. Whose skin is stretched. Whose career is in a nuclear winter of discontent. Who is who is who? You're all invited to come round to Delfern Drive afterwards. I'm sorry I can't make it, but I've got a bit of a grilling coming up.'

He smiled and waved, then snapped his fingers, cueing the trundling forward of the casket.

It was a sensation, as was the party at Delfern Drive. People who had never been allowed access to his estate before crowded in, and April found herself bombarded by various mourners demanding to know, 'Who designed that funeral? Who designed this room? Where can I get hold of him?' Which is how I *really* got going.

Most touching and surprising of all was Syd's last will and testament.

Marga and I were bequeathed the guest house.

Ling got the Silver Cloud.

April married her personal trainer and took up t'ai chi.

▶▶ FAST FORWARD FIFTEEN YEARS ▶▶

# SOME LIKE IT HOT

'Vyvian?'

'Georgia!'

'I've had it. I really, really mean it this time. I ask myself, I'm asking you, for Chrissakes, and you're not even in showbusiness, I ask myself, *what* the hell am I supposed to do to survive this bloody deal, huh? How many movies have I made? I'll tell you, thirty-nine. Thirty-nine is not exactly slouching it. Am I right or am I right? Look, I'm sorry to call you so late, but I really, really need to talk to somebody and you're the only soul I know who won't penalize me for exposing myself *or* charge me by the damned hour. I just realized that I have been in therapy for God knows how many years, and come the end of my hour Dr Fronkenschteen NEVER fails to clock me off. You'd've thought that after this many years in service I might just get lucky and get offered *some* free bonus time or *something*, but no, who *knows* who might just be lurking in the antechamber? A Julia, or a Goldie or a Sandie or a Demi? I ask you, how come these witches who have so much money and success *need* to see a 'Schteen, when there's me with *real* problems? I love the way the house looks, though, and everyone who comes says it feels so right. I just wish I could find someone to do the same for me. Redesign my mind, wouldn't you? I tell you, what you can do, is ask Marga if she could come by and give me a rub down. I've still got that dull ache in my lower back. In fact I could even come by and pick her up, if you like?'

'Georgia, you know I can't let you do that. I'll get her cabbed over to you.'

'What is this with you and "you know I can't let you do that" bullshit? Huh? How long have we known each other? How many

38

times have you rearranged and altered and fixed my houses and never once have you asked me over?'

'You know that that is part of my deal. It's just better that way.'

'Says you. I thought we were friends—'

'We are.'

'Yeah, but on your terms. What's the big deal about doin' a Garbo? What are you scared of?'

'Georgie, we've been here and done this, it's just the way I have found best to operate. Suits me and keeps things clear. But as I've said a million times before, you can call on me any time, anyplace, just not at my place. I've said it before—'

'And now you're gonna say it again – you're "in service". Well, I discussed you with Fronkenschteen and he thinks you're in some kinda denial.'

'C'mon. He, me, we're both in service. Let me ask you this: how many times have you been round Dr Fronck's for dinner and some poolside chats?'

'That's *my* business.'

'Precisely! Does he know, for instance, that you call him Dr Fronkenschteen?'

'Are you kidding me? Of course not. He'd go ape.'

'So what's the difference? As I said, we are both in service and that's the line.'

'That is so goddamned English of you.'

'Isn't Dr Fronk an American?'

'I think he's a sadist, is what I think. I mean, how do you figure listening to human horrorshow all day *by choice*? I asked him why once and he said it was an inappropriate question.'

'I don't want to go down that road, Georgie, it's too late.'

'You always "Georgie" me when you wanna get out of things.'

'I'm not the enemy.'

'Don't go noble on me. I *know* what it is. It's because I'm just not famous enough any more.'

'Georgia, don't.'

'It's true. Let's fucking face it. When I met you, I was splashy and noisy with the stuff, couldn't move without reading about or seeing me someplace fabulous. Now, if I'm *lucky*, someone *might* give me the old "stare" treatment, but now most times the folks who I think are recognizing me are usually just myopic or insane or whatever else is going on, and I've started doing random checks on this. Keeping my increasingly non-vital statistics on record. I got a notepad in my bag and one in the car for drive-by recog-sightings, and things are not looking too good. I honestly think I am becoming more and more anonymous by the day. Like each day is doing its own eclipse job on my prospects. And this is not just the paranoids. I can tell. D'you wanna know how? – I *never* get through to my agent any more. He's always otherwise occupied or on a plane or a set or somewhere other than available to me, and I get fobbed off with the assistants, who change on a weekly basis, so much so that I never even bother to learn their names, cos the parade of Chondras, Lukes and Amys is too much to keep up with. And *these* are the people in charge of my professional life. I reckon that if I can't keep up and remember *their* names, how in the fuck are they gonna know *mine*? This is *not* paranoia, these are the facts of my life. But you can bet your sweet macaroni that if Sigourney or Sharon were to call, his Highness would be on the line in seconds. Though to be honest, things have not been going that well for Sharon lately, but at least people know who she is. She can at least ride the Benefit, Tribute and Charity express. Me – I swear to you – I am becoming more ordinary by the minute. In fact I'm gonna test myself right now, right here—'

'Where are you?'

'Tower Records.'

'Inside?'

'What does it matter where I am, people are people, right?'

'On a mobile? Inside or out?'

'In front of Joni Mitchell. What is it with you?'

'What d'you mean, Joni Mitchell?'

'I.am.standing.in.front.of.Joni.Mitchell.As.in.her.section! Keep up, Vyv!'

'Aren't you talking rather loudly for inside?'

'Damn right, 'n' don' give me that hoity-toity "rather loudly" bullshit—FUCK OFF!'

'OK.'

'NO! Not you, HIM.—Yes, YOU. YES YOU!! ... Well, do you have it in stock or dontcha? Jesus, what do you want it in? Mexican? Huh? I asked a simple question and you're givin' me this load of horseshit!'

'Georgie?'

'SHUDDUP—(Don't go) No, *you* go back through the door once more and see if you can find *any* stock, but don't just stand there, giving me this ' "I can't help you, ma'am" crap, cos I've just about had enough of you guys already, d'you hear me?— VYVIAN?!!'

'I'm still here.'

'Can you fuckin' believe this? Jesus blow me down – I come into this store, how many times? Huh? How many times do you think I have come into this cocksucking joint of assholes to buy stuff, huh? How many times? DO YOU MIND, I'M ON THE PHONE!'

'Probab—'

'Exactly, probably for ever. How much money do you think I have laid over the counter, stuffed up the register and paid for some dumbfuck's drug habit strapped to his beach condo? A lot, right. A whole lotta bucks. Right? RIGHT!!'

'Geor—'

'Listen to me, Vy, you are not getting this. I'm telling you, I have HAD it. Holy Maloney Baloneysville.'

'Let me come and get you.'

'Don't be fucking ridiculous. I'm not a child. WHAT?—(Vy, don't hang up.) Excuse me? Do you have ANY idea who you are dealing with, young man? Call Security? CALL security. Go ahead. I'd like a word myself. The customer is always right, RIGHT? Right? Answer me my question, am I right or am I right? I come in here, right, LATE, right, it's not your busy busy busy time, right? Nuh-uh, it's after midnight, it's Monday, it's way past most of this town's fuckin' 10 p.m. executive distress curfew hour, right? I am a regular customer here, OK? You've seen me in here before, RE GU LAR LY, right? All I am asking for is a LITTLE respect, a little cooperation, a little recognition, call it what you will, when I HUMBLY enquire as to whether you carry ANY copies or even one copy of a movie I starred in, SOME years ago, called *Topanga Canyon*, and what I get is, what I *get is*, some guy with a dope-eyed "nah" and a filthy fingernail and nickel-skulled knuckle ring jabbing a fucking computer key and after a fuckin' Deborah-Kerr-to-Eternity time lapse, I am told, "No, lady, we have no record of the movie soundtrack at all. Are you sure you got the title right?" AM I SURE I GOT MY OWN TITLE RIGHT? What IS this? Is everyone in on this thing or am I truly losing the plot here? Huh? Vy? (Hold on.) I got a friend of mine on here who can verify for me – take it. I said take it.'

'Geor—'

'What do you mean this isn't regular store policy, GET your hands off me! I SAID GET YOUR FUCKING HANDS OFFA ME. WHAT DO YOU THINK I AM, SOME FUCKIN' NORMA DESMOND NEVERBEEN? I AM GOING! WATCH ME GO!!! YEAH YOU, YOU, YOU PUBLIC YOU, I AM ON MY WAY. Vy, are you there, I can't hear you breathing.'

'Haaaaaaaa.'

'OK, I'm walking outta this place. Right now. Yeah yeah yeah, you see that Austrian guy's flick, you know, where he says, "I'll be back," well, you just watch me, kids, cos I'm never coming back. Yeah yeah, laugh. Clap your little hands, reach out and touch yourselves, the lotta ya. Vy, I'm walking towards my car – if I can get this fuckin' alarm thing to work ... Don't go. Don't lose me. OK? OK?'

'OK ... Georgia?'

'Can you hear me?'

'Lost you there a minute.'

'Stay with me. I just gotta change batteries here, it's bleeping an/ / / / / osing you/ / / / / / / / / / /————Vyvian?'

'Still with you. Are you all right?'

'Am I all right? Am I ALL RIGHT? I sure intend to be. There may be static ahead, but while there's moonlight and Spago's and egos instead, why go to bed.'

This is not sounding good.

'I'll be coming up that mountain, here I come. I'll be comin' up your mountain, here I come. I'll be comin' up this mountain, I'll be entering Wolfgang Puckdom, I'll be coming down this mountain when I'm done. Hi, guys!'

'I'm sorry, but we're closed, Ms Sepulveda.'

'Well, at least you got my name right, it's just I'm desperate to use the bathroom and know you won't turn down a damsel in distress, right? Right. Hi, starfuckers, yes it's me, I know it's late and you're the last of the midnighters, but when a gal's gotta go, a gal's gotta GO!'

'Miss Sepulveda!!'

'/ / / Geor / / / gia!'

'Going in the can, Vy, hold your breath————I'm leaving, diners, don't you worry 'bout a thing. I'm leavin', on a Gulf Stream, don' know when I'll be back again—'

'Miss Sepulveda!!!!'

'The sun'll come out, toooomorrow, bet your bottom dollar that tomorrow, there'll be something about me in the *National Enquiraaaaaah*! GET YOUR HANDS OFF ME, SUNSHINE!!!!!!!! I'm back, boys. You may as well go home, nobody in there worth waiting for, but if you wanna get some really good snaps, paparazzi your way after me. Because Georgie baby is goin' on the ride of her life, this little ol' Monday midnight hour on Sunset. VYVIAN?'

'Georgie, I am begging you not to go any further with this!'

'Beg away, baby, Georgia Sepulveda is on her way down this little motherfucker of a slope, and headed for her car.'————/ / / / / / ————

'Transferring you to speaker mode. Can you credit this? I got in my car, a half-hour ago, to pick up a little chicken salad from Chin-Chin, dropped a right into Tower parking lot and first thing, some Neanderthal security guy leans over and says, "Are you a customer for Tower?" To which I say, "Hey, man, no, I wanna use the bathroom at Spago's – of course I'm a customer. You ought to know me by now, if not by car, by at least *one* of my fucking performances, in *one* of the mere thirty-nine movies I have made, buttfuck."'

"You called security a buttfuck?'

'Of course not, buttfuck, not to his face. Anyway, I park the motor, get my ass inside the store, am just browsing around like you do, feeling like a Jurassic cos I'm the only one in here over twenty-five, without Gothic make-up, dyed black hair and multiply pierced body parts, and it's clear to me that none of the stragglers recognizes me from Adam— Hold on, I gotta go left on this light – JEEZUZ – doesn't anybody drive right in this town? GO. GO. GOOOOOO!—Vy?'

'I'm still here. Where are you headed?'

'Blockbuster Video, where d'you think? Where was I?'

'Adam.'

'Right. Right ... Adam ... mmmmhmm ... oh yeah, so I'm walking down the aisle, just browsing, you know, and between here and there I end up in front of the soundtracks selection. Like you do, right. So I'm browsing and flicking through the discs, and finger my way past *Tequila Sunrise*, *To Russia with Love*, Top*fuck-ingkapi*, readying to see myself on the cover of *Topanga Canyon*, right? A little confirmation. You know ... a little midnight lift, a little, "Hey, kid you're in the movies too" reassurance, right? Only it's not there. Right? So I tell myself, "Georgie, you went too fast. Backtrack a little. You know how it is. It's midnight, post the weekend, chances are the order of things got a little out of order. Go back. Keep calm. You'll be there." Only I'm not. Not even a *Topanga* plastic title card and note to say *currently out of stock*. Nothing. Then a Towerite slouches up and mumbles, "Can I help you with something?" and I am *you sure can*ing and giving him the particulars of *Topanga*, and he sloths us both to the computer pod in the middle of the aisle, and punches in the title. Screen bleeps back a blank. Next he's telling me, with some authority, that the movie either has a different title, or has been deleted or whatever, and I ask him to call the video store across the road to see if they have it. *This* request gets his head doing the side to side *I don't think so, lady* look, but give him his due, he does it. So while I'm waiting with him for the other store to pick up the fucking endlessly non-answering phone, I ask, "Where's Buffy?"—Says "Who?" and I'm getting a little steamy-stressed here now. "Buffy – you know, film-'Buffy', the guy who knows every credit and obscure movie ever made Buffy." Fuck me if he doesn't say, "I dunno who you mean." This is when I start losing it—What's the cross street for Virgin?'

'I think it's Crescent Heights—'

' "Whaddya mean, you don't know who I mean?" So I open it out to the room and ask, "Has ANYBODY heard of Buffy?" and I get zombie eyes staring back at me and a load of "I'm new here" from the Goth and no matter who or how many times I ask, seems like Buffy and I never existed. Till I give a detailed description of Buffy, which as you know I am *forensically* gifted at, and some slouch bent over doing a stocktake sticks her head up and says, "I think you mean Ray-monde." Next thing she's saying he got taken by the plague, and I'm like "You have got to be kidding me" when the douchebag over in Video picks up and gives it the "Can you hold?" and within seconds is back on line saying, "Movie must have another title. No record of it." Never mind a copy. At which point I admit, I got a little out of hand and started hollering, "Has ANYBODY seen this face before?" and whoever else is in here is now looking super-intently at disc covers and would you believe it, NO ONE pipes up. Not one. Except this dweezil threatening Security. Which is when you called me.'

'You called me, Georgie.'

'Whatever – but you musta heard the way they were dealing with me? Is that anyway to treat an Artist? I ask you, am I going insane or what? Do you think I was being unreasonable?'

'Well—'

'EXACTLY! Jeezus, I've paid my dues, you know that. Can you credit this? Can you fucking credit THIS? Those photographers are following me! Look at THAT?'

'What?'

'This billboard. JEEEEZUS! Meryl Streep's profile for *Savages*. Give me a fucking break. How many parts does this woman WANT?'

'GEORGIA— Re-route! Didn't I warn you not to take this section of Sunset?'

'Relax. I can't be in billboard denial my *whole* life.'

'Drop parallel onto Fountain.'

'Fuck Fountain!'

'Have you passed Alta Loma?'

'—AND she's happily married with fifteen kids and five Oscars, can't she just retire already? JEEEEZUs NO. NO. NOooooooooo!'

'Georgia? GEORGIA. What's happened? Speak to me!'

'I'M GONNA KILL YOU. I'M GONNA KILL YOU—MOTHER-FUCKINGSONOFACUNTFUCK, LOOKWHATYOU'VEDONE-TOMYVEHICLE?'

'*GEORGIA!*'

'SHUDDUP!!!!!GETYOURFUCKINGHEARSEOUTOFMY-WAY.'

'Are you hurt?'

'What happened?'

'ONE AT A TIME. WHO DO YOU THINK I AM, ROBIN WILLIAMS? AM I HURT? WHAT KINDA QUESTION IS THAT. I'M A HOLLYWOOD ACTRESS AND YOU'RE ASKING ME AM I HURT? ARE YOU MENTALLY RETARDED? YOU DRIVE YOUR FUCKING CAR AT A RIGHT ANGLE INTO MINE, TOTAL MY VEHICLE AND YOU'RE ASKING ME, AM I HURT? YOU BETCHA SWEET ASS I'M HURTING.'

'You jumped the lights, lady.'

'DON'T YOU "YOU" ME. I DID NOT JUMP THE LIGHTS, ASSHOLE!'

'That's abusive, lady.'

'Don't you keep *lady*ing me, sonny. I got a witness on line, Vy
– you still there?'

'Here, Georgia.'

'See, he heard the whole thing, so watch whatever you say cos
Vy's got the memory of an elephant HERD. Right? Right. YOU
jumped the lights. YOU totalled my car. GO AHEAD, BOYS.
FLASH AWAY. THIS IS THE *ENQUIRER* LIVE!'

'Lady, I don't know what you're on, but this is something we
have to let the law decide. I'm calling the cops.'

'No need, they're coming right behind you.'

'Lady, you had your head out the window, looking up at the
billboard—'

'Don't be ridiculous!'

'I drive for a living, it's my business to observe.'

'MINE TOO. THE TRUTH. THE WHOLE TRUTH AND
NOTHING BUT THE TRUTH. It's the foundation of my artistry,
puppyfuck.'

'I don't appreciate your tone, ma'am.'

'Well, FUCK YOU, CHARLEY.'

'My name's Chuck, and I've been driving this Deadline Tours
limousine for five years, ma'am, without incident. It's my
livelihood.'

'ARE YOU KIDDING ME?'

'Excuse me?'

'I am in collision with Deadline Tours?'

'Here's my card.'

'Oh boy. Oh, boy oh boy oh boy. My career's in turnaround
and what do I get? A fucking hearse up my ass. Do you have any
idea who I am?'

'Excuse me?'

'You're an actor, right? Driving tourists to pay the rent, right?'

'How'd you know?'

'TRUST ME! How old?'

'Twenty-four. This is incredible, how'd you guess? This is
incredible, are you like psychic?'

'Yeah! You ever see a movie called *Topanga Canyon*?'

'Can't say I have, why?'

'How about *Grace and Favour*, *Inside Omaha*, *The Beverly Connection*?'

'Saw *The Connection*, yeah, wait a minute, you . . .'

'Yeah, that was me. Blonde wig, but me.'

'I can't believe this. Of all the things— I never thought—'

'You'd crash into a movie star, right?'

'Right!'

'I'm lucky you didn't kill me. You woulda had to add me to your itinerary!'

'I can't get over that you recognized I was an actor. Did you catch my showcase at the—'

'STAND BACK. STOP FLASHING! LAPD – anyone injured? Driver's licence and insurance papers, please? Are you the driver of the grey hearse limousine? If so, please return to your vehicle and switch on your emergency indicators. Stay in the vehicle till we have taken a statement. Please step out of your vehicle, ma'am.'

'I'm on the phone to a friend of mine, officer.'

'Ma'am, it's an offence to drive and mobile at the same time.'

'Look, officer, it's on speaker phone. Hands free. Vyvian, are you still on line?'

'Let me call you later, Georgia.'

'Don't move a muscle!'

'Excuse me?'

'Sorry, officer, not you, him. On line. He is a witness. You might wanna get his statement?'

'I don't think so, ma'am.'

'But he was on the phone when the crash happened.'

'That is not relevant, ma'am. Please step out of your vehicle.'

'Vy, looks like I gotta obey the law here. Do you know who I am, officer?'

'Georgia Sepulveda.'

'BULL'S-EYE!'
'You're under arrest.'

I get into a suit and tie and rip-speed east on Sunset. There is already a tailback to Le Dome, so parallel down Holloway, up Olive, and park as near to Sunset as I can get. Run. Up. I can see where it is because a copter is hovering overhead, spotlighting proceedings below. Sirens. Old folks in nightgowns, unusually craning their gizzard necks from the sidewalk (cos they generally only come out for a quake). Cacophony of car horns. Gesticulating cops. Chateau Marmontites looking down from balconies and windows. Copter wind thrashing trees. Epi-centre stage in the mangled 'manger' of her own making radiates Georgia Sepulveda: surveying her own immaculate conception and rebirth-by-publicity. A glaringly overlit Hollywood Nativity all her own. Presided over by the giant Marlboro Man cut-out. Photographer's flashing and the guy in grey chauffeur's uniform and cap posing on the hissing bonnet of his crumpled hearse. Above the noise, intermittent shouts of 'Sepulveda' from the crowd. I never get close, as they've cordoned off everything.

By the time I get back to my car, the late-night DJ is revving up some breathless 'just-in news flash' revelations, detailing a 'confirmed horror-crash on Sunset Boulevard, involving a veteran movie star in collision with a Deadline Tours limousine. Details to follow as and when they come in. The Police Department has requested drivers to avoid the area at all costs.' (Pity me her 'veteran' post-mortem diatribe.)

'Alanis Morrisette kicks off this next half-hour of non-stop music with "Isn't it Ironic?" – and we'll have more news updates for you on the Sunset crash as soon as we have it. You're listening to . . . the Koast, on—'

Dawn, and the phone buzzes – Georgia at top volume. 'Where *are* you?'

She is in as near a state of mesmerization as ever I never heard her. 'Speaking to you, Georgia.'

'When did we get cut off?'

'Bull's-eye.'

'You'll never believe this, Vy. I've been arrested,' crowed with the conviction of a born-again Jehovah's Witness. 'The guy in the other car is not pressing charges, but wouldn't you just know it, the fuckin' paparazzi have given statements claiming I was leaning out my window and gesticulating at Meryl Streep's billboard – would you believe?! – and driving in the middle of the road and causing a collision. They have gone even further and claim that they have pictures of me giving Meryl the two's-up sign, as if I would, which will be developed and on an LAPD desk within the hour. It's just insane. I REALLY identify with Diana and Dodi, let me tell you. These guys are SCUM!'

The breakfast channels are *all* covering the crash. Turns out that the chopper pilot was en route home from some assignment in the Valley and, wouldn't you know it, just happened to happen to have his video camera to hand. And a mega-sized spotlight on the undercarriage. Hovered, and handheld his way to fifteen seconds of fame. Here he is suited up and smiling his 'I couldn't believe my luck' story for *Good Morning America*.

'Vy? – put the TV on. I'm on. Or at least I'm gonna be.'

'Gotcha.'

'Can you please tell me WHERE these people get their drugs to make them THIS peppy E.V.E.R.Y. fucking morning, come hurricane or hellfire?'

'Did you get any sleep?'

'Are you kidding me? I'm in victim bathrobe mode. I'm gonna hold while I wait for myself to come on, OK?'

Looks like the pilot is not the only one handy with a camcorder. Two elderly women have different-angled footage, taken from a third-floor balcony, and yep, they're going to be on 'after these few messages'.

'JEEZUS, who ISN'T on my case? Hold on, don't go, I got someone on the other line.'

(Publicist, agent, shrink, futurist, manicurist, secretary, *National Enquirer*, lawyer, assistant, aunt, doghandler, masseuse, estranged sister, dry cleaners, wrong number?)

'You'll never believe this.'

'Try me.'

'It's my publicist *and* agent on a conference call. Both of whom I had given up for dead. I've got them on hold, I'll call you later.'

The adrenalin spritzing through her vocal cords is the verbal equivalent of Spielberg lighting. You know how his movies always look like they're going to have an ET arrival – that smoky, glowing, through-the-shutters incandescence? (Well, how else am I supposed to describe it?) The vocal equivalent is shoobedoowah silking down her cords right now. Realize just how long it's been since I last heard it. Too long. How her voice had worn itself down, along with what was left of everyone's patience. If everyone is just 'one phone call away', her calls were being relayed via the Siberian wastes. Till now. Even if the clamour is for all the wrong reasons, it's better than deep-freeze. Better than entry on the 'Where are they now?' page in *Premiere*.

I'm now running late, so excuse me while I just grab a bite and get going.

# A STAR IS BORN

Now, today you're going to meet a 'comer': Connor Child.

This year's John Grisham hero. Hasn't been around long enough to know how honeymoon-sweet things actually are for him right now. Fresh. Friendly. Foaming with prospects and smiley hopes. It's endearing for sure. Almost hokey-pure.

He saw a house I did for friends of a friend of his. (Best recommendation at twice the remove.) Please forgive my forthcoming gear change, but this is the perfect opportunity for you to observe the rules by which I operate. Turning left now.

The reason I had to leave so early was to get out here to Malibu, which at forty-five minutes is never a guaranteed clear run. But managed it, just. Misty this morning. Don't allow myself to be put off by the garage-door like façade. Most of these million-plus condos look like trailer-trash from the back. Buzz. Dog bark.

'Is that you, Vy?' (Very few call me Vyv, and certainly no male clients.)

'Morning. Hope I'm not late.'

'Not a bit. Come on in.'

I do. Be-do-be-do-waaaaaaah, 'What a view!' (Dog's is crotch up-close.)

'No kidding, good to meet you again. Down, Doug! – I'm so grateful you could make it out here so early, it's just I got a whole lotta stuff goin' on and I feel like my life is in overdrive.'

(Note the built-in assumption that mine isn't.) The 'kid' has a knuckle-buckling handshake that could only have been bred in the Midwest.

'And you want me to—'

'Make this place feel like home. I had no idea Jake and Marta's place had been *decorated*—' He italicized like it might be some contagious bubonic. I *heh heh heh*d some testosteroid support and assured him, 'That's the way I work. I'm really glad you said that, because I now have a concrete idea of what you don't want.' (Words like 'concrete', 'structure', 'architectural' and 'engineered' are talisman's talk in these situations.)

'No frills.'

And within minutes we are macho-ing forth into the uncharted waters of this near-total stranger's most intimate ebbs and flows.

'I only have about a half-hour, so why don't I show you round the place and maybe you can get some ideas.'

'Lead the way, Connor,' and up the stairs we go into the bedroom, where a fuck-off sized TV is blaring, 'Live coverage of a "situation" developing that has the nation gripped – we'll be back right after these messages. Don't go away.'

'You hear about this?'

'No, I was in the car.'

'I tell *you*, *only* in Hollywood. There's some actress had a head-on on Sunset in the middle of last night, some guy got actual footage, which they just showed, and now they've got the driver from the totalled Deadline Tours limo being interviewed. But they're getting interrupted by this actress who is honking her horn outside the studio gates hollering that it's *her* life story and everyone else is hijacking it and if they don't let her in to talk, she's gonna blow her brains out. Simultaneous criss-cross live coverage!'

'What's her name?'

'Sepulva-something. I know her face, but you know how it is. There's just so many famous people in the world now, it's hard to keep track of 'em all.'

'You bet!'

'Jeez, my old man always used to say that. That's . . . that's a good sign.'

'You bet!!'

'It's weird, it's like I've known you a long time already—Uh oh, she's *on*!'

'Welcome back. We're crossing live to the studio parking lot—'

'D'you mind watching this a second?'

'Not at all.'

'Oh boy.'

'—ulveda is holding a gun to her head and—'

'God damn it, I missed her name again.'

'Georgia Sepulveda.'

'*THAT'S* it!'

'—Anchorman Chuck is on his way over while Security is trying to negotiate with the actress – apologies for the sound, but as you can see, our microphone guy is running alongside Chuck, who let me tell you is looking amazingly fit on this beautifully clear sunny morning here in the City of Angels, and it looks like he'll be with the car any moment. Chuck, can you hear me?'

'I can, Don. Hi, guys, can I get through here?'

Chuck is being led through the crowd of onlookers, which is getting bigger by the minute as people from all over the lot are coming to look-see.

'And let's hear what she has to say, over to you, Chuck.'

'Miss Sepulveda, please wind down your window. Good morning! You're on *Good Morning America* live, and we'd love to hear your version of what happened last night!'

'What, here? In my car?'

'Would you mind lowering your weapon, it's just a, uh . . . little unnerving.'

'How can I trust you?'

'Trust me.'

'Do you have *any* idea how many times actors in this town have been asked to do that?'

'Why not come into the studio and we'll get your view proper?'

'Lemme park.'

Even Chuck, the seen-and-heard-it-all guy, is looking directly into the camera with a look of 'so what happens next?' stupefaction.

'Well, you heard it from the lady herself. I'll hand you back to Don and Laurie.'

'Thanks, Chuck – well, Laurie, she really is something, huh? Don't go away. We'll be right back with the Sunset Crash story as if unfolds, right after these messages.'

'D'you know her?' accompanies Connor's side-to-side head shake.

'We've met – now, I know you're pushed for time. I've just had an idea. If you had any old photo albums or pictures of your childhood home or anything to clue me in, then I might get a clearer idea of what it is precisely you're after.'

'No problem. I've only been in this place a coupla months, so everything is kinda upside down still, but I think they're in a box in the kitchen somewheres. Excuse the mess. What I'm really after is a sense of space and size. To bring the outside in, if you get my drift?'

'Gotcha.'

'This is *really* weird – that's exactly what my pa woulda said.'

'The structure [see?] is quite narrow, but – and this is only off the top of what you're saying – I reckon we could push through this whole front section to bring the ocean in?'

'I'm with you.'

'And possibly go up and out as well, by removing the roof, glazing it in, so that you access both sea and sky. Combining two fundamental elements from without, while within, earth and fire complement and balance everything. Yet maintaining the structural integrity of the original architecture. For instance, you might like to have a fireplace made entirely of reinforced industrial [I warned you] glass, positioned in the middle of the ocean-window – no logs or coals, just a flat sandbox with gas jets. So that for all intents and purposes – d'you mind turning the TV off? – it is almost non-visible. But when fired up, especially in the evening with the ocean backdrop, the flames will appear as if out of nowhere, like a mirage, affording a magical juxtaposition of fire *in* water. Operating as the centripetal force on all eyes that enter. But all this can be sorted in good time and perhaps it's best to do drawings and mock-up photo collages first, to give you as many options as possible. If this is vaguely in the direction you want to go?' (All the above accompanied by a veritable ballet of bold, definite, strong arm movements and marchings about. Reassures.)

'God damn it, that sounds just incredible. Man ... Jeez, incredible, no vaguely about it, YEAH!'

'In effect, a glass cabin in the sky.'

'Incredible – you just described something that has been a dream of mine for years, without even knowing it. When can we start?'

'Let's go downstairs, get the albums, I'll take some snaps. I'll have plans drawn up, and a costings estimate done and we can go from there.'

'*Gotcha!*'—expressed with the glee of Archimedes' 'Eureka!' If things seem hyperbolic, relax. Hyperbole hangs over LA like smog.

So intimatey are we, Connor leaves me, an almost total stranger, behind in his home, while he jeeps off into the fast lane of his life. I ask you, I've asked myself this many times, how do you *know* when you're well and truly *in*? You just do, don't you?

Most folks will admit to a little bathroom mirror-cabinet reconnaissance when visiting another's home, agreed? Well, imagine my pig-in-shit curiosity-fix given carte blanche to do so in the name of my trade. I call it 'reconnoitring with intent'. If Nietzsche believed 'God is in the details', then that is the altar before which I worship. But I'm also gagging to tune into the Sepulveda channel.

'—it for this morning, folks, but we'll be back same time, same place tomorrow morning with the latest and greatests, and we'll keep you posted on, what for me, has been quite an unusual morning, Laurie?'

'Thanks, Don, well, Chuck, she sure was a fiery lady—'

'Sure is, Laurie—'

'So from all of us here, take care, have a calm day and see you tomorrow—'

I switched off my mobile on the way over here, knowing that

the scriptures according to Sepulveda would be lengthily recorded for replay without my having to endure her interruptory bleeps. Not that I feel any disdain. Not at all. I have been here long enough to understand how logical the path to pressing the self-destruct button is for actors in general and Georgia in particular.

Now is *my* inhalation/exclamation time – the pre-construction, free-of-restrictions period before any work has begun. Bliss.

Free to indulge the insatiable curiosity I am blessed with. For me, there can never be enough details; it is from their myriad that the pyramid of personality is assembled and deconstructed. And I even surprise myself sometimes, with the way in which, in the midst of an all too public crisis, like right now, I have the ineffable ability to zone out and focus on the immediate project in hand. Despite the fact that I have eschewed analysis thus far, having seen the neutering results of over-shrinkage at close range. To give you a specific – I had an exceptionally emotionally deranged studio executive client, Randy Rottweil, who lost his temper more frequently than Sharon Stone changed clothes in *Casino*. Anyway, to cut a long, I expected a run-in around the high-stress time of promised construction completion (always a quagmire), to find instead this totally calm zombie persona. Randy could not wipe the mild grin off his face, no matter that the paintwork was incomplete and half the furniture had been waylaid in the Panama Canal en route from *Europe*; *nothing* ruffled the former goat-horned ram. I asked, 'Randy, what happened?' and he stretched his short arms wide and said, 'I let go. I Just Let It All Go.'

An image of a once too tightly sprung set of testicles bungee-jumping to the South Pole popped up. Without boinging back. Not unlike the severely landscaped cases of too much plastic surgery (more of which anon) where, hard as you try, it is impossible to locate any expression of the 'former' in the therapeutized 'latter'. I found myself nostalgically longing for a brief return to his old Rottweiller-self, but no, nothing seemed capable of getting a bark out of him.

Haven't you found that abusive behaviour can be quite addictive, whereas staying awake around the 'over-shrunk' is a guaranteed sedative?

I haven't seen Randy in a while, but I've heard that his calm is showing signs of wear and tear as underlings are being fired again, and his housekeeper has been enquiring as to where to get replacements for the dozen Provençal vases arranged in a straight line down the centre of the refectory table in the dining room.

Golden decorator-rule: Always befriend the domestic staff. They will never forget you for remembering their names and for admiring their diligence. You would be amazed to hear stories I've heard of staff neglect. *Every* person needs appreciation. Remember, I spend more time in some people's homes than they possibly do themselves. If you can forge a little of ye olde conspiratorials with the underlings, it oils the way to get things done. Without knipshens. I have tried my damnedest to learn even basic Spanish – staff are mostly from South America/Mexico (with the usual sprinkling of tamed Brit butlers and nannies) – quite honestly not the chic thing to speak among the masters' race. But it goes a hell of a long way 'down below'. I'm surprised, but then again not, by the absence of any staff at Connor's condo. It suggests that he is still in the pre-stratospheric Day-Glo-zone of stardom, convincing himself that 'living on the beach' is the one way to keep in touch with himself and reality. Well, think about it: you're promised, then delivered the world on a plate, paid enough money to wipe out the debt of a Third World country, and told you're shitting gold nuggets.

My contact, more often than not, begins precisely when these folk are mid-mega-flight. But when their movies flop – this is the time when *my* role becomes meaningful. (Mid-decorating, you can't afford to run away.) This is *way* beyond the 'What pattern or colour?' questions.

'What am I doing with my life and where am I going and how do I want to actually live with myself?' are the questions being asked.

My talent for *this* kind of work requires two ready-installed components – ears. Listen, listen and then, when you think there is no more listening to do, listen again. For then you will be privileged to hear true and vulnerable heartbeats.

Java Hall – screen sex kitten on the turn (37½) – has her own theory. It goes like this. Most you and Is have day-to-day schizophrenetic lives: public/private faces. But actors are required to be *four*-faced.

1. Screen face – the many metre high-rise version of themselves in 'character' and blemish-free make-up. (Unless scarred or in wheelchairs.)

2. Supermarket face – the near-as-damn-it approximation of the screen version without professional help or script. Even if in heavy cap 'n' shades disguise, they daren't look miserable, lest a lurking lens picks off a frown, causing the magazine reader to a) gloat at the imperfections b) curse them for not smiling when everyone knows how much they're getting overpaid.

3. Recognize-me-but-I'm-normal-too face – involves smiling discipline. A carefully controlled easygoin' expression that doesn't look a) smug b) stoned c) like an invitation for strangers/fans to chat d) grumpy or manically depressed.

4. Home/homey face – as you really are (albeit moisturized and buffed), the face reserved for your nearest and dearest. Note the true expression of joy at how well it's all going, even when your father/mother/relative asks, 'So what are you doing *next*?'

The naked panic and what-will-this-day-be-like-I-wonder? face is reserved for the bathroom mirror/partner/lover/spouse, who knows not to dial for a paramedic when the Dorian-Gray-in-the-attic portrait says 'Hi.'

Well, this is Java's view, and she if anyone ought to know, passing as she is through the straits of cruelty – post-sex-kitten syndrome.

'Oh, yeah?' yelps Georgia on hearing Java's 'confession' about her age on *Oprah*. '*That* old cat still has fat bones of employment to chew over with her collagen-blown lips. Bones of her ass?—my *ass*. I can't listen to this.' But she does. *We* do, midway through discussing a new colour scheme she has in mind for her bathrooms.

Georgia seems increasingly not to notice any difference between interacting with a live person and someone on TV, quite confidently joining the proceedings in a three-way. This particular session involved my having to restrain her from actually kicking the screen in, which she managed – just – when I reminded her that the insurers swore that after the previous three were replaced, 'That's it.' Which only made her swing round at me and *demand* that I agree with her.

'About what?' – my focus having gone soft.

'*HER!* For Chrissakes. Sometimes I don't think you're keepin' up, Vy. C'mon!'

'What'd she say? Forgive, I was looking at these paint samples.'

'What she *always* says. You have got to go, Vy. I'm sorry, but I'm overheating, I can feel it happening. I don't wanna jeopardize our friendship, but honestly if you can't even listen to basics, I don't know why-which-what-for we're gonna carry on working together.'

This is deep breath time: leave the samples neatly in a row, fold the folders and discreet oh so discreetly out through the door, knowing that before my ignition is once-over'd my mobile will bleat, and that by the time I have reversed in the driveway she'll be standing on the porch, miming her inner turmoil, while neglecting to notice that her words are Sony clear and her Marcel Marceauing mere dumbshow.

'I'll call you,' she mouths, whispering too ferociously down the line.

Why do I put up with this? You know how it is when you've been friends for some years, you go beyond the 'beyond reasonable doubt' stage? She first employed me when her career was going such guns that she thought she didn't need a guy, didn't need anyone to get in the way of her Stalin-for-Stardom five-year plan, didn't want a family – 'When do I have the time, Vy?' – and never had to live a day that wasn't Filofixed.

The ebb and flow of 'friends' in times of fat and flux is so profound in its extremities that there were precious few of us left after her nuclear fallout. (Read: movie actress at the wrong end of her forties.)

I warned her that withdrawal symptoms were inevitable and suggested she get her shrink to help prepare the way, but in the first few weeks she refused to believe it. 'This *always* happens after you get Oscar-nommed. Look what happened to Faye.'

'Who?'

'Jeez, Vy!—Dunaway, who d'you think?'

'But she won in 76.'

'There's no need to rub it in. And don't be so fucking pedantic. My point is, that even though she won, her career went into dead-cat mode. That's not the point. The point is that whether you get nommed or gonged, everyone assumes you must be booked for the next year, so my point is, is that this is normal, that's all.'

Her reality checked in so ruthlessly, and the miniaturized core of her actual friends was so small, she decided to 'expand and reward' herself, 'after all these years of giving, giving, giving' by adopting a baby. 'Someone who will love me, just for me.'

Manless, but moneyed, she found a lawyer and bought one. What precipitated this momentous decision was *Vanity Fair*. (The October '95 Denzel Washington issue, to be precise.)

The magazine was the one 'fix' she could not bring herself to relinquish, despite the stern advice of her shrink ('It'll only tip you over'). Every month, crisp as crackers, it would deliver the bad news of someone else's meteoric ascent, instantly provoking an outbreak of Tourette's syndrome. Her housekeeper knew to get her toddler (Scarlett) out of the way before Georgia began frothing her way through the prose profile, which she assured herself was as good as scream-therapy – 'Only a fuck of a lot cheaper!'

No, for once, rather than ranting, she was initially assuaged by Denzel's broody cover picture, thought he was a 'worthy and true talent' (though in fairness to Denz, the fact that he is male was a significant reason for her preternatural calm in contrast to her mood swings whenever sighting Demi, Meg or Nicole and the gang). But much as she fancied Mr Washington, who had complimented her with 'affecting sincerity' during his 'on-the-way-up years', what really wobbled her aminobenzoic acids was a comment 'made by Julie bloody Andrews, if you please.' Julie Andrews had allegedly moaned to her therapist something along the lines of, 'How many more years can I take doing this showbiz stuff, do I need this, am I ever satisfied?' to which the shrunken reply was, 'Maybe it's because you love it too much?'

MAYBE. IT'S. BECAUSE. YOU. LOVE. IT. TOO. MUCH.

These eight words transmogrified her every sense. Spoke to her direct. 'The Sound of Music of my soul,' was all she could gasp, before being overwhelmed (like Julie) by a volcanic eruption of tears. All over again, when retelling it to me.

'You read this in Vanity Fair?' I asked.

'I've had them engraved, Vy – those eight words. On everything.' She had.

Back to Connor. One scrappy box contained every picture of his pre-Hollywood life. (In case you're wondering if I've ever been tempted to call People magazine or the National Enquirer with such spoils – never. I'm a hoarder.) Here's his mom, dead pa, brother and sisters, horses and all manner of hoe-down on the farm. Sports scholarship certificates, medals, ribbons, his whole life. About to be exchanged for what at best can only ever be a half-life. If he's lucky.

The 'trade' word on him is that he has 'a quality'. Now if, by chance, you are not intimately acquainted with this term, it covers a multitude of options, best boiled down to 'that certain something'. Nothing specific, mind, but bluntly put: 'Men wanna be him; women wanna bed him.' That's the bottom-line aim of his agent/manager/publicist/studio banking big doughball.

The will-he-won't-he? factor will be determined by just how much home-on-the-range integrity he can hold on to in the face of the onslaught ahead. Natural beauty is his insurance at the moment. Likewise, an equally natural absence of any real intelligence, which will be crucial in helping him navigate the swamps of paranoia and piranha press to port and starboard.

Yet he has 'country-smarts', a no-messing-about, from-the-hip persona that is precisely what transmits on screen and chat shows. Going a long way to make up for his lack of business slithy tove and gymble. This is his 'quality'.

Now that I think about it, the fact that he is so stupendously ignorant of most actors' work/history/legend (excepting Clint's) is what so endears him to studio executives. Unthreatening in every way. Comfy as the cowboy chaps he habitually wears. Like this morning. Likewise in the Annie Leibovitz photo-portfolio in this month's issue of *Life*.

Truly a case of pictures speaking louder than words. There aren't any. A brilliant publicity coup. To date, he's only done one chat-show performance, in which he so 'dumb-blonded' Letterman that the gap-toothed maestro misinterpreted his 'duh' replies for wit, and found himself dancing arm-in-arm with Connor, as a consequence of his off-the-cuffing, 'So I guess you know some square dances, country boy?'

In a trice, Connor had him in his grip, resolutely demonstrating the rudimentary steps, utterly oblivious to the potential slur on his masculinity. That was up to Dave, who grimaced and pouted hetero-reassurances to the audience while being whisked around the floor, with mucho heavenward eye-rollings and 'what me?' wonderments, to the impromptu accompaniment of the studio band and foot-stomping, hand-clapping approval from the audience. Concluding with a manly display of 'Arnie' handshakes. For insurance. Place went berserk. As did Connor's dog, who was also on the show.

My brief meeting with Connor this morning is so neurosis-free that I find myself briefly 'stalled' on the edge of his sofa, stroking Doug (his German shepherd/Labrador mongrel) while assimilating this aberrant behaviour. My 'mmmmm' settles for the 'stoopid' option. 'Must be dumb . . .?' Reinforced by my examination of the family photos. What jumps out (and this is not that uncommon with celebrity lineage) is a genetic conundrum – *how* could *these* two have mated and produced *that* anatomically perfect specimen? You can discern traces of each parent in their son, but contrasted with his siblings, he is a genetic freak. They all look like they got the wrong bits (and mostly trailer-trash leftovers at best). But then, he can't be *that* dumb, surely not? These are the questions intersecting my measurement-takings of each room, keenly watched by Doug, who goes apoplectic as the phone rings. Barks his way over to the answer machine, flops down, and cocks an ear.

'Doug? Doug Doug Dougie dog! It's your daddy and I won't be lo-oooong!' The dog, I'm not kidding you, rolls over onto its back and lets forth a werewolf howl.

This is the second time today I find myself taking seated refuge on his sofa's edge. The overwhelming desire to share this information with someone other than Marga (who has *no* interest) is pretty steep. This is the devil's temptation of my work and its heavenly reward in one. I know I have to get back to measuring when my thoughts start matchmaking Doug's master with a poodle I know's mistress.

Irresistible, though, don't you think, to be party to answerphone intimacies even if canine, without anyone knowing? I have at times been accused of having an unwipeable Cheshire cat grin in certain social circumstances, simply because I have had access to what an *actual* domestic situation is, rather than its public persona. Voyeur? *C'est moi. Finis.*

You have been warned, so if you're feeling prone to self-righteous revulsion – revolt and au revoir.

Connor's glass cabin in the sky is a project to cherish. As is Doug, whose health and safety is destined for 'high-priority' status with Connor's management. His chat-show partnership, barks and all, is a publicity asset to be 'built upon' and possibly 'product endorsed'. I could sense someone somewhere saying out loud, 'Hey, you know what, Herb Ritts is passionate about dogs – let's put Herb and Doug together for a photoshoot and headline: CONNOR'S "CHILD" – A MAN'S BEST FRIEND, no words, just pictures, cos Connor's that kinda guy.'

And so it came to pass.

★

Back on the coast road, heading for Santa Monica, I wonder: dare I call in for message playback? For the conclusion to the Sepulveda Saga – or perhaps just scramble to the last message? Uh oh, the tape is full. Do I, don't I? Connor's the catch of the day, so what the hell . . . opt for a random sampling midway through and tune into some hysterical police dept. wranglings of the 'Do you not know who I am?' variety. Fast forward to the end and rewind for her finale.

'Vy, where *ARE* you, man?! You will never believe this. I've got calls from people *I'd* taken for dead. This crash is my comeback. Call.' Click.————

Call my trusty dealers, Harold and Tony, to secure as many antique kennels, in all sizes, as soon as possible. They never ask questions. I always provide answers. Perfect. My synaptic-gap shortened: go 'dog'. 'In fact, include sculptures, paintings, figurines, but no taxidermy.' Done.

Drop films, measurements and rough sketches off at the office to be processed and computerized (Nikki's domain), drive via the craft workshop to check on the Buchinskys' table, buy sushi, answer calls (except Georgia's), get home, fall asleep and am awoken by Marga's hands massaging my neck. Transfer to her trestle-table for relaxation and her post-masseuse-mortem of the day.

Seems that the Letterman dog-and-dance routine triggered off wide-ranging reactions from various mutual clients.

What I still can't get over is that because of Marga's public deaf and dumb act, clients tell her *everything*, secure in her 'silence'. Seem grateful to be listened to, and only occasionally wonder out loud what percentage of sounds are picked up by her hearing aid. This prop was her idea, in response to folk trying to test just how deaf she actually was. Such is her self-imposed commitment to silence in public that her nightly conversation seems to be increasingly cryptic.

'Vyv? Doug – why?'

'What have you heard?'

'Non-stop. Client-gripe – actors.'

'Specifically?'

Her usual Morse swelled into whole sentences – all about the dog – why the hell didn't *I* think of a pet as a publicity *ploy*, *everyone* is talking about it, sort of thing.

'What's your speculation, Margs?'

She rubs some peppermint oil into her palms, Lady Macbeths her pause up a bit, then dead-eyes me with: 'Gonna be a run on Sheps and Labs. Invest.' Turns and goes into the bathroom, leaving me nursing this verbal bomb, *knowing* just how much I dislike pets in general, and large farty dogs in particular. Knowing that the opportunity of sniffing out a business angle will keep me whirring away too late into the night. Must persuade Connor to let me design the dog's publicity campaign. Make a note to call first thing. Marga, en route to bed, relays— 'Randy says he's gonna pitch *Rin Tin Tin: The Return*, as *Die Hard 4: The Dogs*. For Doug. G'night.'

'Hold on a minute, you worked Randy *today*?'

'Last call.'

'He say anything about the broken Provençal vases?'

Can't see the point of caring, so she doesn't answer.

'Margs?'

'What?'

'You're beautiful, you know?'

'Stop it.'

'You can't keep this up. It's been fifteen years. Relent for once. Have your dermabrasion done. It's what we came here for. You're beautiful. Forsake the mask.'

'Vyvian, we've been through this a hundred times. I've told you before – the day someone falls in love with me, pockmarks and all,

66

will be the day I book in for surgery. I don't care how many years I have to wait.'

'Marga, nobody even knows what you look like behind that damned thing. Nobody's ever heard you speak, apart from me. You've cut down your options really drastically.'

'Precisely. Whoever wants me will want *me*, deaf, dumb, mask and all. He will be the *one*.'

'But you're living the life of Rapunzel!'

'That's my choice. Everything in this place is based on image. It's why you're as rich and successful as you are. I want someone and something that's beyond all that. Goodnight.'

'You might end up an old maid.'

'So be it.'

'Goodnight.'

Shower and flick through the faxes and e's and see Georgia's.

MARGA — 11TH HR. CANCELLATION. FORGIVE. MY LIFE IS NEWS. LOVE G.S.

Channel surf, pondering the last time La Sepulveda *ever* conversed with such cryptogrammatic economy. Probably her trio of 'I Do's.' To bed.

To dream a scheme for Randy's refectory table, possibly a phalanx of antique kennels, starting small and getting bigger. Making a 'statement'. All that remains is to convince him that it is his idea in the first place so that it becomes a natural conversation piece, an extension of his personality. Calling him 'quirky' never fails to get him quietly ecstatic. *This* is my synaptic-snap. Sleep.

# THE MIRROR HAS TWO FACES

'I want his sperm.'

'Java! It's five a.m.'

'Isn't it beautiful? So quiet. So calm. It's the *best*!'

'Whose sperm?'

'The cowboy on Letterman. D'you see it?'

'Yes.'

'The dog was adorable. He's the guy we've all been waiting for. I reckon if he treats his *dog* like that, I'd be prepared to lick *his* balls any ol' time.'

'Can't this wait till dawn?'

'I called everybody else and nobody knows the guy. But I know you must?'

'Java, I'm going back to sleep. I'll call in daylight.' Click. Unplug fast.

Slip back into slumber? About as much chance as Malcolm McDowell had in *A Clockwork Orange* when he had his eyes prised open with those miniature forceps. Walk about the darkened house, onto the terrace, wondering what daymares lie ahead for the inhabitants. No wonder *The X-Files* are big. Their mutants make movie stars seem human.

I'm just going to get my laptop file opened to remind myself of my most recent encounters of the worst kind with Java Hall. Scrolling down fast through some old stuff. Here we are:

> Java had persuaded me to pay a flying visit (she paid) to a remote location in Canada where she was filming something in period costume. 'At least my ass won't be visible beneath the bustle,' was her quipped reason for accepting the role. My brief

– to discuss details of the remodelling of her guest house. Met by her driver and taken directly to the set and into make-up where I was told to await her arrival 'as she is running late on account of personal problems'. This information *sotto voce*d to me by an anxious-faced second assistant. If you want to assess the emotional temperature of a film set, I suspect there is no better place to divine the level of mercury than the make-up trailer.

Brenda Bowen is *in situ*. Hers is a face many people recognize but haven't a clue where from. That is her tragedy. Which she plays out in five acts wherever and whenever she can. She is a sixty-something 'character actress' (euphemism for 'too ugly for leads') who has played a couple of nannies in her past, now doing so for real for Java, who has engineered her casting in this picture for two reasons. Firstly, she is a surrogate mother-figure and fulfils the needs of Java and her four-year-old daughter, Mona. Secondly, she unofficially acts as an entourage of one; fatter, older and much uglier than Java (even at her worst), she always makes Java feel and, crucially, *look* better.

As I entered the make-up bus, I refrained from going beyond the makeshift curtain dividing the interior from the driver's seat (this being a no-budget production) because Brenda was mid-scourge. From which I gleaned she was playing a housekeeper – 'With only about a dozen lines – *me*, a veteran of over a hundred features, I ask you! And d'you know who I blame? – YOU! – You fockin' [left Ireland in her youth] bitches! And the reason for that is that it's fockin' bitches like you who *never* accentuate my best features – always make me look the same which is why I never got the leading roles.'

Totally serious. Totally barking. In the arctic silence, I chose to pop my head through and caught the zipped expressions of the make-up and wig gals, in their midriff-sporting twenties, clearly mystified by this old goat's rage at the dying of her light. The instant Brenda clocked me, purged of her bile, she was all sweetness and smiles and colleen-quiet guiles and 'What, me? Oh, don't trouble yourselves' asides. Relayed a lengthy saga of how Mona's natural father ('not natural to me, if you're askin'') has been on the phone all night harassing Java about visiting rights. Hence her absence from warpaint duties this morning.

Assistants were headless-chickening their way back and forth between the production office caravan, catering and make-up trailers, in mobile-phone pursuit of her expected arrival time.

When she did appear, it was a sorry, puffed-up sight. A million miles away from the drop-dead-gorgeous and give-her-a-contract image she projected in her first film, *Ashes and Embers*, fifteen years ago.

The time it had taken me to get up here didn't even merit a 'So how was your trip?', such was the nuclear fallout of her family and career. She declared, 'I am in a crisis of beauty,' at her reflection as she slumped into the chair, initiating an 'all hands on deck' scrum of artisans committed to salvaging whatever they could before the schedule slipped further into old age.

Just thirty-six, having coasted through twenty leading roles of questionable quality, notable, more often than not, for how many times she slung off her bra, she now faced the terrors of playing 'the Mother'. Of a spectacularly gorgeous twenty-year-old who had just entered the bus for final make-up checks.

'Christ, I look like a woman of thirty.'

No sooner had the soubrette been powdered down and out the door than Java inhaled too loudly and let loose a roar of tears and rage, accompanied by contorted facial contractions requiring emergency replastering and paintwork from the team, ice packs and New Age music.

The irony, of course, is that the character she had been cast to play was suffering this precise sea change herself. But we all have our mirror face, and she was incapable of accepting the truth.

'Last role I was the sex kitten, this one I'm the old cat.'

Finally, after much miaowing and pawing, she was led to the set, where the director was rehearsing the ingenue in the most intimate one-to-one mode this side of actually licking her all over. Announced, 'Right. Let's go for a take!' prompting Java to yodel, 'What about me?'

His eyes momentarily flickered recognition of her existence, looked quizzical and decided, 'No, you're just fine,' turned on his Cuban heels and moseyed towards the monitor.

She managed to make it halfway through the take, succumbed to internal pressures and combusted. He of course was clueless as to why she was causing such a heap of fuss and declared, 'We'll take five.' While we entouraged back into the trailer for round three of Ms Hall's horrors.

'I will fuck *anyone* who wants me – drawing the line at married men,' was the rhetorical statement she uttered over the heads of the four supporting actors currently being prepped. Eyelids flickered and froze when she confirmed: 'I haven't had a fuck in four years. Not since Mona was born. To be exact.' Not that we were asking. The nineteen-year-old blushed visibly (this being his first day), any star-struck proximity compromised by this real-life threat. In them, she had a captive audience, which is what saved her day. I watched, riveted, as Java deployed her vast arsenal of seductions, like an overused spider. Spinning up interest. Beauty had always been her power base, ergo the panoply of eyelid flutterings and dulcet-toned orders that have successfully commandeered suites, men, service, cash, contracts and attention – till now.

Her sell-by date was up, and everything was now underpinned by questions of 'But can she really act?' which her beauty had so far enabled her to transgress. Her ageing sex kitten scenario went beyond mere director dismissal and suggested neglect on a profoundly cosmic scale for the puss.

'What we all need is a joint!' accompanied her finger-wagging command to pass over her bag. Lit up, inhaled deeply, then stood and planted her lips on the nineteen-year-old's and exhaled. We all watched as his eyes bulged and his lungs heaved. Accepting and rejecting her offer in a coughing fit.

'You've just been kissed by Java Hall on day one, and it's not even ten o'clock yet,' was her triumphant declaration.

'Attagirl, there's life in the ol' boiler yet,' bulleted from my maw, and silenced all.

One, two, three, four, five – and her stunned expression erupted into laughter, mercifully taken up by the chorus, and in that instant I realized that teasing her was a totally foreign concept. Was this the route to her salvation? She checked with her shrink over the phone during lunch. Affirmative. The director thanked me that evening 'for doing the magic'. Flew home. Potentially insulting a client in public is not my usual modus vivendi, but if the boxing glove fits . . .?

Click. Save. Switch off. Dawn.

7.40 a.m.: mid-Granola munching, Georgia is on line one. 'Morning. D'you hear the news? I've been asked to do Jay Leno's show tonight! Love you. Bye.' Nikki has faxed a list of missed calls, most of which concern yesterday's crash and when replied to will no doubt cover tonight's resurrection. Confirming my view that everyone knows everything.

Line two – Mr Buchinsky: 'Vy, it's Mort, listen, I know this is not strictly business, but whaddya know about Georgia Sepulveda – Kitty said she thought you might have done some work for her?'

'Good to hear your voice, Mort, yes, I do know her a little – how can I help?'

'I'm in the middle of casting my next picture and Kitty says she'd be perfect for one of the roles, but to be honest with you, I can't remember what she looks like exactly – is she the one who looks like Karen Black's sister if she had one?'

'*Topanga Canyon* is her calling card.'

'Yeah, yeah, I know, but I jus' can't remember her too clearly. Has she had a lotta surgery since then?'

'I wouldn't say so.'

'Kitty taped some stuff off the news, but she pressed the wrong channel, so all I got was dolphin footage. Sorry to bother you so early.'

'Not at all, it's always a pleasure to talk with you. I saw your table yesterday – it should be ready by next weekend.'

'What table?' – Line blanks momentarily – 'I'm gonna put you on to Kitty.' Click over.

'Hi, honey,' Kitty's voice is two octaves below basso profundo, 'don't mind Mort, he's in pre-production and *nothing* gets through. And I've been married to him for thirty-two years. I saw the coverage of that Sunset crash and her interview on *Good Morning* and she is *perfect* for Mort's movie. Even though he doesn't know it yet. He just can't remember who she is. I told him *Topanga*, but he just blanked, so I thought if anyone could help, it'd be you.'

'Wasn't she in *The Lotus Eaters* that he directed?'

'Oh my God, but that was thirty-four years ago. Oh my God, of *course* she was.'

'I think she's with ICM.'

'You're a doll. I'll have him call Jeff.'

You might be wondering whether I spend all my time on the phone – I do. It's a phoney culture. Whereas any other city has a centre of sorts, LA doesn't. The sprawl is so vast that with all the driving you have to get through, the phone is symbiotic. At every level. The network of actors' phone lines (numbering one to multiples depending on which rung they are clinging to), connected to their agents, managers and therapists, would resemble Gulliver, in his strapped-to-the-ground position, criss-crossed with cord.

Daily, these invisible lines conduit so many variations of humiliation of the 'I'm so sorry, but it's just not gonna work' type, that I can only conclude thespians are fitted up with sadomasochistic DNA. I have not found any other explanation for this phenomenon. If you don't believe me, think back to any Oscar acceptance speeches, personality profiles, chat shows – they are veritable rollcalls of rejection, reworked into anecdote. 'I've been so lucky, if he hadn't fallen down dead, I never would've gotten this break, just happened to be in the right place at the . . . through bad times and good, I never stopped believing, everyone has been so loyal, I'd like to thank at least ninety-seven people by name, you know who you are, if it wasn't for my family, and just in case, I wanna thank God.' I think I can hear Lionel Ritchie tuning up, or is that Whitney Houston about to shatter glass?

My experience of designing for actors is that as much as they feel compelled to thank Mahatma and the multitudes, they *know* that no one else got them 'there' other than themselves. The naming of names is the equivalent of placing offerings to appease the gods for hubris.

My approach is this: every successful actor possesses a unique 'talent'. You don't see it, so much as feel it. Mine, you see. Of which I ask – 'How do you price my eye?' I like to put it like this to them: 'This is your home, your money, your vision, your dream – hire my eyes like midwives.' Money is never discussed. I have a set consultation fee, and then Nikki draws up an estimate which is sent to the client's business manager, accountant, lawyer, whoever. I never sign a formal contract. Drives their lawyers nuts. 'How can we do business with you?' they regularly yell down Nikki's line. Appreciate that this city has a concentration of mega-wealth that out-sultans Brunei. And an army of lawyers to contract and get everything on the dotted line. 'But what if we wanna sue you?' they whine.

That's precisely it. I can walk away. At any time. I've had clients who don't want to pay— 'What's in an eye?'

Walk away. Makes 'em real mad. No amount of money or threat can change you. Call it honour, integrity, talent – what you will. Ironically, actors are the first to recognize these parallels. Except they have to sign their dotted lines. And just as they have to love the character they're cast to play, likewise I aim to fall in love with their home like it was my own. I've had clients ask in all seriousness, 'Am I allowed this?' as if the Style Police were about to impound the item in question, to which I always reply, 'That is a question no client of mine should ever have to ask.' Which is not to say that I am not faced with interior-horrors on a daily basis. I am. Galvanizing all my persuasive powers to rid houses of their owner's abhorrentia, sans insult, is my art form. Especially difficult when a client is colour-blind. The 'I love that red' guys, who, however many variations of the spectrum from dark brown through to pale orange you offer up, resolutely assert, 'But they're *all* red.' Think Kissinger, 'The Persuaders', Carter, Moses – any of the great negotiators – and you'll get a glimpse of what a trick it takes to get them retuned to my tastes.

An indispensable word is 'osmosis' – 'Making *your* life better makes *my* life better. So let's begin by auctioning off some of your less treasured items [kitsch monstrosities] to make room for new masterpieces.' Practically speaking, it's either Sotheby's or Butterfields auction dumping houses or actual charity/trash dumpsters. Requires some sensitivity. Not unlike clearing cupboards of the dead. In particularly delicate cases, it's best to put the junk into storage, replace it with something beautiful and in no time memory has rearranged and dispensed with what was once 'irreplaceable'. Sound philosophical? It works.

My singular triumph has been the inclusion of a 'memory room'. This is a room of modest proportions, hidden from all public access. (Modest simply because most actors tend not to be born into wealth, and making space to honour their humble beginnings is something to which most of them respond.) Within which their past is contained. Tangible keepsakes. It requires some discipline in that every item has to be particularly charged with memory to merit inclusion – or that's what I recommend – be it a chair, bed, print, piece of fabric, toy or chotchke. In the non-celebrity home, for the most part, the past forms part of the accumulated itinerary. Sure, stuff gets discarded, but there are always objects that you can date all the way back. Every home has its Little Shop of Horrors.

The celebrity home is almost never like that. If anything, the past is erased or reconceived in nostalgic rosy-glowing terms. The reason for this is to do with scale. If for instance you are dragged up in a trailer park and within eins–zwei–drei years of leaving you find yourself being paid millions to star opposite Sandra Bullock, chances are that your Winnebago is going to be bigger than the house on wheels your entire family grew up in. Flying ducks, crocheted toilet-roll covers, ceramic dogs, cocktail-drink umbrellas and Uncle Andy's matchbook collection are not going to make it into the bigtime rooms you now have at your disposal.

It was while working with a young client, panic-stricken at the thought of having to fill his new home, that I suggested the creation of a Memory room, rather than just dumping his four boxes of possessions in storage. Hence my asking Connor for his photo albums. At best, these hidey-holes can be places of meditation, wherein a client may trace her/his route from nowhere to somewhere. And they are particularly useful if visited by folk from the distant past, who are always Dobermann-keen to sniff out whether their lives are still connected to yours. It's a form of modesty-insurance. No one can accuse you of severing ties. Even if they sneetch that your past is kept under lock and key, the very fact of its display reassures. Helps too in ballasting the overwhelm experienced by the non-celebrity entering the halls of Holly-Halla.

My other genius is for scale. The nouveau fortune sings a one-line lyric: 'It's gotta be bigger and better than this!'—NOT. In my experience. Which is that you can only eat so many meals, sleep in so many beds and visit so many bathrooms in a day. A fourteen-bathroom house is no happier than your regular two- or three-. Keeping things intimate is my most common challenge. Unless a client is insistent on a dining room that seats thirty-six, I try and guide them towards a series of smaller interconnecting rooms that get used, rather than showpiece caverns that get visited twice a year like old people in homes.

This too is dependent on the size of the star entourage. If a family of four is multiply attended at all times by payrolled relatives, assistants, walkers and talkers, laughers and cocktail makers, chances are you're going to need the fourteen flushers. Chances are I'm going to get fucked over by too many cooks spoiling for broth.

Two areas that defy this diktat are crucially male-dominated interests: art and sound systems. Men will spend *anything* to achieve state-of-the-art sound. In the pool, up a tree, down a chimney, under-floor, anywhere and everywhere. Whenever I encounter prejudice regarding the machismo quotient of my work, I segue into Sony's latest, and it's guaranteed boy-bonding time: industrial, hardcore, solid, black, shiny with plenty of twirly knobs; fat instruction manuals, wires, plugs, tweeters, drums, volume density and multiple control panels that seem light-years away from fabric and wall colour coordinates.

The collision of Man and his femininity manifests itself perfectly in Art. Big-buck collections spread throughout the home proclaim an artistic sensitivity (crucial to mega-loaded producers unable to sing a note, write a line or act – even woodenly) and investment sensibility. A smart collection stamps prestige on a home, wherein publicly acknowledged masterpieces are privately housed. And on its master. No matter how extensive and expensive the index, you are guaranteed never to be accused of ballroom vulgarity or multiple pool and tennis court excesses. Art = Class.

More significantly, it can be traded and upgraded endlessly. There truly is no limit. Publicize that it is destined for museum public domaindom post death and you're halfway to canonization in your breathing years. Its other attribute is 'enigma'. Like perfume, it imbues the possessor with mystery and unmined depths of intellect and passion. Never mind the crater in your doughball of dollars. My art historian guise has proved an invaluable calling card.

My other innovation is the Press Pond. Again, this idea, like the Memory room, was prompted by my being in the house of an actor on the day that bad news faxed, e'd and delivered itself in every media form into his home: diabolical reviews. For a project he believed in and supported with religious zeal from its inception as a one-page article in the *New Yorker* through the development hell of scripting and raising finance, getting greenlit, filmed, distributed and critically dumped on the day of its nationwide release. Killed before any punter had even paid for a multiplex ticket. Not a good day to be remodelling interiors at some expense.

I found him squatting in the lotus position beside an ornamental pond, whose fountain I had wandered over to inspect, desultorily plopping pebbles into the pool and intoning a mantra— 'Fucking sticks and stones can break your bones, but words can never harm you,' to which I interjected, 'I totally disagree with that. I've always thought it should go, "Sticks and stones? You can fix your bones, but words will always harm you."' He looked at me as if I was Solomon and said, 'Yeah,' really slowly, really quietly.

I asked for the name of his worst critic, picked up a pebble from his pile and offered him my felt-tipped indelible marker pen from my top pocket. Without a word, he wrote the offending name on the pale stone, threw it into the water, leaned forward and watched as it sank into the green slime. Looked up, smiling with epiphanic gratitude.

# ONE FLEW OVER THE
# CUCKOO'S NEST

I wonder what's happening at Sepulveda Central? After what you've heard from her already, you could be forgiven for wondering whether she is in fact nearing destitution. Not a bit of it. Despite having entered the Sahara desert years of her career, she has had the sense to marry three seriously rich men in a row, each even more dysfunctional than she. Their departures were blueprints of one another. Each paid her substantial, and I mean superstantial, alimony, conditional on her never attempting to contact any of them. No matter how desperate her future circumstances might be, on no account were any of these three victims ever to be pursued. Roy, her last licensee, contemplated face-altering surgery, lest he accidentally bump into her somewhere. But there was little chance of this happening, as they were, curiously, all in the rag trade, so their social paths never crossed.

'You are Chaos Theory personified!' was Roy's parting shot.

Not that you could have discerned this from the house itself, which is an immaculate Spanish villa on three levels, with terraced gardens, small olive grove and Press Pond, the piles of pebbles bearing the names of all who have done her wrong resembling so many pyramids.

Apart from the three-metre-tall iron gates inscribed with a giant-sized 'S' among the metal filigree, there is nothing to denote any notion of disorder as you approach the house. As you enter, there is a full-length portrait of Georgia to greet you, painted in Rockwell realist style, which has the unsettling effect of making visitors feel as if there is no place to hide. Her painted eyes seem to follow you everywhere. Then, above the curved staircase rail, guarding the first-floor landing, is another huge portrait, Lempicka style. Each painting is perfectly lit, day and night. The round centre table in the hall, groaning under a Leviathan of flowers, is also home to a field of framed portraits of baby Scarlett. The short passageway through to the living room is crammed from floor to ceiling with portraits of her mother, from every magazine cover she ever graced, giving you a visual trip through the seven ages of Sepulveda. Her fireplace is guarded by her life-sized sculpture, in bronze, while on the coffee table her bust stands sentry, in head-tossed-back mode, as though the rest of her body were imprisoned within the wood below. Just when you thought it was safe to sit down, the sight seen as you face the west wall is a Warhol multiple silk screen of her face in every colour variation he ever produced. Far from being persuaded to distribute these throughout the house, her instruction to me way back when was to group them together 'for maximum impact', to which I responded by suggesting a grid of recessed spotlights each in a different colour according to the dominant colour of the print, with the result that the pink is pink lit, the red, red and so forth, giving the overall a vibrancy and colour density that overpowers everything else. 'That's *exactly* what I wanted.' Are you getting the idea?

The guest bathroom is wallpapered with her signature, repeated in multiples as a pattern. Writ large. I should point out here that this is a highly unusual interior style – the ME ME ME look. For the most part, the actors with whom I work quite consciously avoid anything that smacks of self-promotion. Even the Oscar winners discreet their statuettes on a bookshelf or mantelpiece. Whereas Georgia, had she won one, would doubtless have had it enshrined centre stage and laser-lit. Her home is a shrine to the cult of her self. You might assume this is an ego in overdrive, but knowing her as I do what mitigates everything is her chronic lack of confidence. This personality cocktail about sums up the genetics of most thespians: large ego, low self-esteem.

'If I can't see evidence of myself, then who the hell else will?' trails her conversation like vapour.

★

Outside her gates is a chaos of cars, including television vehicles with satellite dishes on top and cables snaking up the drive. Security hulks on walkie-talkies waving me away. Wind down the window and it's 'Move along, please, sir.'

'I'm a friend of Ms Sepulveda's.'

'Sure you are, please move along, sir.'

Do so and finger the mobile. Motor away from the gates and park next to the ubiquitous no parking signs. Ring the house. Engaged. The housekeeper – engaged. Her mobile – 'Please leave your message.' Bleep.

This is too good to miss. Must be. The house hasn't seen this much activity since Serena McKinley overdosed here in the early seventies. No option but to walk it. With a large wallpaper sample book from the back seat.

'Good morning, I'm under contract to the owner. Interior design. I'd be very grateful if you could radio the housekeeper to verify my credentials.' (What the hell *are* you s'posed to say, especially as Georgia's gates are known to her friends as 'Open Sesame'.)

'What's your name?'

'Vyvian Cork.'

His left eyebrow has Roger Moored north.

'Excuse me?'

'Vyvian Cork – as in bottle-stopper.'

He can barely suppress his guffaw when he crackles through to the house. 'I got a guy here calls himself Cork.' *Heh heh heh*ing into the plastic. Luckily, Miguel is on the other end and vouches for me. He and his wife Maria operate as gardener and housekeeper and most significantly as surrogate parents to Scarlett.

The Moore eyebrows are now fighting each other into a disappointed frown. He reluctantly points his walkie-talkie at me, then prods it in the direction of the house, just as the Home of the Stars tour bus rears into view, stargazers' eyes all saucering towards the live action.

Walk up the winding drive towards the front door, which is ajar and jammed with people and lights. Smartly dressed sprites who can't get a look in are pacing the lawn on mobiles. *Awesome*s and *unbelievable*s assail the air. Make my way through the door beyond the garage and enter via the kitchen.

'Oh, Señor Vyvian!' hand on hearts Maria, her emotions in confusion as to how to react to all this action. 'So many cups of coffee for so many people. Señora Georgia she very h'exciting.'

'You will go straight to heaven, Santa Maria. No question.'

'Oh, Señor Vyvian.' She is nearing imminent tearfall.

'Where's Scarlett?'

'Scarlett, she with Miguel in poolhouse. Better there.'

'Good, I'm going to go up the back stairs to the landing and I'll be down to help you in no time. Lock the garage door.'

Belt up the narrow service stairs and slow down upon hearing Georgia holding forth below in the oval entrance hall, which is klieg-bright with TV lights. Ease my way forward so as not to be seen by the press pack below.

'You see I've fallen from Grace and Flavour,' prompts over-generous laughter from her audience, during which I prostrate myself and inch forward in *Full Metal Jacket* mode till I can just spy the proceedings. Which look like this: wall to wall press, photographers, microphones, lights, TV cameras, all of them vortically fixed on Georgia, seated centre stage, in front of her vast portrait. The revolver, revolving idly in her left hand, redefines the phrase 'a captive audience', giving this impromptu press conference a unique frisson. For once, the pack look genuinely respectful, as one would when faced with a live, unscripted actress toying with a loaded weapon.

'Is this what it takes? I'm asking you,' she fires to no one in particular. Again, the laughter is that tad too forthcoming, like the canned stuff they hit every joke with on new comedy pilots.

'I know why you're here. I know what you're thinking. You think I'm some dumb cockamamie lost-it-in-the-last-quake saggy-faced old maybe-been – don't interrupt – star of *Topanga Canyon* gone gaga who's gonna blow her brains out cos Tarantino didn't ride into ICM on his charger and butt-fuck her agent into salvaging her career like he did with those other fucks. Am I right or am I right?'

'Right!' squealed one in a panic attack of sisterhood.

'SHADDUP! What you haven't taken on board is that I've got a daughter to support, so I ain't about to splatter myself all over my beautifully distressed designer walls like some scuzzy summer blockbuster. No way. They keep telling us we can't cut the action-picture cake. To which I say one word. SIGOURNEY. Go quiver. Yeah, yeah, sure, sure Meryl did some good sturdy river rowing, and Demi did seventy-four thousand push ups a day for *G.I.* – but lemme tell you all something, when it comes to out-smarting the smartlings, there is nothing, and you better write this one down, cos I'm only gonna say it once, there is nothing like the power of the pudenda. With a capital P. We *are* the cake that baked you!' And she's up on her feet, approaching terminal velocity, the eyes of her audience fixed on that lolling hand.

'Now many of you boys will not be familiar with this power-point philosophy of mine, but the ladies here know exactly what I'm talking about. Am I right or am I right? Right.'

'Right! Right!' round-twos the former pretender.

'*SHADDUP!!*'

She does.

'Now, I'm going to let you all in on a little pearl of wisdom I was gifted with by Julie Andrews, yes her, which she learnt at the sty of the swinish pigs who run this town. You see that brass plate up there? Look above you, I'd like one of you to read it out loud. Don't be shy,' she commands while aiming her barrel above their craning heads.

Silence.

'C'mon!'

More silence.

'Maybe. It's. Because. You. Love. It. Too. Much. I wanna hear someone say it.'

Ever so tentatively a nasal twang attempts to accommodate. 'Maybe . . . it's—'

'*Louder!*'

Dense silence.

'*C'mon!!*'

'You're kidding us, right?' ventures a young brave, instantly shushed by an elder tribesman.

Serious silence. Of the cosmic kind. Within which all sense of time and place is suspended. Each to his own impending panic attack. Shattered by her single gunshot, which goes straight through the left-hand glass panel in the cupola high above. All eyes split-second shift up, see my wide-eyed stare looking down, body prone on the landing. They assume I have copped it, and all collapses into chaos and hysteria.

The door crush to get out is pure Marx Brothers in *A Night at the Opera*, until this diva bellows, '*NOBODY LEAVES TILL THE FAT LADY SINGS!*' Now it's the grown-up version of that kid's game where everyone freezes on cue waiting for the music to start up again.

'And just where the hell do you think you're all going?' Curiouser and curiouser. To a man, woman and in between, they all slowly turn, look and listen.

'You don't think that after all these years of oblivion I'm gonna blow it right now, do you? Uh-huh. I'm a reasonable woman. I've been around the block a couple of times. I know the score. I'm not going to blow anyone away only to get *myself* put away for the rest of eternity, now am I? Am I right or am I right?'

The resident rhetoric opts not to try her luck a third time.

'Besides, didn't you know that I'm booked on the *Jay Leno Show* tonight, and if there's one thing *everybody* knows, that is something nobody forgoes. Whole careers have been remade at his confessional altar. If you've done bad, or if you've done good, his is the desk before which all can be forgiven and rewritten. And you can bet your sweet asses he's gonna get good ratings tonight after you get back to base and file your little ol' reports on the latest Sepulveda scenario. "Mad actress shoots at press. The barrel of Beverly Hills. Georgia's lost her mind." Am I right or am I right? Now, before we all say our goodbyes, I'm gonna make this a whole lot easier for you . . .'

Will she/won't she blow us all away? scream their eyes. Georgia sits. 'Someone, stick up your hand and say slowly after *me*, *clearly*, "MAYBE. IT'S. BECAUSE—"'

'You love it too much, Mommy,' is not the piping-voiced reply anyone expects to hear at this juncture, emanating from behind a forest of trousers from which Scarlett emerges, calm, poised and clear-sighted as only a four-year-old used to comforting her Barbies can be. Her entrance is hypnotic.

'Scarlett, I want you to say hi to all these people who've come to visit us.'

'Put down the gun, Mommy, please. Hi,' she commands and greets as she climbs onto Georgia's lap. Georgia obeys. The tot gives the assembled throng the once-over and enquires: 'Are you friends or foe?'

'They're the press, honey!' Georgia's laughter coincides with that of her audience. An avalanche of post gun-toting relief combines with a frenzy of camera clickage.

Salvaged by her daughter's self-possession and tender ministrations, Georgia cannot hold back her tears. Hugging Scarlett tight, she stands and pardon-mes her way through the front door and into the garden, followed by a scram of press, all captivated by yet another perfect photo opportunity as Scarlett says, 'Mommy, hold still, you got a piece of glass in your hair,' retrieves it and delicately places it in the outstretched hand of a hack. All to be shown on *Entertainment Tonite*, no doubt.

I return upstairs to find five photographers scrabbling to get their most dramatic close-ups of the glass-strewn floor, gun among the photo frames and the overturned chair, which one of them is artfully arranging on its side in order to capture the essence of the drama in still-life. Another is placing the largest shard of glass he can find against a mother-and-daughter framed picture, a shot which looks like a *National Enquirer* cover-exclusive in the making.

★

Tonight I'm watching Georgia's late-night chat-show date with Leno. It is a triumph. Sporting a bandaged arm, he hobbles out on crutches, quips his way through her Death Tours collision, waves his toy gun while recounting her *Good Morning America* encounter with Chuck and tops off his opening monologue with some stunt gunshots over the heads of the studio audience. Who go wild. He concludes with a gun-to-the-head threat to a guy in the front row, asking 'Would *you* wanna mess with this woman?'

His 'Hell, no!' is retorted by Leno's, 'Well, *we're* going to meet her.' On cue, the plastic pistol-packed band slam-bams into a rendition of 'The Good, the Bad and the Ugly' accompanied by gunshot sound effects, which so up the ante that a standing ovation has developed by the time La Sepulveda makes her *entrada*. Instead of the host's customary handshake, he holds Georgia up at gun-point and fires a cloth-written 'BANG.'

She falls down, chugs some breaths, rolls her eyes, 'dies', gets up and from then on can do no wrong. Which, considering the fact that she was invited on with nothing to promote, no song to sing, no scenes-from-her-latest-flick to show, with nothing, in fact, other than her career-becalmed self, is pretty impressive. For to admit failure is tantamount to walking with a sandwich board proclaiming your LEPROSY in the middle of the Hollywood freeway.

But here she is, Miss Affirmative Action in person, bonding with the audience of 'never-beens', who cheer her every detailed harangue about injustices suffered at the hands of the studio honchos.

'I'm not gonna take this sitting down any more, Jay,' and she is up on her pins declaiming her new manifesto, whipping up audience support. 'What began for me last night as a quest for my soul in Tower Records is today a search for my star that has been dimmed for too long. And in the words of the almost late but still great, Rolling Stones, *"I CAN'T GET NO SA-TIS-FAC-TION!"* ' Somewhat off-key, but in tune with her audience. Band obliges and the crowd goes its own 'Mexican Wave' way, all the way, with her. Marga, for once, is struck off-duty dumb watching this. 'I dread her now. Dread . . .' she mumbles as she unloads her miniature tape machine and hands its daily 'confessions' to me. 'I'll need more tapes just for *her.*'

'Who'd you do today, or did you remember to label them?'

'Richard Eagles, who never stopped blathering. I never took in a word he said, but it should all be there. G'night.'

'G'night and thanks, Margs. You're a real star.'

Marga's interest in celebrity has always been in inverse proportion to mine. Hers registers at around minus fifty, while mine, well guess for yourself. Hence the taping services she willingly performs for me, having become irritated beyond endurance by my former multiple cross-questionings. It was she who suggested I kit her out with a miniature recorder so that she could do her masseusing without having to remember anything clients chose to warble about. This arrangement combines personal pleasure with business insights. I have access to innermost intimacies that, combined with my designing skills, give me the edge over every other stylist in town. Every tape is transferred, labelled, catalogued and coded, so that it can be accessed from the index on my computer at any time.

# WHERE EAGLES DARE

Richard Eagles live and kicking on tape? My curiosity compels me to install the miniature into the converter tape deck, press the duplicating tab and settle right down, right there and then.

Just in case you have been 20,000 leagues under the sea for the past decade, Richard Eagles is *the* American movie star who effortlessly assumed the mantle of Monty Clift and Paul Newman three decades down the line, usurping all other Dean-gonna-bes with a string of nineties box-office hits, garnering an Oscar nomination for his role in the based-on-a-true-story Vietnam War movie, entitled *War!*, and starring in a roster of all-round homeboy roles that placed him in various states of international jeopardy. He is an acute businessman-artist who manages to pull off an outward show of total accessibility, convincing audiences he is their best friend at all times, while ruthlessly guarding his privacy at Fort Knox level. He is married to Swedish-American Kyla Bergman, who played the nurse in *War!*, on which set they met. They were married in Bali at the end of the shoot. Like any successful movie-star coupling, they are held up to the public as an example of a Hollywood marriage that works, while brutally bombarded and backstabbed by the film 'community', which, repulsed by the triple whammy of their fame, fortune *and* true love, generally responds with, 'Makes you sick, doesn't it?' Yet these selfsame disgustees make a beeline for them when they appear, perhaps hoping that by proximity they too might be brushed with the magic wand of their apparent happiness.

It was while doing research for his role as the navigator in *War!* that Richard Eagles was put in contact with Marga via his personal trainer, in order to get the gen on the deaf-mute scene.

If you remember, Richard played a deaf and dumb fighter navigator forced to fly the plane when the pilot was hit, managing to save his shot-up squadron. He really impressed Academy voters by learning sign language fluently, shaving his famously thick black hair and actually flying the stunt plane himself in a simulated crash landing that was shot with multiple cameras. However, being just thirty-one, he lost out to Harrison Ford, who finally claimed the Oscar, for his portrayal of Howard Hughes in his reclusive years.

Such was the outward show of generosity coursing through Richard's veins on Oscar night that when Harrison's nomination was announced and the clip shown from *Hughes*, the cameras caught Richard apparently spontaneously applauding his main rival. This unprecedented camaraderie was compounded when the winner was announced. Whereas we are usually treated to the riveting/revolting spectacle of five tense nominated faces awaiting the winner's name, and the four crestfallen collapsings which follow, when Harrison was declared the winner, Richard was the first on his feet, applauding with his hands above his head. Watching this, one was momentarily tricked into thinking one had misheard, or that Eagles had done so, and was about to disgrace himself before two billion viewers by bounding forth in the belief that *his* name had been called out.

Replaying this moment on video with a bit of stop-start and pause work confirmed that Mr Ford too thought that his moment was being stolen. Stumbling slightly as he made his way towards the podium, he half-looked back as if to check whether he was mistaken. But no, Richard Eagles was merely the first to lead what quickly became a standing ovation. The first time another nominee had ever done so. Much of the press coverage focused on Ford's breakaway performance, trading in his action-packed heroics for incontinent, old age, bearded and overgrown-fingernail character work, but the emotional impact of Eagles' spontaneous generosity became in many people's minds inextricably linked with Ford's win. So much so that, while talking about his artistic achievements,

Harrison was relentlessly quizzed as to how he felt about Richard's first-on-his-feet ovation. 'He's that kinda guy. Unique.'

Such approbation from on high cannot be bought. The curious fallout of this Oscar incident has been the growing impression that Richard Eagles did in fact *win* the Academy Award for *War!*. What he actually won was iron-clad icon status as an all-time good guy.

Excuse the somewhat haphazard nature of what you are about to hear, but it is the one-sided conversation Richard Eagles had with Marga earlier today. In many ways Marga is the perfect audience for an actor/director/producer: captive, silent, uncritical, incapable of indiscretion, warm and comforting, cheaper than a shrink, and gifted with serenity and skilful hands that signify all is well – *shhhhhh*.

So here we go. Richard Eagles. Midmorning. Massage.

'I don't wanna do it any more. Just can't. I've got so much money, so much, you can't, I can't even begin to comprehend it. You know when Sting bust his accountant for siphoning off six million and didn't even notice for some years, people were going, "But how could he *not have* noticed that six mill. had gone missing," and I'm trying to find people who know exactly how and why that could happen. And here you are just pressing and pummelling and you know, Marga, it's got like you are the only soul who doesn't want something. It's almost like you are a guardian angel saving sanity sometimes. Truly. I don't know anyone who doesn't *want* something, just wish you could know that. Vyvian assured me that you wanted for nothing, but I couldn't help myself, and I have to tell you that I have set up a trust fund for you, and I have nominated him to take charge of it so that you will always be secure. No matter what. Because what you give cannot be counted in cash terms. I know you cannot hear me, but I want you to know something. Here, let me put your fingers on my eyes. You feel the wet? My tears? If you register, give me some sort of sign, because sometimes I swear you are like a psychic being, press my cheeks if you feel what's coming out of me? – Wiping my tears. Wiping my tears. I am a grown man and this stranger is wiping my tears. Do you know why I'm crying? Kyla, my beautiful Kyla, got the results of my sperm test, that I secretly had done when we were on holiday in Rajasthan – you would just love that country. Nobody knows me there. Us there. We could go anywhere, everywhere – just beautiful – and my sperm are dead. No count. Zeros. We cried and cried, and the beauty and the simplicity of the people we met only made us cry all the more. Kyla is so convinced that we will have a child that she has gone so far as to let her publicist know that "something" is going to be coming our way in the near future. I said, "Honey, I am as good as a dead man to you," but she is having none of it and says that a child is our right. Says it is our RIGHT, vehemently. Nature. Destiny. Deity and such. It's making me crazy. I don't even know if I can trust the publicist any more, cos our lawyer called yesterday and said not to worry about the new Website that just appeared on the Internet about us, claiming we have been to some ashram in Pakistan to find ourselves. Now nobody knew we were going there. The Website claims we are both gay and used the Indian trip as some kind of smokescreen to go our own sweet way with local savouries, and other insanities. The idea that we could be together for so long and not produce a baby, and worse still, show one another affection in public, has become "proof" that we are not what we say we are. Can you imagine that? That they convince themselves that our happiness cannot possibly be true, cos it's simply too *good* to be true. So what do we *do* – *not* show affection? *Not* spend time together in other people's company? *Not* look like we love each other or find each other funny and fascinating? Doesn't seem to matter what we do, they rumour-monger and find clues in our innocence that become an indictment. It's as if they can't wait for us to fall apart. We've even laughed about doing it for a joke. But it's not funny. Hurts my family, you know. They get calls. Snooped around. Odd sentence in passing from someone who has met each of us once becomes a *National Enquirer* front-page revelation. We don't want to adopt,

Kyla says no way, so I'm asking myself if it's just the money and the fame, is that enough? But it's not. Nowhere near. It's biological. I want us a baby so bad, and not all of our millions can get even one of my little sperm to swim. I am a dead man. My last hope is the faith healer we met at the ashram – that's the real reason we went. He laid his healing hands on my genitals, and the heat was unbelievably intense. He's a fertility guru, and he assured us that within a month my testicles would be reborn. Marga, I am a man travelling. Travelling with the highest hopes.' Click.

Curiouser and curiouser.

Of all my clients, Kyla Bergman is conspicuously absent from my list of female 'hard-hitters'. You might think this sounds improbable, but I have yet to make it through a whole commission without being propositioned. Those who assume me to be gay, bi, A, or just plain God knows what are as resolutely tempted to test my waters as any of Bluebeard's wives were when given that key and warned never to open *that* door. But Kyla – by consensus, one of the most beautiful women on the planet, whose number of *Vanity Fair* covers alone testifies to her charismability – has always been impervious to my charms. And so lovingly devoted and supportive of Richard is she that she finds herself regularly pilloried for being so. '*Too* perfect, if you ask me,' is the gist of the SMARTIES' complaints (Sophisticated Middle-class ARty IntellEctualS). This does not however dampen the ardour with which they accept invitations to circulate with Mr and Mrs Eagles/Bergman. Quite the reverse. Not to be invited to one of their soirées is tantamount to A-list social suicide. Which is in the arena of a box-office catastrophe. Something never quite recovers.

So when I thought I found myself being 'approached' by Kyla last week, I dismissed it as the frothings of fantasy – the scenario whereby you so *will* something to happen that you believe it is about to. But her husband's sperm soliloquy has made me wonder. My close encounter with her went like this.

Walking round the newly painted and decorated shell of their fifth home out in the Palisades, Kyla got personal. I have known them as a mega-successful movie-couple for the past decade, worked on all their houses, and more recently overhauled the interior of their Lear jet. Richard has never been anything less than the sum of his totally impeccable diplomatic parts. He is the guy whom the public like, love, worship and adore, as do the folk that work for him. His technique is simple. When in public he will meet, greet and shake hands with everyone, rigorously maintaining direct eye contact for the duration of each exchange, reckoning that when in contact with ordinary mortals he owes them his undivided attention. Such is the chemical combustion that occurs in the brain of the fan that pheromones or some such are released which have the effect of slowing everything down into a slow-motion state of grace. What in fact lasts seconds is thus elongated into hours by a chemical trick in the cranium, which is why anyone relating the details of their encounter with a mega-celeb can talk at such length about their conversation, which shades into delusion only when the invitation – e.g. to 'come round and spend time with Kyla and me' – is turned down due to the fan's pressing appointment with his orthodontist. As if.

I don't want you to think that Richard Eagles is some kind of manipulative people-pleaser. He is what he is. He is the guy that has made it his mission to know every last person's name on a film crew within twenty-four hours. Now remember that most crews he works with number 100 plus. That's a lot of Hanks, Joes and Mikes. But that's the kind of challenge he seeks in any and every situation. That all-important 'common touch' is actually a competition with himself. And it makes him one of the all time good-guy bores, so approachable that sometimes you wanna Cagney a grapefruit into his charming chops. But chances are, he'd willingly find that the funniest thing that ever happened to him. This is the quality that made him one-man-band his ovation for Harrison Ford while the remaining nominees popped Prozac suppositories to get through the rest of their miserable night.

However, what he lacks in apparent guile Kyla makes up for by the snowload. Whereas his ambition projects as a struggle with himself, hers is perceived as the manipulative manoeuvrings of a Swedish She-Minx, despite the fact that she is three generations State-side removed from her Stockholm stock. Her reputation for being 'cold' seems unshakeable. Not unlike the royals, she's charming, attentive but aloof, somehow conveying the impression that she'd rather be doing anything than communing with mere mortals. Which may be why she is privately referred to as the Princess.

When Kyla is being 'normal', your instincts alert you to the fact that she is aware of just how effectively 'normal' she is being. It's as if you can see the invisible *click* when she decides that you are worthy of her attention as she silently rewards herself with Brownie points for being so caring and sharing with her time, confidences, snacks or snippets of gossip.

Yet despite your awareness of all this, at the moment you receive her attention you feel privileged and special, and when it is denied, it's as if a spotlight has been slammed off leaving you feeling duped and slightly resentful. Does not faze *me* in the least, of course, but I have witnessed many a hopeful face go crestfalling when she ices over.

Her usual *modus operandi* is to call me via a phalanx of assistants with instructions, to call back at such and such a specified time. But about five weeks ago I got a call from her direct. I should qualify. When I say direct, I mean her number one assistant got me on the line and transferred me to Princess Kyla herself. Kyla is not the *hi honey how ya doin?* type, but I could sense the full atomic force of her decision to be matey.

'Vyvian! – I can't wait to see you!'

Kyla is not someone who ever speaks in exclamations. That stuff is left for minions, lawyers, managers and agents. And me!

'Richard and I would love to see you for dinner on the ...' Three weeks from now. 'We're doing a kitchen supper, casual, you know, for a dozen or so, and I'm going to cook! ... We're out of town till then, and I'll tell you where we've been when we meet, but in the meantime we thought that since you're redecorating anyway, you could raze the kitchen and refit it in the style you created for the Katzenbergs. But not the same, if you know what we mean.'

You should know that the 'redecorating' was prompted by the discovery of a fist-sized paint smudge above the living-room fireplace. My 'Why not let me have my specialist painter just patch up the blemish?' was dismissed with a wave of, 'Look, we'll be away, and the house could do with freshening up.' I had agreed to a re-coat and de-smudge. But to Kyla's request that I raze and reconstruct the kitchen in three weeks, I had to reply with three words she is not used to hearing: 'Can't be done.'

That submerged iceberg in her voice came bobbing down the line.

'Vyvian, is this about money?'

'Kyla, you know that in all the years we've worked together, we have never discussed money. At the risk of boring you, planning permission could involve a six-month delay, quite apart from removal, construction and everything else you don't want to know about.'

'I'm counting on you.'

'Please don't.'

'But I've already invited everybody.'

'Kyla, the kitchen that's there is the one you dream-designed. The Katzenbergs' design is a whole other concept—'

'I want you to do it for me. I know you can. I'll call when we get back to finalize seating ideas with you. Richard sends love. Bye.'

I now understood my invitation to a dinner party three weeks hence. It would theoretically ensure that the kitchen got completed. I took no offence, however, and was secure in the knowledge that it could not be done.

Fast forward to the day before, and one of Kyla's panic-stricken assistants is bleating, 'But how will she be able to cook for her guests?'

'On the cooker she specifically chose herself before she got this dumb notion in her head to copy the Katzenbergs'.'

95

'I don't like your tone.'

'Too fucking bad! Save your ass and have Kyla call me herself, and I'll explain all over again why it couldn't be done in three weeks.'

Sure as Schwarzenegger does Action, Bergman is on the blower. 'Are we still on for tomorrow night?'

'Absolutely.'

'I knew you'd do it.'

'I haven't, Kyla.'

Imagine the audible equivalent of a polar front.

'What am I going to do? I've promised everyone I'm cooking for them in the kitchen!'

'Fake it. Get caterers.'

'This is not a joke, Vyvian. D'you mean I'll have to use the cooker I already have?'

'I'll tell you what, I'll drape the kitchen in dustsheets, rig up some scaffolding, stuff the place with cushions and candles, hire in a barbecue grill and you can tell your guests that you weren't going to cancel for anything, and that they will just have to make do with a construction-site picnic.'

'You're a genius!'

Indeed. The insanity of disguising an immaculate, barely used, six-month-old fitted kitchen with the paraphernalia of a construction job for an impromptu picnic did not register with her for a moment. And of course the collective billionaire guest list ooh'd and aah'd at Kyla and Richard's casual chic, including, from one very famous mouth, the following: 'You two, God damn it, you know what this reminds me of? How I got started in this business, when I was renting space from a slimeball in New York and we had to eat off the floor and live like Bedouin tribesmen. Going back to basics. I tell you, we forget so goddam quick, and I'd like to propose a toast to the most beautiful couple in the world, Kyla and Rich, for keeping us in touch with who we truly are.'

Later on, Kyla and I walked around the house, inspecting each newly painted room, and she invited me to the window to admire the view. Side by side. Facing out. She said, 'Do you ever want to have children?'

My demurral was answered with, 'But you've got such beautiful genes.' At which point she put her arm round my waist and squeezed my left butt cheek. Equatorial contact. So out of 'perfect couple' character.

'You've got a really tight sticky-out ass,' she giggled.

'Steatopygous.'

'What!'

'That's the technical term for it. Particular to Africans.'

Instead of giggling off, her hand held fast. God, I love my life! Oh my God! Oh my God? Oh my God! . . . God, I love my life!

# MISSION IMPOSSIBLE

2.27 a.m. Private line call. 'Yes?'

'It's me' – me being Technophobe.

Not his real name, of course, which is Ted Moby, but that's what I call him, as there is no division between his condition and his personality. They are at one with each other. Whereas most phobics spend all their energies avoiding their *bêtes noires*, he is the opposite – embraces and is engulfed by his techno obsession.

He is a middle-ranking movie star who pops up in every other late-night rerun of something. Known but not celebrated. Dependable and familiar, like what's his name. He lives in – how shall I put this? – a junk-joint: floor to ceiling, wall to wall, up, down and sideways techno-cram. When I first visited, every gadget and domestic invention with knobs on was stacked wherever you looked. Televisions, monitors, cameras, videos, miniatures, satellite dishes, tape decks, radiograms, transistors, wirelesses, hi-fis, fax machines, printers, cassettes, eight tracks, reel to reels, Playstations, phones and, in one room, typewriters. Only typewriters. A down the ages trot through every conceivable machine ever invented. The distinguishing characteristic of the entire collection? Nothing worked. Sure, wheels turned, machines hissed and spluttered, screens snowed and flickered, radios jumbled a cacophony of signals, but not a single appliance functioned normally. The kitchen table was stacked with TV, satellite and cable guides going back years. Visual and aural hell.

However, in a small ante-room, the very latest, most expensive hard- and software the Japanese have come up with was arranged in a conflagration of cross-wires and cables on a wide counter. Here, everything worked. Simultaneously. Three walls were a jigsaw of televisions, all on, like the *Man Who Fell to Earth* interior of David Bowie's house. Laptops, video monitors and a plethora of PCs were all scrolling information. In the midst of which, Technophobe swivelled back and forth on a wheeled chair with screwdrivers and tools in each hand, trying to decipher his own way into the unknown. Hence the piles of damaged and distraught machines whirring away in every other room. He claims he is at the cutting edge of the future, but has thus far succeeded only in squandering his savings on the latest machines in order to replace the ones he is in the process of rendering dysfunctional.

The do-it-yourself nightmare man. 'I hate technology, but I'm damned if I'm gonna let it get the better of me,' is his attitude. His position is further complicated by his reputation for being the guy who will get your technicals back in order should they short circuit.

This began when he offered to 'fix up' Elizabeth Taylor's sound system a couple of centuries ago. All that was required was the reconnection of some speaker wires that had come loose, but such was the collision of the legend's joy with his own sense of achievement when, without the aid of a minion, the music came on again, he did not have the heart to explain how simple a job it was, as he revelled in her violet-eyed gratitude. And so it came to pass that a man incapable of mending a plug without risk of electrocution became privately known as the guy to call if ever anything technical went wrong. Rather than getting in an expert, movie folk invited him round to give faulty fixtures a fixing. He couldn't, of course, so he would tinker around till they crashed and then fork out a fortune replacing them. When people marvelled that their returned machine was 'as good as new', that was because it was. The cache and kudos of this 'sideline' was so seductive that he could not go back. At the time that we met he fixated upon my Smith-Corona, sight unseen, in the hope that it might be the Holy Grail end of his quest to master at least one machine.

'What can I do for you at two twenty-seven a.m.?'

'I just failed to end my life.'

'Uh huh?'

'This is no laughing matter.'

'I'm not laughing, it's two twenty-eight a.m.'

'Have you seen my reviews? Of course you have. This is the first lead I've had for some years and the bad news is coming at me from every means of communication known to man. E-mail, fax, Website, phone, courier, telex, radio, cable, satellite and terrestrial TV, oh and the guy that delivers the groceries. Gives me the sorry spiel like I'm terminal. I have signed contracts stipulating that my image shall be protected and copyrighted in all media forms existing and yet to be invented. But I have NO protection from the INFORMATION. [This word attacked as though it was loaded with lethal mamba poison.] Nothing to stop the INFORMATION coming at ya. It's a wonder they don't do whole billboards of my bad reviews. I've resorted to telepathy to try and reach my friends, all of whom have answer services on—'

'Well, it is two—'

'Vy, I need to talk to SOMEONE. Even the answer machines are out to torment!'

I'll spare you the grislies of his failed DIY electric chair immolation. Suffice it to say that Burt Reynolds' faulty PC suffered the explosion and plastic meltdown he'd planned for himself. 'I am in an SOS situation here.'

'But these are *reviews* you're worrying about. Nobody else gives a damn. Believe me, when Siskel and Ebert croak, they'll be climbing their family trees to find anyone that cares. You are a star. [This is last resort stuff, but I sense self-esteem collapsing fast.] A STAR. A TRUE STAR. [Career requiring wholesale transfusion.] ONE OF THE GREATS.' Seems to be working, as '*Maybe* . . . fever' sounds like it's taking hold.

'Maybe I should change my agentmanagershrinknutritionist-Fengshuiacupuncturist.' I am editing here, as he has a paragraph's worth on each of their particular shortcomings. What he is not prepared to relinquish is the detailed description of all things technical by which he attempted to execute himself. These include computerized hosepipes and shotguns, medicine cabinets and gas mains, fingers in plugs and hairdryers in the bathtub. And this is the guy who laughed away my proposed Press Pond. Till tonight. 'You know that Press Pond idea you were telling me about? Well, I'm thinking maybe, maybe there's some way you could design me a Tech-pod pool?'

'Believe me, anything is possible, it's just a little early in the morning for me. I could speak to your therapist and between us we might arrive at some mutually agreeable solution. How does that sound?'

He is obviously only half-listening as there is a sudden crackle of machinery in the background.

'What's happening?'

'Shit, I'm just channel surfing, sorry.'

'I'm going to suggest something truly radical. Are you ready for this?'

'Vy, you are speaking to a desperate man, a man at the very edge, Christ, man, you're not even my shrink, but listen, guy, I'll try anything right now.'

'OK, now here's what I suggest we do: this is a big, big commitment.'

'Fire away, chief.'

'I'm suggesting you follow my idea all the way through, no questions, are you ready to hear me?'

'I already told you, give it to me straight up. OK.'

'I want you to – hold on, are you on a mobile or attached?'

'Mobile.'

'Good. Walk yourself into the kitchen. Do you have any candles?'

'I'm on my way, I'm going with you on this. Candles? I don't think so.'

'Well, have a look. Everywhere.'

'Yeah, yeah, yeah! I got one. Now what do I do?'

'OK. Light it.'

'Done.'

'OK, now walk your way to your Tech-pod and switch everything off.'

'You're kidding me!'

'Do as I suggest. One switch at a time. And – this is important – before you flick it, turn the volume control to the max, then fade it down till it dies, then kill it.'

'Oh, oh, man, this is too much.'

'Are you giving up?'

'Never. I'm doing what you say.'

I hold the phone away as each machine crosses the sound barrier and then back again to silence.

'How're you doing?'

'I'm doing it. But it's like you're asking me to kill my babies.'

'Not at all, just putting them all to bed. That's all we're doing. Where have you got to?'

'I can't stand the noise. Can't I just switch them off?'

'Absolutely. But do them one by one. How do you feel?'

'Freaked.'

'Good. You could go for the big one, you know, if you're feeling brave enough?'

'What do you mean?'

'Go downstairs and find the mains lever. You still got the candle?'

'Sure. I'm going downstairs. You want me to wire myself to the mains?'

'Don't be daft. Are you there yet?'

'Going, going . . . I'm there. I mean here. Now what?'

'Hold the candle in your left hand, and flick the lever up with your right. No questions.'

'Oh, Jesus. This is too much. I got so much stuff connected—'

'Flick it!'

'Vy, this is a really tough call, you know?'

'I know, but trust me on this. Flick the fucker.'

'I wish I could still believe in God. This is gonna kill me.'

'No, it won't, we are talking about a small hand movement that promises psychic relief. Isn't that what you are longing for?'

102

Silence.

'Hi, you there? I think you are suffering from pre-millennial techno-overload anxiety syndrome.'

'That's what my therapist thought too.'

'Well, here's your chance for some instant relief.'

'OK. OK. OK! I'm gonna do it! JESUS!!'

Silence.

'You there?'

'I did it! I did it!! Christ, it's dark in here, Vy.'

'Got the candle?'

'Yeah, yeah, got the candle. Now what?'

'You did it! Congratulations. Upstairs. To bed. Oblivion.'

'Vy, the silence is fucking freaking me!'

'Go with it. It's a lever flick away. You want the nightmare back?'

'No way. But this is fucking freaking me all the same.'

'Put your hand out front, and candlelight your way back upstairs, get into bed and then switch off your mobile. I'm going to send Marga round first thing to give you a workover. Then we can make a plan for a whole new deal, OK? I'm talking techno-free rooms, save for a Bakelite phone and an old Smith-Corona typewriter in perfect working order.'

'OK. OK. Maybe, maybe. I feel like Dracula.'

'Goodnight, Count.'

Click.

# STAR WARS

From *Variety*:

> PARAMOUNT PICTURES AND WARNER BROTHERS
> PROUDLY ANNOUNCE PRE-PRODUCTION FOR
> CO-PRODUCTION TITLED *ZEITGEIST*. TO BE HELMED
> BY MORT BUCHINSKY AND Jj DAGNEY. WITH MEGA
> ALL-STAR CAST.
> Veteran maestro Mort Buchinsky will co-direct with MTV
> techno-wizard Jj DAGNEY what promises to be the Space
> Buster to end them all. THE POSEIDON ADVENTURE meets
> ALIEN. Shooting in LA and the Mojave Desert. Casting Direc-
> tor – Howie Lollapaloosa.

My phone system is blinking all systems agaga. Now you might
wonder why I am not comfortably swathed beneath a pile of
furnishing fabrics, coordinating colour schemes somewhere quiet
and peaceful. I am, it's just that the humans demand and dement,
and the more people I know and work for, the more possessive
and territorial they become.

The anvil chorus of this morning's calls hammering every
airwave above LA demands: 'Did you see *Variety*? Co-production??
Co-direction??? WHICH Stars????' This news obliterates everything
else off the scanner. Bosnia? Middle East? Alaskan oil spills? Don't
get me wrong, these affairs are not generally omnipresent on the
collective conscience around here, but come an announcement like
this and everything else is blipped (apart from among the old stars
who have become hardcore CNN junkies).

Everyone in this town can give you a rundown of the weekend
movie grosses with the glazed eyes of an automatic pilot, from gas-

station attendants to the dental fraternity, who offer a sideline in film financial forecasts. All are riddled with this announcement.

The magical word is 'pre-production', with its promise and implication that anyone and everyone might get a shot at being involved. No technicians have been set. No actors actually cast. Nothing is signed and sealed. No one's excluded. Yet. The conjuring coup is the *co*, as in co-production. Translation: doubles your chances. Studios going to bed with one another is unique enough. But co-directors? It can only mean one thing. Trouble. Billboard size. Mmmmmm! The question is, who do YOU know? Mort or Jj?? Already, around the breakfast meeting tables and banquettes, hotel lobbies and bungalows, mouths are watering with the permutations and possibilities. Here's a soupçon of my reconnaissance at the croissant joint on Sunset Plaza.

Two fit fifty-year-olds, blue-jeaned and pressed into immaculately laundered white collarless shirts, hair groomed to within an inch of their lavishly moisturized necks, are sipping freshly squeezed orange juice and tucking into yolk-free omelettes, tut-tutting about the *co*.

'Who the fuck is this Dagney guy anyway? And what's with the big J small j business?' says one, his irritation concentrated in his left foot, tapping Morse with a Gucci loafer.

'MTV guy, it says. I'm amazed Mort'll stand for it.'

'He won't. Guy's got an Academy Award for fuck's sake.'

Their ponytailed and goateed waiter offers to elucidate.

'He's a comer. Trained in graphics, master technologist and computer artist Buddhist, a cyberspace visionary. More juice?'

At an adjacent table, two unknown actors wearing sunglasses in the hope of being mistaken for knowns are film-buffing their way through Mort's oeuvre, ticking off who the likely casting suspects will be.

'Who do you reckon for the Shelley Winters role?'

'Roseanne?'

'Nuh uh. She's over. Cathy Nijimy, I'll bet. Unless they get Midler to pad up?'

105

'Nuh uh. Did that already – *Hocus Pocus*.'

'Maybe Cathy's too young.'

'How about Liz? Didn't Buchinsky direct her in . . . you know, what was it called?'

'Nuh uh. Can't swim any more.'

'Whaddya mean she can't swim any more? She can walk!'

'Nuh uh. Insurance wouldn't cover her.'

'Why'd she have to swim? It's set in space.'

'Nuh uh. *The Poseidon Adventure* – all happens at sea.'

'I know that! Only it's not set at sea, but in space. As in outer.'

'Nuh uh. It's a remake of *The Poseidon*. Believe me. I read the book. Paul Gallico. Boat goes belly-up and Shelley has to swim for her life.'

'Lenore! It's written right here, it's called *Zeitgeist*, for Chrissakes.'

'Nuh uh. They always change the title for the remake. Anyway, Liz retired.'

'Did not.'

'Did *The Flintstones*, played the grammy.'

'Nuh uh. As in, I didn't see it.'

'So whaddya saying – just cos you didn't see it, it didn't happen?'

'Nuh uh. Will you calm down already? All I'm saying is, I don't think Mort's gonna go with Liz. Maybe they'll go postmodern and have Gene Hackman play Ernest Borgnine's part and have Brad Pitt do Gene's?'

'Borgnine wasn't in it.'

'Nuh uh. You're wrong. He was.'

'He was in *Marnie's Adventure*.'

'Nuh uh! *Poseidon* – he played the cop who was with the hooker, played by Connie Stephens. And it wasn't called *Marnie's Adventure*, just *Marnie*.'

'Will you stop saying "Nuh uh" all the fucking time?'

'Nuh uh. But I'll tell you something for nothing; I saw Connie Stephens on the Home Shopping Channel the other night, talking non-stop for an hour about some crappy bracelets, and I said to myself, "How the mighty have fallen." Take note. A whole hour. Non-stop. We couldn't do that. A whole hour's improv about a bracelet? Nuh uh! No way.'

'At least she's working. An hour's longer than either of us have been on TV.'

'Nuh uh.'

'Lenore! Will you stop that? I asked you once already! Anyway, it wasn't Connie, it was Stella.'

Lenore's nuh uh was muffled by a choke-sized bite of croissant covered in sugar-free preserve that he was shovelling down his throat. Shook his head instead.

'Lenore! I'm telling you, it was Stella Stevens. With a v. Connie's is a ph. Stella has two l's. Stevens, Lenore! Stevens. As in S.T.E.—'

'I gotta call my agent. Get me seen for the Red Buttons or Roddy McDowall roles. Do you know Howie Lollapaloosa?'

'Nuh uh! Oh, Christ, you've got me doing it now.'

Get into my car and overhear the valet parking attendant explaining the meaning of zeitgeist to the delivery biker from Chin Chin's takeaway counter.

'. . . means second sight, like that character had in *Zardoz*.'

Stop off at Tower Video to pick up an order, and am met by a gaggle of desperadoes arguing about where they can buy a video copy of *The Poseidon Adventure* as Tower's sole copy is rented out and their two for sale copies 'were snapped up, like that, man,' says the store guy, snapping his fingers for emphasis like he was about to segue into a scene from *West Side Story*. 'Like that, man, gone.'

'Last copy of *Alien*, guys!' the Goth at the cash register yells, waving the nugget in the air. A chorus of hands and voices begins an impromptu bidding war.

The store has only just opened, and as I leave, more eager-eyed Poseidon Aliens, clutching *Variety*, are cramming through.

'Who for the Michael Caine role?'

'He wasn't in it. Never been in any of the *Alien*s. Or space.'

'Not *Alien*, you dumbfuck. *Poseidon*.'

'Never been in either.'

'He was. With Sally Field.'

'Listen – *Poseidon* was Pamela Sue Martin, Carol Lynley, Gene Hackman and that guy with the teeth. Got eaten by rats in that other movie.'

'You mean *Willard*? That was Ernest Borgnine.'

'That's him.'

'He wasn't in it.'

'He was. I saw it. With my own eyes.'

'Not in the sequel, he wasn't.'

'What sequel?'

'The sequel to *Poseidon*, dumbfuck. Sally Field and Michael Caine!'

'How could there be a sequel, they all got out, 'cept for Shelley Winters who drowned?'

'Shelley didn't drown, she got a heart attack after her big swim.'

En route to deliver the Smith-Corona to Technophobe, the following news announcement scores through the misery:

'. . . and Georgia Sepulveda has landed a coveted role in the forthcoming movie, *Zeitgeist*, following her show-stopping turn on *Leno*. Sounds like she did get satisfaction after all. Remember. You heard it here first. And now it's over to Donny with the traffic news.'

# DR NO

Technophobe's home is situated on a side road off Mulholland Drive, chosen for its altitude access to satellite and airwaves. He is loading up a hire van with ancient amplifiers as I pull up. Beaming. As if coked to the sky.

'Oh, man, oh, man! Vy! You have saved my life.'

'Steady on. I'm no saviour. Here, let me help you with that stuff.'

He shakes his broad grin from side to side.

'No way. No way. I gotta carry my own shit out. You know something? I've been living my life like some kinda snail. Carrying this burden on my back, and it's nearly killed me. You wanna know something else? I am a free man. Free. *You* have freed me.'

'Nonsense. What are you going to do with all this equipment?'

He laughs his answer. Nodding and bobbing his head in a knowing mime indicating that this armful is destined for the dumpster, then throwing his head back in the direction of the house, laughing further encouragement for the rest of the stuff to follow suit.

'You don't think you're being a little rash?' I venture, attempting some damage limitation should he change his mind and issue a lawsuit.

'I feel biblical. Lights shining down. Machines going out.'

His gardener, housekeeper, driver and a couple of others I'd not seen before are staggering back and forth, trailing severed wiring and the muddled guts of machinery. Maria, who'd endlessly endured giving service while tormented by techno-hiss and crackle, is smiling so profusely that I can't help wondering whether she has been intravenously drugged in the early hours. But no. Just glee-filled at seeing all these horrors being elbowed out.

'Let me help you with that, Maria,' I offer as she totters out with a particularly brutal TV.

'Oh, no thank you, señor. I bin waiting a long, long time to do this.'

Room after room has been cleared.

'Where have all the gadgets gone?'

'This is the fifth truckload. I'm keeping the typewriters – the ones that aren't electric – and using the remaining hundred seventy-nine to line the garden pathways with. I'm also going to have the house disconnected from the electricity supply.' This announcement is accompanied by a hefty kick into the ass of a Toshiba. 'I've had this brilliant idea. Came to me in a dream last night. Clear everything out save for a Bakelite phone and a single typewriter that works, perfectly placed in the middle of the living room. Candlelight everywhere. I want empty interiors to match my inner being.'

'But what about hot water?'

'Gas!'

'Sounds sound to me. I'd like to suggest you stall on the electric cut-off till we've had the rooms all vacuumed and redecorated. Any colour scheme in mind?'

'Lunar,' is his beam-me-up-Scottie command.

On my way out, I check with Pablo which dump all this gear is headed for and call Tundra, the conceptual celebrity sculptor, to let him know where he can pick up the raw material. Tundra, being monosyllabic, is one of the few friends Marga and I share. He says, 'Secured,' which I assume means 'Thanks a lot, O valued friend, for providing me with such rich info and access to valuable raw materials that I would otherwise not have known about; I am truly, deeply indebted to you for your kindness, consideration and unstinting generosity.' Secured.

I like Tundra. Probably as much for his brevity of speech as anything, which in a town of Big Talkers makes him unique. He does not have an agent, lawyer, manager or manicurist. Answers his own phone – when he feels like it. Silently. This unnerves most callers and undermines all attempts at sycophancy. Think about it. You call up asking, 'What have you got?' or 'What are you working on?' or 'Can we do a deal?' or 'You're the greatest artist living and breathing on the beleaguered planet at this point in time, Pablo, Leonardo, Michelangelo and the boys take a back seat, Tundra, you're our guy,' – but his silent response will eventually strangle your tonsils and have you going existential on how empty and full of shit your life is.

Not that I have ever done this. I just happen to have been in the studio when such calls have come bleating through. The way he deals with them is to put the caller on speaker phone, so that he can walk away and carry on working. When the poor caller has bleached his heart of all pleas, Tundra will calmly walk over and issue a well-hewn one-word answer. More often than not: 'NO.'

His monosyllabic reply has the enigmatic effect of a haiku. No prizes for guessing how popular he is with Japanese art collectors. His 'thing' is refusing to sell anything to anyone, which has created an unlimited state of frenzy about his works. If he refuses to sell, what do people do?

RENT.

A near-revolutionary concept. Stymied many a business brain at first.

'What do you mean, *rent*? Rent Art? But we want to *own* it.'

'RENT.'

Eventually, a dealer finally agreed to rent, and immediately got his Mont Blanc at the ready, demanding terms. Tundra offered him that facial expression most of us keep in reserve for when we find our shoes have squelched into shit. The dealer got so freaked that he offered a vast amount of money for a year's rental.

'NO.'

And our man experienced that spritz of panic that causes your body temperature to soar and water to seep out in all the wrong places, leaving tell-tale circles around armpits and Calvin Klein fronts.

'What do you mean, *no*, it's not enough money, too long a rental period, maybe too many art works?'

'YES.'

'No disrespect, Tundra, but yes to which part?'

Tundra's turn away blew a cranial circuit.

'OK. OK OK OK OK OK. Here's what I'm offering—' and he blathered out a doubled dollar count, nine-month rental period, going off at some tangent to do with *that's how long it takes to make a full-grown baby, like your Art,* and agreed to rent only one piece of Art at a time. I should point out here that this dealer is not a man reputed for panic. On the contrary, streamlined minimalist calm-person is his persona. It was reassuring to see him as desperate as the rest of us can be.

Tundra is not a sadomasochistic torturer, but you might have been forgiven for thinking so when he walked away from this frenetic, sweating adult and carried on doing his Art as though the man had not uttered a word.

Dealer-man was getting really steamy now and bulgy about the eyeballs when Tundra turned to him, pointed to a work, smiled, paused and said: 'DONE.'

Thus began Tundra's style of Art dealing, which as far as I know remains unique. The idea that no one can own an artist's art proved a difficult concept for consumers to assimilate initially, but such is Tundra's status now that there is a snobbery about how long your Art-rental agreement is. The shorter the better – i.e., the more pricey.

Weird? I tend to think so. But, you will appreciate, perfect for my line of trade. Tundra ensures that nothing is ever stagnant. Once the nine-month rental is up, that's it. Return to sender time. Pity the poor star who attempted to secure an extended rental on a particularly beloved sculpture (of himself), provoking the dreaded double negative: 'NO. NO!'

Tundra struck said star off his list, and the social stigma of not being able to rent a Tundra hurts. Deep.

In case you are not familiar with his work, it might help if I describe his most celebrated pieces. As I said, his studio is his showplace so there is no backstage frontstage distinction – no subtle concealed lighting, receptionists or shop-window enticements. The warehouse is a vast windowless space with a glass roof, which floods it with natural light. It was here that Tundra came to public attention with two sculptures, the first, entitled *BIG-small*, a neatly assembled pyramid of numbered sandbags (handbag-sized) printed with weight details, and significant dates. Plus names. The names were those of Elizabeth Taylor's husbands and movies. The weight numbers correlated with the yo-yo weight gain and loss experienced by the star throughout her career. Visually, this divided up into a shockingly substantial heap of sandbags bulging to the left, representing her excess poundage. On the right, a forlorn pile of smaller semi-filled bags represented her reductions. In between the piles, a narrow factory conveyor belt rattled and jerked, transporting movie-titled bags on a continuous cycle.

The second work stood in a lonesome corner: a table buckling under the weight of a large metal crate-box with the letters E.G.O. stamped industrial-style on all sides, in black ink, overlaid with standard-issue FRAGILE stickers, bearing a graphic of a broken glass in silhouette. Beside the table an upright half-ladder was kitted out with boxes in descending size, getting progressively smaller on each downward step. At the ladder base the boxes trailed round a table leg till your eye stopped at the tiniest box, which was painted with miniature, elongated letters: Avant Garde-S.E.L.F.E.S.T.E.E.M.

These two seminal works instantly established Tundra and are currently in the homes of Georgia Sepulveda and Mort and Kitty Buchinsky. I guess you can guess which one suits which. Randy Rottweil is gagging to get his chance to rent *BIG-small*, but thus far, Tundra refuses to rent to any agents or executives as he deems them NONS – non-creatives. Which causes grief.

Tundra's latest work doing the rental rounds is entitled *Eat*. A wire-mesh and porcelain array of film stars is welded around a circular table, with outstretched arms gripping each other's guts. The cast list includes Clint Eastwood, life-sized in red porcelain, plunging his hand into the fifties-sized Marlon Brando, who is constructed of wire and papier mâché scrunch-balls and whose left fist in turn is stuffed into Mae West's arse. She is bending over the table looking surprised, but smiling, cast in white porcelain. Her right hand is strapped to Sophia Loren's left breast, cast in black porcelain. The translucent glaze has the effect of rendering her as a three-dimensional Tretchikoff. West's left hand is gripped round Jack Nicholson's privates – a pair of golf balls. His entire form is sculpted from golf clubs, putters, gloves, irons and tees, his face a replica of the Joker from *Batman*. Marilyn Monroe is the table; legs and arms forming the supports, with Marlon's right hand cupped round her left breast, Clint's other hand on her crotch, and Sophia's hands cradling her head. Sound grotesque? When you actually see it, you might change your mind, as it manages to be both beautiful and humorous. So we say.

*Theft* is one of my particular favourites: ten figures, of descending size. The front figure, a life-sized actual of Dustin Hoffman, papier-mâchéd with scenes from *The Graduate* covering every inch of him. Behind him, a smaller figure of his Razzo in *Midnight Cowboy*, rendered in black and white newspaper flesh with transparent holes arbitrarily placed here and there. Behind him, a reduced figure of his Little Big Man role, crudely cast in red clay, with whole chunks missing. And so forth, till the tenth figure, merely hand-sized in height, while still recognizably Dustin, is completely transparent. Sculptural proof that being photographed steals the soul. So we say.

When Java Hall first saw this, she wept. Shrieking, 'This is my life!' and promptly booked Dustin for nine months. She was particularly touched by Tundra's concern for her, manifested by his silently hugging her from behind while holding her breasts in each hand, till her tears subsided. On the way out she ventured that his embrace was 'Performance Art in itself.

'He never even touched my nipples. Just expressed total empathy. Can you believe that? I feel honoured.'

Imagine then her stupefaction, when he sculpted her breasts, 'From memory, Vy, from memory!' The work required a large, uncluttered space, as her sculpted mammaries easily equalled the measurements of two big family-sized igloos. Entitled *Natural*, they have proved a conversation stopper and starter wherever they fetch up. Curiously, a curmudgeonly director, famed for his philistinism, was converted to art at an instant upon seeing *Natural*, and during his nine months' rental placed the awe-inspiring pair at the far side of his swimming pool. They were hoisted in by crane and a mysterious tip-off ensured that the installation made the tag end of the evening news around the country. What is so joyous about Tundra's gift is that with this particular work, he appeals to both male and female collectors, especially the latter, who have identified the centrifugal force of the Maternal in his gigantism. So we say.

Java is currently in possession of *Mmmmmmmmmm*, Tundra's celebrated sculpture of Barbra Streisand's nose. Standing at just under two metres in height, the length and bulk of a five-door Landcruiser, its volume required meticulous planning to manoeuvre it into her house without incurring damage. The surging status of Tundra's work has necessitated the incorporation of at least one vast, minimalist gallery space in every interior I design. Such has been the growth of serious private collectors that this epic space has been deemed 'a classic' by those kind folk at *Architectural Digest* and *Interiors* magazines.

Java claims that running her hands along Barbra's curvaceous nose-bridge every morning has given her comfort, calm and, more importantly, continued inspiration. No denying that it's an impressive and exciting work. Java is especially honoured that it is destined for nine months at the Guggenheim, post her tenure. Though it'll likely be sorely missed by little Mona, who loves nothing more than to clamber all over it, and hides herself in the left nostril to delay bedtime.

Just as I'm musing on all this, the mobile rings.

'VYVIAN?'

'Java!'

'What the fuck is going on and is this what it now takes to get a gig in this town, that you gotta threaten to blow your brains out to get the publicity that's then gonna get you the part in *Shitegeist*? I thought it just took a couple of Academy Awards, knee pads and some serious tongue and casting-couch work to secure a role. What's wrong with the old ways? And! When last was this Sepulveda in anything that anyone ever heard of or that made more than a "straight to video" dime? Has Mort lost his mind or what? I tried to get through to Kitty, but her assistant said she was out someplace. And!! What's the deal about two directors? We are talking an Academy Award winning artist here, Vy, we gotta draw the line somewhere, for fuck's sake.'

'Agreed.'

'Agreed? Is that all you can say? Don't you go Tundra on me. It won't work.'

'Java, I'd love to talk, but I'm about to go into a consultation.'

'Listen, you wouldn't happen to happen to have a copy of *The Poseidon Adventure*, would you?'

# THE EAGLE HAS LANDED

11 a.m. appointment. The Pacific Palisades Eagle–Bergman compound is a small community within itself, peopled by assistants, accountants and business managers, script readers, chef, gardeners, housekeepers and a miscellany of lurkers, all immaculately turned out in Donna Karan black crêpe suits. Four houses have been combined to provide guest accommodation, editing suite, sound studio, gymnasium, meditation pod, games room and security quarters. There is an unmistakable cohesion among the staff, who value their privileged position, having been chosen to work with, rather than for this mega-couple, to whom they collectively offer unstinting loyalty, bolstered by privacy contracts stipulating watertight secrecy.

'It's like a home from home' is its courtiers' rap. I slip my specially designed ID card into the camouflaged gate slot, wait for a couple of seconds, am asked by an unseen voice to say my name for voice identification and then am allowed to drive up to the main house.

The atmosphere of which is a kind of constant carol service to itself. Hum 'Silent Night' and you'll get the idea: *All is calm, all is bright, round yon virgin mother and* – there's the catch. There ain't no holy infant.

Their Maria greets me, offers juice and seven types of mineral water, then buzzes an assistant. 'Hi, I'm Flo, I'm new here. Welcome.' She walks me through the just-painted series of rooms with the territorial exuberance of a Lottery winner, cinch-waisted suit and just-this-side-of-censorious rumpty-tumpty walk to match. Into Kyla's office. Kyla turns from her desk and pointedly pierces Flo with a 'thank you' that leaves the recipient in no doubt as to the desired speed of her exit. With equal incisiveness, she wheels towards me, takes my arm and sotto voces, 'I've got something I want to show you.' We are almost through the door when she does a sudden U-turn, closes the door behind her, grips my head with one hand, kissing me violently, while roving with her free hand for my surprised, but flattered cock!

'What ab—?'

'Richard's out. I want you! In!!'

She sucks my tongue so hard it is difficult to form a syllable, besides which my bloodrush south is so ferocious that I really have little choice other than to succumb completely, vaguely conscious that should she guide my now throbbing *Titanic* into her iceberg, I would definitely be sunk. Reinforced by our tongue-tied slide down the door, onto the custom-made carpet. Kyla on top. Kyla down below. Gaskets and cylinders, boilers and pistons, shafting and combusting. Oh, God, I do love my life!

Her hands dispense with my clothing with bodice-ripping dexterity, and all prior experience of female foreplay (of the prolonged variety) is swept away by the most intense display of fellating skills I have been lucky enough to encounter. Though I am compelled to admit that while I am delighted to be watching, albeit through slumped eyelids, my familiar old chap being slurped and imbibed by a goddess usually paid millions per picture to merely kiss other stars, Kyla's personalized tour around my nether world in eighty glorious ways is not quite the agenda I had in mind for today. Not that I'm complaining. Kyla's furious up-down dedication is fast approaching meltdown, and a synaptic leap synchs two thoughts: 1) why? and 2) why not let's get truly biblical and share and share alike? I bypassed my first broad query and opt for reciprocals, panty-snatching fast, only to discover that she isn't wearing any, wriggle round and bury my mouth in her clump. Mmm!

Now, you know and I know that comedy and copulation are not ideal bedfellows, laughter being the sure-fire antidote to maintaining erectitude. Kyla is giggling. Gagging. Then gasping.

'God, Vyvian, but I thought I thought . . . you were . . . ohmigod . . . you know . . . ?'

I am not in the best position to reply, fixed in tongue-in-groove mode, so to speak.

'Oooohmigod . . . you have done this be . . . fore!'

I marvel at my capacity simultaneously to gorge on her vulva, flick tongue her clitoris and consider the implications of what she is grunting on about.

'We thought you might be . . . OHMIGOD . . . Asex . . . ual!' coincided with frontal entry. Her foot banged and jammed the door. Tongue to tongue-tied. At each other. Crotch for crotch.

My elbows are experiencing premature carpet-burn, prompting a roll-over and sideways variation. Get my breath back. Venture a bit of— 'So . . . what . . .'s this all ab—'

'Fuckmee!'

The penis has a one-track mind. What it is capable of is obeying blunt orders. Especially, 'Fuckme!'

'To the very hilt, madam,' it single-mindedly obliges.

In the moments succeeding our mutual snap-crackle-'n'-pop, possibilities stalk through the sticky stuff, the most immediate being discovery by door or window. Eyes revolve around the familiar room, from a distinctly unfamiliar angle – i.e., from the floor, entangled betwixt the snowy legs of the wife of the most powerful player in town.

A soft knocking at the door clamps my orchestrals.

'Yes?' Kyla replies, icily composed and controlled.

'It's Flo. Devonia has your delivery in the entrance hall. You said to alert you.'

Kyla gets up, straightens herself out, fixes her pale lipstick and says, 'Well well well? Whose bush have you been hiding under all these years?'

'Yours,' is the only reply available.

'See you in five.'

I am somewhat relieved that the Dobermann eyeing me through the glass door into the garden is incapable of speech. Its eyes never waver as I attempt to salvage some sartorial dignity.

'I think the kitchen plans might be a mistake after all,'

announces Kyla on her return as she opens a Fedexed parcel of videotapes.

'What have you ordered?' I ask, trying to reclaim my baritone notes from the basso profundo post-coital growl that makes me sound like Kitty Buchinsky.

'Four *Aliens* and two *Poseidons*.'

# HIGH ANXIETY

Heading for Malibu for my next appointment, I wonder whether what has just happened to me happens to Connor Child on a regular basis? Didn't Java Hall say *I want his sperm*? And don't gals always get what they want? And wasn't I feeling a little used and baffled by so willingly obliging Kyla Bergman on the floor of her study that I had personally designed and had decorated?

'Vy? It's Nikki, where are you?' The voice of work crashed through.

'In the car.'

'I know that, but where?'

'En route to Connor Child's in Malibu.'

'Turn around. Georgia Sepulveda's shot herself.'

'Mortally?'

'Not sure.'

'Nikki, I'm not designing funerals any more. Not since Syd.'

'For God's sake, Vyvian! Get over there.'

'Why me?'

'Vyvian! You are practically the only friend she has left.'

I swerve and speed back inland. Try the radio:

'Beautiful sunny day here on the koast. Highs in the mid-eighties, lows in / reach out and touch, somebody's / killing me softly / wishoo be doowah / Dow Jones index dropped / and the Lord said unto / burritos when you're / Big Mac for only / shigga dugga doggy beulah / White House today / cleans and reclarifies / rangers in the night, exchanging glances / at only $9.99 / right back after these messages.'

'Can't be dead. She'd have alerted the media,' I hear myself saying out loud as my finger stabs the off button and dials her house. Engaged. Try Maria. Ringing.

She is less than her usual calm self and claims that Scarlett called the paramedics, who are currently attending to Miss Georgia as we speak.

From what I can decipher from Maria's gabble, it seems that Scarlett came sauntering into the kitchen covered in blood, calmly got up onto the bar stool and dialled E for emergency services, having been drilled by Georgia to do just this in the event of an emergency since the day she could walk and talk.

Maria had fainted, hence her confusion, but, 'No worry, Señor Vy, paramedics all here now. Fix me up.'

As I arrive, a phalanx of white-coated medics are hoisting a gurney into the back of an ambulance. Georgia out for the count.

'Shot herself through the left hand. Lost a lot of blood. Taking her down to Cedars-Sinai for further transfusion and possible surgery.'

I assume responsibility for Scarlett. This is getting too TV movie-of-the-week for me. Quickly put into big-screen perspective by the hypnotically controlled performance given by Scarlett. Ever see *The Omen*? Well, this four-year-old is giving a consummate performance of the Damien role. She takes me by the hand and leads me through the action.

First into the living room, re-enacting with supreme calm the moment when Georgia threw her arms into the air and declared, 'I AM HEDDA GABLER.' Seeing this tot effortlessly aping her mama's dramatics, without the histrionics, makes it all the more chilling and arresting. Especially when she deadpans her voice and features for the Big Bang moment. Crouching down, she mimes the action of trying to pull her mother up from the floor, demonstrating how her clothes became covered with blood. Then leads me into the kitchen, retraces her stool climbing and describes how when Maria came in and saw her blood-splattered clothes she screamed and fell over, Maria nodding and smiling her corroboration of events.

'Then I dialled E like Mommy said I always should and said, "Hi, my name is Scarlett Sepulveda, I live at [discretion prevents me] and I'd like to report an emergency. My Mommy just shot herself. It's a hole with lots of blood. She's lying on the floor. And our housekeeper, Maria, she is also lying on the floor. But in the kitchen, not the living room. Oh, and I'm four, can you come quickly. Thank you.'

This is Tatum O'Kneel and receive an Oscar time. Where are the panic, shock and horror all hiding out? Visions of Salem's finest briefly witch through my thoughts, till I remind myself that she is the daughter of an actress, and that four years is sufficient time in which to attain immunity to dramatic stunts.

Considering Georgia's penchant for my-career-is-dead proclamations, it's possible that little Scarlett might even suffer post-traumatic-disappointment syndrome upon discovering that her mother has survived this shooting. But that's one for her therapist.

Java gets me on the mobile en route to the hospital, crowing, 'That child's performance on the emergency recording beat anything her mother ever acted in her entire career.' The tape has apparently already been played on the news.

My, 'But, Java, this doesn't become someone of your stature,' is bulldozed down by her conviction that: 'The kid'll have an agent next.'

'Funny you should say that, cos I've had Randy on the phone.'

This actually causes a moment's silence. An unusual phenomenon, to be sure.

She then goes jugular.

'Infertile old cunt!'

My turn to take up the momentary silence option.

'Java, Randy dances on the other side of the ballroom.'

'What the fuck are you talking about?'

'His fertility is not in question. He's gay.'

'I *know* that! I'm not talking about *him*. I'm talking about *her*.'

'Who?'

'Sepulveda, that's who! Sacrificed her ovaries for a career that got her nowheres. All she got was one fucking Oscar nomination to cuddle up to in the twilight zone of her non-career, then she spends her cash buying a child. Wouldn't take the time off to conceive naturally. Oh no. Cunt waited till her career had collapsed and then decides to have herself a little companion. Bitch got so old, she had to buy herself one. Cunt.'

'Rage is not healthy,' I told us both as I narrowly avoid being demolished by an articulated five-tonner changing lanes.

'What's that honking?'

'I've just narrowly avoided being demolished by an articulated five-tonner changing lanes.'

I know that Java is not the remotest bit concerned for my health and safety; she is merely annoyed by the hiccup in our conversation.

'What's Randy want?'

'To know if Scarlett has an agent.'

'What for?'

'He's an exec on *Zeitgeist* and is thinking of casting her.'

'You've got to be kidding me! What about Mona? I've had her in improv class since she was two and a half. Got her own agent. How old's this Scarlett?'

Need urgently to get this conversation into a lower gear. 'Same as Mona. Four. But you know Randy, he's going for the publicity angle. Kid has been on TV a couple of times, so he's thinking Tatum and Anna Paquin at the Oscars.'

'Who?'

'The kid in *The Piano*.'

'Never saw it. Campion refused to audition me.'

He's just being Randy. You know what he's like. Whatever's news ...'

'Well, if he's casting four-year-olds, I'm gonna make sure he sees Mona. But isn't Lollapaloosa casting this movie?'

'Officially, but it's the usual inside-track job, as you know.'

'Lollapaloosa one of Sepulveda's ex-husbands, then?'

'Not that I'm aware of. But as I said, she's been in the news threatening to shoot herself, went on *Leno*, and as a result she's landed herself a role in *Zeitgeist*. Today she's actually shot herself, so in terms of pre-publicity from Randy's point of view, it couldn't be better.'

'Couldn't be worse, Vy.'

'How's that?'

'They will never insure the cunt.'

At which, she triumphantly clicks over and out.

★

Java's point is being reinforced by Randy's whispered précis of all the actors historically refused roles on the grounds of mental instability into Georgia's right ear, the tail end of which I catch as I cleave through the hospital security staff controlling the press gang outside her ward.

'You CANNOT uncast me, Randy!' hurtles from the prostrate patient.

'Keep calm. I'm not saying you're gonna get uncast. It's just that having shot yourself, the insurance people are gonna be problematic. But it'll be sorted. Trust me.'

I understand completely the depth of Georgia's fear upon hearing that dreaded 'Trust me' placebo as her eyes widen in horror. I think she might be about to take a bite out of Randy's hand, currently stroking her cheek, but mercifully her career revival instincts prevail, and she opts for verbal self-defence rather than cannibalistics.

'But, Randy, I was working on a scene from *Hedda Gabler*. She uses a gun.'

'Gabler who? Who's doing the picture? Is this an *Alien* thing? Is Sigourney pencilled in to do this?'

Georgia's jaw locks. I have never seen her clamp up before, but I know it doesn't bode well. Cue for me to motor in with some cultural reference triple-bypass surgicals.

'Randy, it's our old friend Ibsen.'

I'm hoping that my *ha ha ha*ing will divert the dolt and give him sufficient seconds to make the connection. For I have spent a not inconsiderable amount of my time (and his money) assembling a comprehensive library of antique books for him and compiling abbreviated lists of basic info so that he will never have to read any of them, but will be able to fake his way through rudimentary highbrow chatter when required. However, his executive plot-pitching instincts take precedence, as his brain evidently conjures up an *Alien* sequel starring Ms Weaver as Gabler, himself as executive broker *extraordinaire*.

'Old friend Ib—?' At which something somewhere clicks and he swirls round and smilingly says to Georgia, 'Of course! *The Doll's House*. Forgive me, honey!'

Sepulveda manages the tiniest gasp, quickly superseded by Randy's full-throttled declaration, 'Hedda Gabler and her Doll's House. God damn it, how could I have been so dumb? She goes nuts with a gun, right?'

The nurse notices that Georgia's face is turning purple and rushes forward with a hypodermic. While the medics force her to start breathing again, Randy monologues his way up his own stream of consciousness, telling her that she need not worry. 'When I explain about your rehearsing and everything for Hedda and her Doll's, we'll prove that a real gun had been mistaken for a toy.'

Satisfied with this summation, he bends forward, kisses her cramp-stricken cheek and leaves, assuring her, 'I'll call you in the morning, honey.'

The nurse stoically endures Georgia's explanation that *Hedda Gabler* and *The Doll's House* are separate dramatic entities written by a Norwegian playwright suffering manic depression, though by the time Georgia is essaying her theories about northern hemisphere light deprivation as a possible cause she is quietly easing her way out of the door.

I park myself at her bedside and hold her un-shot hand till she has rambled to a halt. She draws our hands to her face and kisses mine. Sniffs. Looks quizzical and Clouseaus me with: 'I smell pussy.'

Ah!

My turn to freeze. I attempt to withdraw my paw, but she vice-grips it and dilates each nostril in turn, inhaling the perfume of Kyla's pudenda. I hear myself mutter something about crackle-glaze varnish in a voice too quiet to carry anything like conviction. Fortunately, my soft-spoken lie coincides with the onset of her sedation, and she seems satisfied, loosening her grip and near-whispering:

'Vy, this is my last chance. You have to steer me true on this one, right?' In her post-gunsmoke calm (albeit drug-assisted) Georgia's plain-spoken plea is as sincere as a Tom Hanks Oscar acceptance speech. 'I know this is it! For me.'

At this precise moment, she is as close to that primordial state of release that precedes death as I've ever witnessed. Pure. Unorchestrated. Direct. Her eyes lock on mine, and for once it seems as if she isn't putting on a performance. Her features look softer, taking on an ageless serenity that alongside her speech renders her quite beautiful. Reminding me just how and why she became a star in the first place. I realize how long it has been since I have seen her like this. Too long.

Somewhere along the help-line of her life she has lost her volume control button, and it comes as something of a revelation to hear her speak like a shy person once more. I hold her hand and can sense the approach of wobblyscope-into-memory-mode undulations, as favoured by directors of sixties kitsch-and-sink dramas. But before I've had time to segue nostalgiawards, she beckons me closer and whispers, 'That's exactly how I'm going to do my dying last words in *Zeitgeist*.' Misting off to sleep and allowing me to scarper home.

To Bel Air and bed.

Nikki has rescheduled my aborted Connor Child visit. Kyla has left seven messages with specific instructions to call a mobile number I do not recognize. Connor and dog bark halloos. Randy waxes harmonious about replaced Provençal vases. Java asks for Scarlett's acting coach's number *re* Mona. Kitty and Mort Buchinsky invite me to dinner on their new table. Technophobe manages to cut himself off halfway through his message. Tundra just breathes heavily and manages a Tun.

# GUESS WHO'S COMING
# TO DINNER?

Kitty and Mort are legendary hosts. It's been my privilege to design and coordinate whatever extras they've required, simply to be in their company. For their home has not really altered much since it was done in the early sixties in a style that can only be charitably described as Hideous. However, such is the retro nature of things that, like flared pants, it could be mistaken for postmodernist chic, if you were thus inclined. Which Jj Dagney is, and on arriving for dinner is outspokenly impressed with their interior from hell.

Kitty is thrilled, if a little taken aback, when Jj admires the room's authenticity. 'It's so Sinatra–Kennedy!' he exclaims, getting very excited about a push-down ashtray on a pole stand that whirrs round and swallows ash and butts. Kneeling before the totem, he feels the base and decides that, 'This design is something I think we could incorporate into *Zeitgeist*.' To which Mort agrees.

'Do you smoke?' asks Jj, looking up.

Kitty and Mort exchange charged glances and mutually decide to risk it.

'Only in our own homes.'

Jj, rather worryingly, shakes his head from side to side, then, reaching out his hand, says, with the utmost gravitas, 'Let's shake on that, man.'

A Hollywood *tableau vivant*. Whereupon all three reach into pockets, procure cigs and light up.

Mort's relief is expressed through an exhalation of smoke. 'I was worried there for a moment, Jj.'

Jj laughs a laugh that signals a *you're an OK cool old guy* respect that he clearly never anticipated experiencing this evening.

For this is an ice-breaker dinner date between the two directors, without studio heads or executive interference. A getting to know you number, to which I have been invited as neutral ballast.

Kitty is positively gleaming as her carburettor vocals roar out an invitation to 'raise our glasses to *Zeitgeist* and all who sail in her!'

I must admit that this flagrant display of whiskey and tobacco sailing south down their oesophagi lends the occasion a historical aspect, as it has not been seen for some years in this town. Or not at this social level.

Post the clink clink clinks, we go through to the dining room. Kitty shakes a well-worn Nepalese table bell, its tinkling signalling the entrance of 'Maria', pushing a hostess trolley. This warming oven on wheels draws even more admiration from young Jj, who somewhat undiplomatically cries, 'That's exactly like the one my grandmother used to have.' His enthusiastic nostalgics avert possible insult. But Kitty is oblivious, her heavily bangled wrists in mid-percussion as she wrangles some serving spoons, joined-at-the-middle twin-spooned pincers that fleetingly make her look like a dressed crab.

Maria removes each lid, liberating a flourish of steam as Kitty offers to serve.

'Now, Jj, I wasn't sure, but we assumed you might be vegetarian or vegan, so we have a stir fry with rice ... or ...' She looks up and pauses.

Jj asks, 'Or?'

'Well, Mort and I still love a pot roast.' Kitty grins without apology.

'You know what? I feel like I'm in Mary Tyler Moore Land! Nothing I'd love better than a pot roast.'

I strangle my, 'But I heard you were a Buddhist,' and opt to chopstick it alone. Kitty pays Maria a culinary compliment and then limps through some instructions in Spanish. 'A hostess who serves her own guests?' notes a particularly impressed Jj. Kitty is purring on all cylinders, extolling the virtues of Maria, 'who has been with our family for thirty years and is practically family.' Such was the ease and charm of the old puss that any anti-feudal polemics Jj might have entertained are dissipated instantly, and in any case he is being diverted by Mort, who is topping up Jj's crystal tumbler with another whiskey sour. So swimmingly are things progressing that Mort spreads his arms and announces: 'A *Titanic Poseidon Adventure* in outer space.' The purest pitch before the plunder. 'That's *Zeitgeist!*'

He then flawlessly details the staggering global success of Jim Cameron's *Titanic* and how *Zeitgeist* will be its worthy successor, 'So long as we honour the classical structure of jeopardy drama: a trapped cast of characters aboard a vessel in terminal distress. It's a *gift*.' Delivered between mouthfuls of roast and potatoes. 'It's a tradition going back to *Grand Hotel* in the thirties.'

'*Ship of Fools* in the fifties,' adds Kitty, 'and *Airport* in the seventies.'

Mort lays a forty-carat grin of devotion in her direction.

'We cannot fail! So long as we honour the doomed romance at the centre.'

They are licking their lips in anticipation. Chewing up to speed.

Mort chooses this moment to address the issue of co-directing, opting for full-frontal diplomacy.

'Jj, *Zeitgeist* is a unique opportunity for us both. I know and have worked with 'most everyone in this town and know nothing about acting other than Do I Believe? Or Not? I love actors, haven't a clue how or why they do what they do. But they trust me. Technical stuff, computers, morphing, generating, blue screen, green screen, compositing – I'm like the waiter in *Fawlty Towers* – I know nothing. You, Jj, are the man. At the helm. Into the future. Out there.'

I am wondering whether this blatant avuncular tone will be welcomed. But so far so good. Noddings and smiles all round.

Kitty fuels Mort up with a sizeable second portion, and after some eyelid batting and rattling of her bangles spoons out more for Jj.

What I so love about Los Angelian life is the way that my presence is both utterly accepted and ignored. Post-introductions, Jj speaks through and past me as though I am a pane of glass. The acceptance of people just being there to fill sofa space, laugh and applaud as and when appropriate, is unquestioning. Of course, were I an unknown actor or wannabe, being ignored would be unbearable. But visible invisibility is my chosen ideal. Like my designs. Just as well, considering what transpires . . .

Mort is now filling us in on the *Zeitgeist* plot. 'As in *Titanic*, a group of wealthy passengers embark upon the maiden voyage of a futuristic, state of the art spaceship, which like *The Poseidon Adventure* goes belly-up on New Year's Eve. In outer space.

'The craft is attacked by an unseen alien. Havoc and hell ensue in an upside-down setting. Majority of passengers are frozen, while a core group, corresponding to the *Poseidon* cast, survive and try to escape. With the addition of a doomed romance between a pair of Winslet–DiCaprio-type young lovers to balance out the Shelley Winters–Jack Albertson oldsters, to ensure cross-generational appeal.'

Mort wipes his mouth with an antique linen napkin, takes a slug of his sour and proceeds to present his ideas about casting.

'Problem I had with *Poseidon* was this – the crowd was too anonymous and the main cast, with the exception of Gene and Shelley, too character – too character typey – Ernie [Borgnine], Roddy [McDowall], Red [Buttons], Jack [Albertson] and Stella [Stevens]. My point is that we can up the ante if the audience can relate to and care for everyone, not just the chosen few. And by everyone, I mean instantly identifiable star names. Of all ages. Because if the *Titanic*'s original passenger list were to be duplicated today, it would be a list of the most rich and famous people on the planet embarking on the inaugural flight of the most luxurious passenger craft bound for outer space. A galaxy of stars. Which'll satisfy the two studios financing us as they can poster byline the picture with something like *See more Stars than there are in Heaven on a journey into Hell.*'

Kitty interjects with an, 'Or *Hear everyone scream in Space.*'

The three of us are focused on Jj for his initial response. Kitty's bangle jangle is the only challenge to the silence.

'They'll never pay for them,' Jj challenges.

Mort is ready for this. 'Jj, I have worked with the lot of them, and for a set fee. I think we can get a Rolerdex-load of twinklers to participate. It would only be a week's work maximum, for the actual crowd, and believe me, none of them needs the money. They have enough of that to salvage Russia. They all get a set fee as I said, appear and play themselves, wear their own clothes, choose whom they want to sit with, and get to party. New Year's Eve party.'

Jj's brow furrows. 'I have a problem with stars. Period.'

Kitty chants, 'Don't we all, honey!'

Mort joins in her *ha ha ha*ing, and points out, 'If they're all massed together like this, you'll get ego equilibrium. No one daring to out-diva anyone else.'

Jj does a lot of negative *well, maybe, possibly* non-agreement.

When he finally looks up he makes no attempt to disguise the dread in his question as to whom Mort has in mind for the lead roles. Due to Mort's elder statesman status and two Academy Awards, he has contractually given casting power and approval over the head of the young techno-wunderkind, hence this upstart stickling.

Mort pauses and drains a full glass of still water, dabs his mouth, clears his throat, smiles and leans conspiratorially forward.

'Jj, if we go with this star crowd idea, why not let's cast the lead roles with the most powerful players we can get?'

His rhetorical tone is bluntly rejected.

'Why?' Jj looks sulky about the chops.

'Why? I'll tell you why. Because it's never been done before, that's why.'

Jj, determined to thwart, counters with a dismissive, 'C'mon, man. Every disaster movie that's ever been has been full of stars, and they've all been fucking embarrassing. *Earthquake, Towering Inferno, Orient Express* – the reason why *Alien* and *Titanic* have succeeded is because they have *no* stars. The story of the disaster and the technical vision of how realistically that is achieved is the star.'

Jj leans back, puts his hand behind his neck and gives himself a couple of cricks as if adjusting and releasing his head from a vice.

'You're right. Every movie of this genre has been star-studded. What I'm saying is that it's always been a top-heavy talent formula, without the support of a star crowd. I'm suggesting we get everyone. Stars wall to wall.'

Kitty bangles up and busies herself with serving dessert.

'Like who?'

Mort grins determinedly, knowing that if he gives way he is done for. Knowing that his last two movies have made less at the box office than this sulky young whippersnapper's. Knowing that he has to woo the little shit, else he might stab him through the gizzard with his serving fork.

'Richard Eagles, Kyla Bergman, Java Hall. And Georgia Sepulveda in the Shelley Winters role.'

Kitty places a bowl of home-made vanilla ice cream in front of Jj.

'Who are these people? They aren't real. Everyone knows that. You can't have movie stars pretending to play blue-collar characters any more. Pretending to get excited cos their screen character is excited about getting fifty grand a year, when everyone in the audience knows that their real-life salary is in multiples of millions. It's just insulting. I'll go with the idea that you get the old star-farts to play themselves –' he does a fake yawn for emphasis – 'but telling me you're gonna get Kyla fucking boring Bergman to do the Sigourney Weaver role, I mean, what's the fucking deal? Every movie she's done she's been in a fucking hoop skirt and corset. So now it's her new career trajectory and "character-arc" bullshit we're gonna be dealing with. Look at Kubrick's *2001*. No fucking stars, only the ones that are legitimately in the night sky. Actual stars are only dead planets of well-lit mud. I just am finding it hard to get a hard-on about Kyla Bergman, acting like she's lovesick over Richard Eagles. I mean, c'mon. When last did you see a married couple who you wanted to see act like they wanted to fuck each other on screen? Doesn't work. It's like watching other people's bad home movies. Too fucking boring. I'll give Bruce and Demi that, they never made that mistake. Just doesn't cut. Make 'em enemies, and the audience can get a kick outta seeing how they maybe kick ass at home, but fall in love? I'd rather—'

Mort attacks with an avalanche of agreement. 'That's a brilliant idea! – I agree. It was never my idea to have real-life partners playing out a screen romance. Rarely works.'

'Never, man.'

'Well,' countered Kitty, 'it did with Bogie and Bacall.'

'Doesn't count – that was last century.'

'Kitty, Jj's right. His idea about stars at each other's throats is a stroke of genius. It'll blur the line between fantasy and reality. It's brilliant. If we use stars, let's not pretend they're anything other than who they are. The rivalry between Kyla and Georgia, Richard and young Connor can be played out for real under the guise of the characters-in-jeopardy situations. They are themselves, aboard this maiden voyage into space, and when the craft goes turtle, it's the survival of the fittest. It'll be perfect. Every star is in a semi-Olympic state of fitness and nutritional perfection, so getting them to do the impossible won't be that implausible. The script will only need minor adjustments according to casting, but essentially the relationships between the original *Poseidon* characters will work. Jj, this is really, really exciting. Truly original. Your way we get to have stars from top to bottom.'

Jj cricks his neck in the opposite direction as he tries to work out just how his objections have suddenly metamorphosed into genius. He has clearly come with the agenda to detonate any star talk into some distant stratosphere, convince Mort that Indie actors with integrity and zero global recognition are the casting ticket, yet has been U-turned by the wily old Buchinsky charm.

'So, you're not agin the idea of Eagles and Bergman, then?' asks Mort, diplomatic patience incarnate.

'I'm not dumb. The financiers want 'em. If they're fighting each other, there's an interest. Not huge. But at least some. I saw this old black-and-white on TNT last night with that Burton guy and his fat wife. The pre-film intro explained how they were a big love match way back and what a big deal it was for them to be seen fighting on screen. What I'm saying is, I think if we cast for that kind of conflict, then we might get something, but no ways else.'

Mort, God bless him, fires up a cigarette and congratulates Jj for his blinding insight.

'Georgia Sepulveda will be perfect. Did you see her on the news?'

'Never seen her before, but yeah, mad as a box of snakes.'

Kitty pulls her chair closer to Jj, puts her hand on his Dolce e Gabanna PVC'd shoulder and miaows that Morty directed Georgia in her first picture thirty years ago. 'She is supremely, and fabulously, insane.'

'You know, Jj, your concept of star-couple casting is a bull's-eye. Really perceptive.'

'Thank you,' Jj gruffs, clearly disconcerted. 'How do you see the New Year's Eve party?' he queries, not looking up.

'Tracking shot − a mile long, down the dinner table.' Mort looks at him dead centre.

Jj's 'Oh yeah?' attempts a so-what nonchalance, but he is clearly surprised.

'Longer than *Goodfellas*, *Henry V*, *Kane*, Hitchcock, Greenaway, *The Player*. Epic track with every star you ever saw in your life. As themselves, or however they wanna play it. Own clothes. Own friends. So you get incongruity of people sitting schmoozing that you'd never cast in any other circumstance. Like Clint Eastwood and . . . you pick. And as we are in a co-production with these two studios, why not raid their vaults and access their classics for scenes from the past that could play on background screens. You've heard of The Beatles, I take it?'

Jj has completely dropped his sulk and is laser-focused on Mort's casual display of ideas.

'You mean like the *Sgt. Pepper* cover?'

'That's it.'

'You mean, computer-generate dead stars and mix them in with live ones? I always wanted to do that, man.'

Mort has him by the scrote.

'Yeah, but there might be a problem combining the still living with their dead partners. For instance, Lauren Bacall as she is now, partnering Bogart then, forty years ago, would be a no-no.'

Jj is *yeah yeah yeah*ing his way through the petits fours, very taken with Mort's mile-long track and regeneration stuff.

'I wanna morph and model and computer generate and digitalize everything.' Eating fast. Drinking faster.

Kitty smiles beguilement in Mort's direction, a smile that's been in practice for thirty-five years of marriage. Watching her I see something that I have almost forgotten existed: her face *creases* up when she smiles, revealing every unironed expression of love and ongoing delight. A once beautiful face that has dared to allow itself to become lined. Her forehead *moves*. Her eyebrows *shift*. Her lips have a variety of positions. Her eyes *crinkle up* and almost disappear when she laughs long and hard at Mort's stories. Never ceasing to find pleasure. Or give it. They make marriage seem like it might be a good idea after all.

Mort is the oldest young soul I know, and he slides the following compliment into Jj's side with all the deft skill of a bull-fighting assassin.

'Jj, you are the future. You've got the baton. Teach me. Share with me your vision.' Saving his best for last: 'You're an *artist*!'

Mort is a director who graduated through the school of lowliest odd-jobster, third assistant, second assistant, second unit director, assistant editor, first assistant, till he finally got to direct a B-feature and finally an A. The hardcore industrial route. The idea that anyone in pictures is an artist, namby-pambying about with delusions of genius, is anathema to him. But Mort has cannily put his proboscis to the new world wherein moviefolk perceive themselves as Artists. Jj is his first guinea pig, and judging by the breadth of his smile Mort's flattery has depth-charged the height-impaired ponce's ego, and he is as good as in the bag.

Jj ponders out loud, 'I was thinking about maybe getting this other amazing artist I know to design some stuff for us. Or hire his Art out. He's a conceptualist. Like me. Inaccessible but pure.'

His self-congratulatory head bobbing is proving too much for me, or certainly my subconscious, and I hear the following shoot out of my hitherto shut mouth.

'He's an old friend of mine.'

Jj swivels and dismisses me with a withering, 'I don't think so.'

'I've known him for years.'

Jj is clearly having problems accommodating my insurrection and looks at me as if I have squelched up from the slime of ignominy.

'Tundra?'

I hear myself annexing that distinctly English tone so lethally effective in patronizing a parvenu and reply, 'Oh, Tundra's been a friend of the family for years. He's very close to my sister.'

Jj thinks he has me and asks for her name.

'You wouldn't possibly have heard of her. Mort, I'd love another drink, please.'

'Try me.' Jj is not to be deterred. 'I know all his friends.'

I've noticed this territorialism with regard to Tundra before.

'Her name's Marga. She's a—'

'Masseuse! I know her. Marga's your sister?'

'Fabulous girl,' announces Kitty, obviously entering her 'everyone's fabulous' phase of the whiskeyd evening.

'She is. Why should that surprise you?' I am still smiling at the droid as he attempts an answer but manages only a goldfish O, as silent as if he is trapped in a bowl.

Mort mortars proceedings by claiming, 'Everyone knows everyone! Which is why a totally all-star cast will be perfect for *Zeitgeist*.'

# SILENCE OF THE LAMBS

I phone the hospital on my way home and am assured that 'Ms Sepulveda is sleeping soundly.' There is a package on the hall table when I get in, delivered By Hand. In the living room, Marga is in a towelling robe and the usual vegetable face pack. 'Where'd this come from?'

'I massaged Kyla this afternoon and she said you had left it when you were round there earlier.'

Unwrap the parcel, which reveals a small Picasso drawing. No way round this. Blackmail. Hushmail. Whichever way I look at it. Which is every.

I sit down as calmly as I can and sigh a sigh for all the complications that suddenly congest with the delayed realization that my entire clientele will be working on the same movie. I'd somehow managed to overlook this during Mort's pitch for precedence over Jj jerk-off.

'What is it you left behind?'

'Oh . . . work. The usual. Did you do Richard today as well?'

While my tongue is routinely *how was your day*ing, panic buttons are pressing themselves in all directions. The what-if-she-finds-out-about-her-who-squeals-about-me-who-doodled-her-way-back-then of my clandestine activities froths up some justified paranoia. Ground myself forcibly with a question about Tundra.

'Just had dinner with Mort and Kitty and a director who calls himself Jj. Says he knows you. You never mentioned him before?'

Marga's eyes have gone saucer-sized. She sits upright and asks for precise details. 'What'd you tell him?'

'About what?'

'Does he know about us?'

'Relax, of course not. I just said that you were my sister. As per.'

There is no hiding the tremor in her voice. 'Where is he?'

'Margs, what's going on? I just had dinner with Kitty and Mort Buchinsky and this Jj Dagney was there. He's co-directing *Zeitgeist* with Mort. What's up?'

Furiously wiping off the face pack with cotton wool, her hands shaking, she demands, 'What's the connection?'

'None. As I said, he's working with Mort.'

'The connection with me! How did my name come up?'

She is really agitated now and stuffing the used cotton wool balls into a plastic disposal bag.

'Jj mentioned he knew Tundra, and I said that he was an old friend of ours.'

'What's all this "ours"?'

'Marga! It's no big deal. I said "ours" as in a friend of our family.'

'Vyvian – we don't *have* any family.'

'He wasn't to know that. The little shit is so full of shit that I couldn't help dumping some high-status shit on his shitfaced little shithead. OK?'

Things are getting marital here. She is now standing face to face, a totally uncharacteristic posture, as she avoids confrontation at all costs. This has to be something.

'You haven't answered my question. How did my name come up?'

'I've just told you!'

'You haven't. You just said that you were a friend of Tundra's.'

'I don't know! Oh, yes I do! The little shit didn't believe that anyone other than himself could be a friend of Tundra's, so he very pompously claimed that he knew all of Tundra's friends, as if I was lying, and I think it must have been then that I said, "Well, my sister is very close friends with Tundra."'

Marga is actually gasping now. 'How COULD YOU? You agreed never to talk about me socially!'

'I'm sorry – but up until that point I hadn't said a thing other than that my sister was a friend of Tundra. That's right, it was then that the jerk asked for your name, still convinced that I was bullshitting. All I said was "Marga" and before I could draw breath he said, "Masseuse? I know her."'

Her eyes are fixed. Unblinking.

'AND?!'

'He said, "Marga's your sister?" – like that, and I said, "Why, does that surprise you?" Kitty chimed in about what a fabulous girl you were and Mort rounded up with some proclamation that everyone knew everyone in this town. Which I suppose is true when you come to think about it.'

'What did *he* say, Vyvian?'

'He didn't. That's what was so weird. He just sort of made as if to speak, and maybe then one of the Buchinskys spoke first and he never actually got to say anything. But I assumed it was going to be something about him knowing Tundra longer than the rest of the human race.'

'That's it?' Her face is crumpling.

'How do you know him?'

Shaking from top to toe, she puts her hands to her face and starts sobbing, a gut-wrenching noise that feels like mercury poured down my spine.

'What has the little fucker done to you?'

She clings on to me and drags me down to a kneeling position, burying her face in my shoulder. I hug her as tightly as I can and rock her back and forth, stroking her hair. Her entire body is racked with whatever it is she is withholding. I manage to carry her through to her bedroom, get under the covers with her, switch off the lights and wait. And wait.

I am so exhausted by the day's events that I know I might fall asleep, so decide to project into some paranoid frightmare of what might happen when called upon to service my varied clientele on *Zeitgeist* simultaneously.

Stars are very possessive. Once you are in their fold, it is best to

141

collude with their fantasy that you are exclusive, one-to-one, even though they know you are a freelance agent. The assumption tends to be that *their* home is the only project on your agenda. So it helps to keep everyone separate, even when one set of folk knows that you have worked for another set. It requires every last corpuscle of self-effacement and tact to ensure that no one's talented toes are trod upon. Which is why my frothing at Jj proved so unfortunate. If I had avoided rising to the shrimp's bait, Marga would have been spared her late-night horrorshow.

'Wake up, Vy, I've got to talk.'

Marga never 'has to talk', so her demand demands unique attention. Her voice utterly calm, she describes how Tundra advocated her services to Jj Dagney with the claim that she had magic hands. She agreed to an appointment based on her total trust in Tundra.

'Hold on a minute, where was this?'

'At Tundra's studio. Jj Dagney was over there hiring Art. He'd suffered a Steadicam back injury or something and asked Tundra's advice. Tundra recommended me, and I was at the studio that day having my hands sculpted.'

'But, Margs, that was two years ago.'

She ignores me and carries on: how she set up her work table in Dagney's condo, lit candles, prepared her aromatherapy oils, laid out towels and left her customary note, as she always did for first-time clients, with instructions to undress and lie face downwards, using the smaller towel provided to cover his buttocks. Inhaling very deeply, she matter-of-factly describes how Jj had done everything according to her rule book with regard to towels and keeping his privates where they belonged. She did think it odd that he had a small TV-type remote-control panel in his hand in a room that had no TV, but realized only too late that it controlled the lock on the door. Jj then began talking dirty, assuming this to be OK as he understood from Tundra that she was a deaf-mute. 'I'd had the talk stuff happen before, and just zoned out. I don't have a problem with that. Then he suddenly turned himself over, grabbed my hands and said, "Do your magic, MAGIC HANDS," pressing my palms onto his thing.'

Marga is both tall and physically strong and the idea that little Dagney could possibly have overpowered her seems ludicrous, until she recounts how he had then pounced with incredible speed, winded her and shoved her forwards onto the massage table. When she tried to fight back, her hands were so oily and his body so slippery that she couldn't get a grip, and the next thing she felt was his digit up her. 'It was like a child's thumb.' After he came he yanked her round and pulled off her surgical half mask (which she alternates with a yashmak of her own design between clients). He staggered back and started laughing, sneering, 'Look at the state of your skin! You look like a fucking lunar landscape. Cover your face up! You make me sick. Now get out!'

These taunts were what profoundly enraged and hurt her, far more it seemed than the actual rape. In the pitch dark her renewed sobbing has a terrible haunted, hounded sound.

'I'll kill him!' I rasp, every muscle constricted and strained. I hug her, hold her tight, rocking back and forth.

'Like a fucking lunar . . .' she can't complete his insult, just whimpers, '. . . scape.'

'I'll fucking well garrotte him slowly.'

This makes her laugh. 'Don't be daft.' She reaches over and clicks on a bedside lamp.

'Don't laugh! I intend to kill the little fucker.'

This only makes her laugh all the more.

'What's so bloody funny?'

'You are!' she says. 'Look at you. I'm the one he pounced on, not you!'

'Why didn't you tell me?'

She got up and went through to the bathroom to run a bath, shrugging. 'What good would it have done? He knew I was deaf and dumb, so he knew he was likely to get away with it.'

'But you're not!' I argue, following after her.

'Vyv. That is our deal. I wanted to be deaf and it's suited our

143

needs for me to play dumb. Perfectly. It's done. Gone. It just took me by surprise when you brought his name up . . .'

'What do you want me to do about him, then?' I plead.

She shuffles me out. 'Get some sleep and forget about it. And Vyv? No mention of this ever again, d'you promise?'

I nodded, imagining myself a Caesar in the Colosseum, giving the thumbs down to a miniature gladiator sporting a large J. small j. on his shield staring up at his fate, prior to being disembowelled by some Spartan. But this thought is interrupted by the unexpected stab of her parting shot:

'Your new aftershave smells a bit girly. G'night.'

Case of once smitten, twice sniffened out. Head for the shower for a serious scrubbing of cheeks both top and bottom. To descent Kyla Bergman.

Never again!

# LITTLE BIG MAN

Midway through discussing the installation of the glass fireplace, Connor kneels down and ruffles Doug's coat and, without looking up, announces that he needs to speak to me.

'In private. Not here. There's too many workmen around.'

He pulls on cap and sunglasses and whistles for Doug to follow us out to his jeep. He checks up and down the street, then squints towards the hills for signs of any lurking lenses.

Once we are driving he explains how he is under surveillance – there has been telephoto evidence of his toing and froing in various magazines. 'Not that it bothers me that much, Vy, but I'll tell you this: I just don't get it. Do you know what I mean? I mean, I'm just this guy. You know? I'm finding it hard to stay normal out here. I figured it this way: seems like the people who go to the movies want you to be like them. Sorta. Maybe better looking a bit, but you know, there's a word for it, God damn it I had it a minute ago – accessible, that's it! Accessible. But see, here's where the problems start. It's like they want me to be this regular guy who got lucky, which I did, and Doug, my dog, well, completes the picture. You see? Now here's what I'm still tryin' ta figure out. I've been reading a lot you know, like you do, cos there's all this sitting-round time on the set between set-ups and stuff, and I've been reading actors' life stories. All the greats. And I tell you this, I started underlining stuff. And the stuff I found I was underlining was always about their troubles and their bad childhoods. Which is what's got me so damned worried. Got me thinking about my childhood. And I made this terrible discovery.'

He slows down, all the while checking his rear-view mirror for tails. Satisfied that we haven't been followed, he pulls over and parks on a narrow ridge, the Pacific stretching away below us.

'D'you mind if we walk down and sit near the water a bit? Doug likes me to throw a stick for him.'

He throws a branch for the dog, who goes leaping into the water to retrieve it.

'I discovered that my childhood is totally normal.'

Connor is visibly appalled by this admission. With furrowing brows he goes on: 'Nobody in my family could ever be described as neurotic. Nobody was especially cruel s'far as I can remember – except for maybe the time when my ma hollered at me for dropping a box of eggs when I was seven. But she had good reason to get angry, cos those eggs were worth money to her. And I was growing so fast and she'd say, "Connor, you gotta slow down growin', son, your feet are too big for your legs. Tell 'em to catch up."'

I look down and indeed he has a pair of size fourteens.

'It's just that compared to all the other actors I keep meeting and reading 'bout, all of 'em are troubled. And I reckon if I'm ever gonna be any good at this thing, I gotta get myself some real troubles. I'm just not interesting enough to be really interesting to people. When I'm around the guys I've been filming with and I hear their stories, I can't join in. I feel like an outsider. Just left out. Sorta.'

He has started Scud-missiling pebbles along the surface of the water.

'The only thing that anyone really wants to do to me it seems is take pictures of me coming in and out of my house with a zoom lens, or get a picture of me walking Doug along the beach in my trunks. My mom sent me these pictures and asked me why I was walking around Hollywood with no clothes on? It doesn't hassle me, cos I never see these magazines, but my ma says the folks on the next-door farm say stuff. So I've started to check whenever I come in and out of the condo. My agent suggested I get a therapist cos he thinks I could be in denial.'

He articulates the word as if it belonged in a specimen jar.

'So what do you think?'

'Why are you asking me?'

'You're not in the movie business. Well, you're around it, but you're not *in* it. Plus you're the only person I know who says gotcha. And because of your sister. Marga is just like a girl I grew up with, only she wasn't deaf or anything like that, but you could talk to her about anything. And even though Marga can't hear, I've told her about home and my pa dying and everything cos it just seemed like the most natural thing to do. Which I guess is pretty dumb, seeing as she can't hear anything, but the way she manipulated my back, I swear to you, all the pain I had from my old sport injuries has disappeared. I s'pose I feel like both of you aren't after anything.'

'Connor, I am designing for you and that is work. I'm not doing it for nothing. Same way that Marga's body manipulation is her profession. We are in your service.'

He shakes his head in disagreement.

'Sure, I know that, what I mean is that – you've never asked for anything. Either of you. Outside of what you do. This is hard to kinda explain, but I want you to know that I really appreciate being able to talk to you like this, without ... without having to keep a tab of what I've told you. It's like this – ever since stuff has started to happen for me out here, you know, all this attention, people I have never met before are coming on like they've known me my whole life. People I have met for two seconds somewhere come up and act like we're best friends. And I know it's all bullshit, but I can't say anything, cos I don't wanna hurt their feelings, but it's getting so's I don't wanna go anywhere much. So I've been hanging with the surfin' guys. I found a bunch of guys who never go to the movies. Don't watch the TV, but know everything about the tides and times of the sun coming up and going down. They never ask me what I do, other than when we're next gonna meet and surf. Even when I go away on location for months, there's no questions asked when I show up again. I know that one of 'em knows I'm an actor cos he said something about a billboard once – my face is the size of a car on Sunset Boulevard opposite Tower Records for a movie – but he said it real quiet, so's I wouldn't be embarrassed in front of the other guys. This is the only group of people I know out here who are anything like the folks back home. We don't even know each other's names. We've got surf names which we get given according to what has happened at sea. Like there's this guy called Dumper, on account of the fact that when he got started surfing, he was always getting dumped.'

I interrupt with, 'So what's your name?'

'They call me Feetfirst – cos I got such huge feet and cos the first time I got up on a board, I stayed up.'

'Seems to me that you've found the perfect way for handling stardom. Generally speaking, the way in which people start out maps their navigational course through all the bullshit to come. In other words, if you're an arsehole to begin with, chances are you're going to be an even bigger one the more successful you become. People pay thousands of dollars and spend endless hours in therapy striving to get to where you are. Believe me, if you stay in showbusiness your whole life, there will be torture ahead of one sort or another, but not having a trunkload up front is a huge advantage. Trust me!'

He averts his eyes, not entirely convinced.

'I just don't feel that I qualify, somehow.'

'I'll tell you what. Your next three movies – make sure you choose the worst scripts, crappiest directors and some C-list talent, aim for a trio of box-office bombs, and we'll meet here same time next year and see how tortured you are. Then you'll be a fully paid-up member. Agreed?'

He laughed at me. 'How have you survived it here?'

For once, I find myself stalled. Why? Because while my decorating instincts are plundered on a daily basis, it's pretty rare for actors to ask anything of me that does not directly relate to themselves. I'm also wondering where all this is heading.

'Well?'

'Connor, I love what I do. I never really think about surviving. I've always loved the movies, and as I cannot act or direct this is the nearest way in that I chanced upon. Travelled the world. Met the best people. And worst. And if I chunner on any further, you'll hear symphonic strings playing in "My Way". I love my life. Simple as that.'

'Yeah, but what about when you face a nightmare scenario?'

'Like what?'

'Well, let me ask you something. What would you do if you got an anonymous letter, on a repeat basis?'

Bingo! Like a well-trained performing goat, I get myself onto my hind legs and beg, 'What do the letters say?'

Connor blushes from the base of his neck through to the roots of his streaked long hair, stammering an, 'I can't. It's too embarrassing.'

I oblige with the obligatory pause and opt for the tried and tested Bluebeard manoeuvre, saying, 'Then don't tell me.' How many seconds will it be before he turns the key and reveals all? I begin counting to twenty, but am interrupted at eleven.

'Will you promise not to tell anyone about this if I tell you?'

I throw the dog's stick and nonchalantly assure him not to tell me.

'Maybe you won't think it's that embarrassing?' he fishes.

'Connor – it's your choice. Sounds like you're dealing with her just fine.'

His eyebrows charge at one another and he asks: 'How do you know it's a her?'

'I don't. I just assume that it's more likely be a female letter writer.'

'Well, I sure hope it is a her.' He is frowning with deep conviction.

'You're starting to sound tortured, Connor. Be careful!'

He laughs, takes a deep breath and decides to tell.

'Only if you swear never to repeat this to anyone else, OK?'

My patience is bottoming out.

'I get these one-sentence notes, wherever I am, always the same sentence, but made up of different-sized lettering. Cut out from a magazine.'

He stops. Looks at me like a threatened puppy, prompting me to ask: 'Is it a life-threatening sentence?'

'No. That would make it simpler. It's, it's ... [C'MON!] it's always the same demand and it's the increasing numbers of them that are starting to get me freaked.'

Doug collapses in a pant at Connor's feet. Instead of saying it out loud, he opts for showing me, withdrawing a crumpled red envelope from his pocket. 'Here. See what you think.' He turned away.

I open the folded page and stare:

### I WANT YOUR SPERM

I can't help laughing when I realize who it is from. 'Lucky you. How flattering!'

Connor, multiply blushing, admonishes me with, 'It's not funny!'

'Connor, it's not life-threatening!'

'No, but it's relentless. And how do I know it's not a guy?'

I stand up, and say: 'Well if it is, we'll just have to get you kitted out with some plutonium-reinforced ironclad underpants.'

This gets him laughing, back in the jeep and on our way back to his condo, where we discuss installing an electric blind system for his glass roof, in case of helicopter paparazzi. Before sending me on my way he asks, 'Can you imagine what kind of a woman would be compelled to write me like that?'

I grin and say, 'At a push. Yes!'

Grin all the way into my car, grin goodbye and keep grinning till I turn the corner and mouth two words: Java Hall.

I had actually heard her howl *I want his sperm* over the phone in the middle of the night. Knowing Java Hall as I do, what Java Hall wants, Java Hall mostly gets. What most immediately worries me is the fact that I am the only connection she has with him.

I call Nikki for an update of calls and appointments and wish I hadn't.

'Richard Eagles called twice. First via his assistant and then personally. Says he needs to see you in person, ASAP. And Harold and Tony called to say that they have a shipment of antique dog kennels just in. Do you want me to go see them, or shall I suggest they choose some for Mr Rottweil? I have a note here to keep one aside for Mr Child?'

The cranial expansion induced by Mr Eagles' summons is so appalling that my vocals go on automatic pilot with the kennel requests.

'Yes, uh ... Harold and Tony. Keep a large one for Connor. When did Richard call?'

'Twenty minutes ago.'

'I take it he's at home?'

'Correct. Now there are other calls from—'

'Nikki, I'm going to see Eagles now. I'll call you when I'm done.'

Oh, Jesus! If he knows, he must know, why else would he call twice? And a second time personally? The room must have been bugged, monitored, the dog fitted with a miniature camera on its collar, videoing us on the floor – get a grip! Maybe it was that new assistant, what's her name, Flo? Or is it Devonia? C'mon, Vyvian! You know Devonia. It must have been Flo. She looked at me funny.

She'd never dare.

Kyla tell him?

He smell me on her? Some gardener see us through the windows?

My shirt feels damp all down the middle of my back. Close my eyes, take a deep inhalation, flatten the accelerator and speed towards my fate.

★

Devonia, their longest-serving assistant, ushers me into the screening room, which convinces me that I am about to be confronted
by mine cuckolded host for rogering his wife on the property – I
have never, in all my dealings with either of them, been led into
this soundproofed room other than for an actual screening. And
that is always at night, never midmorning. Every business meeting
regarding design and construction has been held in either of their
offices, or in the living room. Never in here. I can feel my pubes
straightening.

Devonia declines to offer me a drink and leaves, saying, 'Richard
will be with you shortly.' (She is the only staff member on a first-
name basis with her employers.)

The airless, darkly lit room, with its plush seats, feels very
tomblike. Perfect for a shaming. Especially as I designed the room
myself. The implications of my indiscretion are on a roller-coaster
ride of their own, when they are interrupted by the startlingly
silent entrance of my Nemesis.

Richard's voice quietly invites me to take a seat.

I do.

'Thank you for coming by so quickly.'

The lack of acoustic deadens his voice completely.

'I need to talk to you about something very serious.'

It takes all my reserves not to yowl out, 'I can explain everything,' in the pause that follows. He sits next to me, puts his hands
on his forehead and sighs. (Oh, fuck!)

This is it.

'Vy, we've known each other how many years – ten, twelve?
Before I met Kyla, even.'

I just nod, like a fake dachshund in the rear window of a white-
trash jalopy.

'I have trusted you with everything in my homes. Everything.'

This is approaching verbal water torture.

'I have a big problem.'

So do I: I seem to have lost contact with the lower part of my

152

body. It feels paralysed. Perhaps I have suffered a seizure while waiting without knowing it?

Richard gets up, propels himself to the padded wall and punches it with both hands again and again.

'I can't take it!'

He swirls around and looks as if he is about to pounce, but sits beside me, head in his hands.

'Vyvian, I know this might sound dumb, but I'm in a real situation here.'

You can say that again!

'I take it you know about *Zeitgeist*?'

I emit what sounds like a grasshopper's fart, signalling that I do.

'I've been asked to do it, as has Kyla, but I have a serious, serious problem.'

As rapidly as he winds up to speed, so my circulation sluggishly lurches and revives feelings again in my lower half. I am off his hook. Aaaaaaah!

I'm briefly distracted from his 'seriously serious problem', but the overwhelming relief I am experiencing is post-orgasmic.

The gist of his angst, it emerges, is to do with playing in the same movie as Connor Child. Never stated directly, but skewed out of a torturous monologue.

'Connor Child is signed to do *Zeitgeist*, is he?' I query, surprised that he never mentioned this during his beachside confessional.

'As near as dammit. I'm sure Connor's a great guy, but this is the first time in a long time that I have not had casting approval. Mort Buchinsky has never waived his directorial right and it's hard to argue with a double Academy Award winner. I don't have a problem with that, but I had been told that Harrison Ford is going to be playing the *Zeitgeist* captain. No problems with that, he is the captain. But apparently he's passed on it due to role-overlap with *Star Wars*.'

My eyes are starting to glaze.

'Mort thought it a good idea to have the captain played much younger and is thinking of Connor Child. I do have a problem with that. What I'm after, in order to avoid confrontation or contact, is some kind of corridor to get me from my Winnebago to the set, which I'd like you to design. I'll claim it as a privacy, "keeping-in-character" clause. The reason we're meeting in here is that you are the only person I am entrusting this information to. Do you have any ideas?'

I hear the following shunting off my tongue: 'Richard, as always, your words are Secure. D'you remember *E.T.*? When Elliot's house is impounded and they have those chutes for the scientists to get in and out of the house?'

'Not really.'

'You know those metal Slinky toys that kids have that can spool down stairs? Well, if I had one constructed life-sized and covered with parachute silk, it could retract and extend between your trailer and a studio door or set. Like a large caterpillar.'

'Problem solved,' and the famed Richard Eagles screen smile comes glittering my way, accompanied by a virile handshake.

'I have to tell you, Vy, since coming back from India, I want to avoid any chance of bad karma, and as good a guy as Child is supposed to be, his box office ascendancy is like sand in my oyster.'

He has dropped the smile. As we walk out into daylight, I feel as if I have awoken from a nightmare, but the lethal fact of schtupping Kyla still hovers on my conscience.

# THE WINDS OF WAR

*Variety*:

> PRINCIPAL CASTING FOR *ZEITGEIST* COMPLETED:
> RICHARD EAGLES, KYLA BERGMAN, CONNOR CHILD,
> JAVA HALL, TED MOBY, GEORGIA SEPULVEDA AND
> INTRODUCING TIBET.
> Howie Lollapaloosa confirmed that the MORT BUCHINSKY,
> Jj DAGNEY co-production includes an ALL-STAR supporting
> cast. START DATE – MAY 1st.

Technophobe is first on the line, frothing about his return from the twilight zone. He is convinced that by going minimal he has somehow invoked the gods of kind-casting, feels resurrected and holds that I am inextricably linked to his good fortune. He asks whether I am still friends with the Buchinskys.

(One can never assume in this town that because someone is best friends this year or month it will remain the case. It rarely does. And I know – part of my company services is the updating of customer diaries and databases. Downloading information about which numbers a star most frequently uses proves revelatory.

From one year to the next, some remain, but these tend to be mostly close relatives or friends from childhood. The majority of the other numbers are regularly dumped to make way for a fresh intake. It's like an index of who's in and who is going out. The number of times celebrity numbers have to be changed to protect their privacy adds to the confusion and is in itself an indicator of your star status – if you have to change your numbers every couple of months, you are sure to be in a state of Vindaloo career-heat.

Unless you're Technophobe; then your numbers change due to

amateur tampering with the phone equipment and the actual line into the property. And it might not surprise you to learn that Georgia Sepulveda placed an anonymous call to the *National Enquirer* magazine giving them the Sepulveda number, in the hope of being deluged by some 'unwanted publicity'.)

Java calls – 'Who the hell is Tibet?'

I am summoned to lend my outside ear to the casting session, chez Buchinsky.

Jj and Mort have drawn up a list of names, which Jj is now sitting on the floor and reading through. Mort has poured himself a dark double on ice and is pacing about the living room. Kitty sits cross-legged on a deep sofa, listening, both hands cupped beneath her chin, I am sunk into another sofa, listening to the names being dropped and plotting the little perv's downfall.

Mort clears his throat. 'Jj, if we go all the way with this, and I'm talking *all* the way, I reckon we can make the first postmodernist-action-disaster picture for the next millennium.'

Jj looks up at the mention of postmod.

'I hear you, Mort, but I have serious doubts that you'll ever get all these people to show up.'

Kitty pipes up that her old friend Bob Altman had gone through his Rolodex and secured everybody who was in *The Player*.

The little oik emits fresh doubt from his position on the floor: 'Yeah, but, this list is just impossible. Anyway, if it's been done before, what's the point of repeating ourselves?'

Mort is not going to be deterred and revs up to speed.

'Listen, Jj, *everything* has been done before. We are essentially doing a remake of *The Poseidon Adventure*. Except this time around, everyone is a celebrity. This has never been done before. Every other sci-fi flick has been set so far in the fucking future that no one questions how they got up there. In this picture we are going to show that. Show the arrivals. Boarding procedure. Take off. Journey into outer space. New Year's Eve in the new century. At midnight the spacecraft, *Zeitgeist* – nicknamed "The Unstoppable" – is going to get hit by something – meteor, black hole,

Bermuda fucking Space Triangle, I don't know what yet. Whichever is the most dramatic and plausible. It will be the space equivalent of the iceberg that the *Titanic* ploughed into.

'The *Zeitgeist* splits in two, and we stick with the back section. Which plunges back to Earth and into the ocean. The other half, which is carrying the majority of the star guests, disappears in space. Perfect for the sequel.

'Meanwhile, the survivors find themselves in an upside-down craft that has miraculously survived the crash, but is sinking fast. They have to work their way to the top in order to try and get out. A perfect sandwich of *Titanic* and *Poseidon*. With a twist.'

'But, Mort, how in the fuck are you gonna convince a bunch of spoilt, overpaid movie stars to agree to be themselves on a journey into oblivion? They will never agree to disappear. How will you sell them that?'

'Once I have convinced a core group of the top players, the rest will follow. You gotta have a little more faith, Jj. Leave the cast list stuff to me and Howie, and I promise you, you'll have a plate full coping with the technical demands I'm gonna be throwing your way. I'm not questioning how you're gonna get the *Zeitgeist* airbound. Or how it's gonna explode. Or how it'll look mid-plunge. Or upside down in the water. I'm trusting you totally to do all of that. That's your genius. I told you right up front, I know nothing about the technical stuff. You do. I can admire, I can appreciate, but I haven't a clue how to morph or computerize a single frame. We need to be very clear on this before we begin.'

Mort is crunching his ice, always a worrying sign. Kitty, intercepting this, purrs up to him and engulfs him in a hug.

'Oh, Morty – it sounds just marvellous. Marvellous. So exciting!'

She gives him a kiss, turns and kneels down beside Jj, paws him all over and whispers stage-loudly, 'Honey, you are just fabulous! You two boys mustn't worry. It's going to be just *huuuuuuuge*.'

Jj is clearly unused to the idea that someone of Kitty's vintage can get this up close and passionate, judging by his look of confusion. She coquettes her way back to the sofa and picks up the phone.

'Watch me! Morty, do me another Martini, would you, please, honey – be ready to pick up for conference.'

She presses some numbers, looking down the list on her lap. Jj and I watch, somewhat bemused, while Mort sticks a toothpick through an olive and into the Y-shaped glass. Kitty smiles at her boys, and winks. Her voice swoops into 'Hiiiii honey' mode.

'It's Kitty! How are you, honey? So good to hear your voice. Beautiful as ever, how's Tom? Uh huh, uh huh ... Oh I know, we've just been talking about it. Morty has the most brilliant concept going. *Zeitgeist* is going to be just fabulous. We've got Jj Dagney over and he is just so full of ideas and energy. Now listen, you are the first people I've called, and I just know you're both gonna love this idea. But I don't wanna step on my boys' toes, so I'm gonna get Morty to talk to you – so good to find you both at home.'

She is waving at Morty to pick up and thumbs-upping at the same time.

'Nicole? Hi, sweetheart ... Thank you very much. I know, it's gonna be a big one, no question. How are the kids? ... Mmmhmm? Great! ... Now, I know your time is precious, so I'll get to it: *Zeitgeist* ... Uh huh – name of the spaceship. Imagine I'm Noah and *Zeitgeist* is the Ark. I want the greatest star-couplings to come aboard, two by two, as themselves, in their own clothes, for the first commercial flight into outer space. For the party of a lifetime. A party celebrating a lifetime in the movies. With every legend of the past and present participating. I see it as a unique opportunity to gather together every screen icon we have, as an historic record of our time, and our place. It's never been done before and the best thing about it is that it will only be a few days' work, no lines to learn, schedules to commit to, no competition and no press. It will be a unique opportunity to meet the truly great artists of our community, especially those who have been sequestered away for too long. I'm calling you and Tom first, because you are the Queen and King of Filmland. If you agree to it, everyone else will be sure to follow. No question.'

Nicole's reply gets Mort nodding and mmhmming. He then agrees to speak to Tom. Kitty and he top and tail their way through some sincere flattery, till both stop simultaneously. There is a wide-eyed pause, relieved by Mort's verification: 'So you'll do it?'

Kitty's 'We knew you would' seamlessly sews it all up.

They put down their phones and go into the kind of clinch that you'd expect to see from a couple of newly weds. Kitty waves a stray arm in Jj's direction and beckons him up, yanks him into a three-way, then growls, 'Vyvian!' and I join the hugfest. The differences in our heights and ages put me in mind of one of Tundra's sculptures.

Then, from Jj: 'How will these people ever agree to terms on this kind of scale?'

Kitty swoops on him, grabs both his cheeks, flaps them about like rubber gills and says: 'Don't be such a doubter, my little baba. This is just the start. Wait till we *both* get going!'

The momentum of the evening has completely changed gear, and I realize how left behind Jj is only when he tentatively enquires: 'Those people on the phone? Were they who I think they are?'

Mort's satisfaction is disguised by an avuncular grin. He can't resist a little taunting and casually asks: 'Who did you think they were?' (O short-arsed hater of stars . . .)

Jj actually blushes and mumbles, 'Kidman and Cruise?' in a feeble attempt to diminish their power.

Kitty *mmmmmmhmmmm*s confirmation, and declares, 'You gotta do it personally. Never work anyways else. Morty and I will call every name on that list. Tonight!'

Even Morty gulps at this prospect. Jj slinks in with some scoff: 'You'll never get people directly. There's just no way.'

Kitty is already dialling a number and reassuring him that everyone is only one phone call away. Kitty gestures towards the study and says: 'Vyvian, won't you be a honey and go get Kitty some extra pens and notepaper? Thanks, honey. Mel! It's Kitty!'

and before I am back she has Julia on the line, and in the bag.

I thought I had met almost everyone I had planned to already, but their combined star-harvesting is nothing short of awesome. Bale-loads of names are accumulating.

To speed things along, they split the list in half, each calling on a separate line, according to the idiosyncrasies of who is being persuaded: those who won't mind being called by Kitty, those who will respond only to Mort himself. At one stage, they have a multiple cross-way with Kitty saying, 'Hold on, Goldie, Morty's just got Sly on the other line, he says he'll do it so long as he can sit next to Kurt . . .'

★

By midnight, the agreed cut-off point, they have secured promises from almost everyone they have called. At times the calls are so short and fast that each person is given only seconds to decide yea or nay.

'When you deal with the best, you always get a straight-arrow response. It's the B- and C-lists that always carp about the money, the schedules, the who-else-is-signed-up? stuff. Always. Oh, honeeeeey! It's a landslide!'

Kitty is lying on the floor, and suddenly scoops her legs up and backwards over her head, and lies there in this contorted position, still talking.

'So how do you explain Georgia Sepulveda in terms of straight-arrow tactics?' beefs Jj. 'She's hardly A-list.'

Kitty spreads her legs to either side of her head.

'My darling Jj, Georgia is fabulously deranged. Artistically she will fight for what's right, all the way. But as for everything else, like all the greats, it's only the work that truly counts.'

'Do the studios know about this, Mort? I mean – how are they ever gonna pay them all?'

'When the studios see this list, they will not believe their fucking luck! None of the actors needs a dime. We'll do it on a charity basis. Each one'll get a nominal fee that we'll then entreat them to donate to the Actors' Fund. It'll be like Band Aid, but for old actors. Vyvian knows a lot of the old-timers through Syd Shirelle, and he's gonna do the coordinating and design the green room for 'em.'

'I am?'

'Course you are. Best man for the job.'

'It's unfilmable,' declares Dagney.

'Jj – it's *Zeitgeist*. It's UNSTOPPABLE. For once the term *Star Trek* will have real meaning.'

Mort drops the lists on the floor, closes his eyes and starts snoring.

It is 3.20 a.m. Kitty rolls over onto her side, yawns, gets up and drapes a cashmere throw over her mate, kisses us both goodnight and says to sleep in either of the guest suites if we'd like. Dagney dwarfs off into the dawn of his own overwhelm. I pick up the scribbled lists. Here they are:

Tom Cruise Nicole Kidman Bruce Willis Julia Roberts Mel Gibson Tom Hanks Meg Ryan Kevin Costner Goldie Hawn Arnold Schwarzenegger Sylvester Stallone Jodie Foster John Travolta Clint Eastwood Al Pacino Meryl Streep Steve Martin Denzel Washington Cher Harrison Ford Diana Ross Robert Redford Julie Christie Paul Newman Susan Sarandon Joanne Wood-ward Kevin Kline Jack Lemmon Walter Matthau Barbra Streisand Tim Robbins Warren Beatty Mia Farrow Glenn Close Sean Connery Demi Moore Diane Keaton Richard Gere Bette Midler Annette Bening Emma Thompson Johnny Depp Gary Oldman Michelle Pfeiffer Daniel Day-Lewis Sally Field Roger Moore Ben Kingsley Whoopi Goldberg Anthony Hopkins Sigourney Weaver Tim Roth Gene Hackman Liam Neeson Michael Douglas Will Smith Jessica Lange Robert De Niro Wesley Snipes Andie MacDowell Kenneth Branagh Lily Tomlin Keanu Reeves Sissy Spacek Angelica Huston Jeremy Irons Lauren Bacall Tommy Lee Jones Jack Nicholson Uma Thurman Eddie Murphy Madonna Michael Caine Sharon Stone Sophia Loren Jeff Goldblum Dianne Wiest Tony Curtis Martin Sheen Winona Ryder Mary Elizabeth Mastrantonio Aidan Quinn Willem Dafoe Forest Whitaker Alec Baldwin Shirley MacLaine Tom Berenger Julie Andrews Charles Bronson Shelley Winters Mel Brooks Debbie Reynolds Kevin Spacey Robin Williams Anne

Bancroft Alan Bates Kim Basinger Faye Dunaway John Hurt Donald Sutherland Claire Bloom Jim Carrey Pierce Brosnan Candice Bergen Burt Reynolds Gabriel Byrne Leslie Caron Dudley Moore Joan Collins Chevy Chase Jamie Lee Curtis Joan Cusack John Cusack John Cleese Judy Davis Richard Crenna Dyan Cannon Geena Davis Brad Pitt Beverly D'Angelo William Hurt Angie Dickinson Harvey Keitel Helena Bonham Carter Matt Dillon Britt Ekland Jennifer Jason Leigh Peter Falk Rosanna Arquette Andy Garcia Rupert Everett Zsa Zsa Gabor Dick Van Dyke Sally Kellerman Danny Glover John Goodman Cuba Gooding Jnr Helen Hunt Angela Bassett Ellen Burstyn George Hamilton Ethan Hawke Kevin Bacon Sandra Bernhard Ian Holm Grace Jones Elton John Matthew Modine Val Kilmer Christopher Lee Minnie Driver Ray Liotta Robert Sean Leonard Rob Lowe Charlie Sheen Jerry Lewis Liza Minnelli Natasha Richardson Sam Neill Danny De Vito William H. Macy Chita Rivera Joe Mantegna Frances McDormand Laura Dern Gregory Peck Kelly McGillis Malcolm McDowell Dolly Parton Mary Tyler Moore Shirley Temple Ryan O'Neal Peter O'Toole Omar Sharif Sarah Jessica Parker Roddy McDowall Elizabeth Taylor Michael Keaton Sean Penn Joe Pesci Billy Zane Christopher Plummer Sidney Poitier Bill Pullman Sandra Bullock Rod Steiger Dennis Quaid Randy Quaid the Carradine Brothers Jason Robards Mickey Rourke Katharine Ross Jane Russell Isabella Rossellini Jill St John Leonard Nimoy Robert Wagner Matthew Broderick John Savage Greta Scacchi George Segal Anthony Quinn Fred Ward Whitney Houston Jane Seymour Stacy Keach Talia Shire Sam Shepard Bob Hoskins Martin Short Jean Simmons James Spader Miranda Richardson Meg Tilly Stephen Rea Dean Stockwell Roseanne Barr Charlton Heston John Turturro Danny Aiello Kathleen Turner Cathy Tyson Jean-Claude Van Damme Tracey Ullman Jon Voight Christopher Walken Helen Mirren Esther Williams Kristin Scott-Thomas James Woods Alfre Woodard Holly Hunter Michael York Sean Young Ernest Borgnine Robert Duvall Ralph Fiennes Kurt Russell Tom Selleck Mary Steenbergen Ted Danson Christian Slater Barbara Hershey Drew Barrymore Amanda Plummer Tim Curry Robert Downey Jnr. Charles Bronson Michael Sarrazin Elizabeth McGovern Kiefer Sutherland Celine Dion Robert Vaughn James Caan Dennis Hopper Alan Alda Elliott Gould Chris O'Donnell Alicia Silverstone Irene Cara Lori Singer Joel Grey Ed Harris Morgan Freeman George Clooney Daryl Hannah Dan Aykroyd Cameron Diaz Antonio Banderas Melanie Griffiths Billy Crystal Gwyneth Paltrow Claire Danes Samuel L. Jackson John Malkovich Matt Damon Ewan McGregor Julianne Moore

Olympia Dukakis Kathy Bates Juliette Binoche Carrie Fisher Christopher Reeve Gina Gershon Patrick Swayze Richard Harris Liv Tyler Alan Rickman Nicolas Cage Elizabeth Shue Mickey Rooney Woody Harrelson Doris Day Carroll Baker Jackie Cooper Gregory Hines Howard Keel Jacqueline Bissett Ann Blyth Cyd Charisse Celeste Holm Ben Affleck Virginia Mayo Olivia Newton-John Kathryn Grayson Eva Marie Saint Marisa Tomei Richard Dreyfuss Marsha Mason Ashley Judd Matthew McConaughey Jennifer Grey Joaquin Phoenix Molly Ringwald Lyle Lovett Albert Finney Jack Palance Peter Ustinov Karl Malden Jane Wyman Hedy Lamarr Hume Cronyn Douglas Fairbanks Jr. John Gielgud Kirk Douglas Olivia de Havilland Fay Wray Richard Attenborough Harry Dean Stanton Glenne Headly Jane Allen Farrah Fawcett Patrick Stewart Linda Hunt Frances Fisher Christian Bale Raquel Welch.

Let's hope they all live long enough . . .

# TORA! TORA! TORA!

The news of the casting is out, and the following one-way conversation is nitroglycerining down the ear of some poor recipient while I am arranging the antique dog kennels in ascending order of size in Randy Rottweil's living room.

'LISTEN TO ME, you cheap fuck in a crap suit! [For one terrible moment I think he is talking to me.] It can never be done! D'you hear me? Uuh-nuh, no no no NO! Nobody will show for this piece of shit. Mort fuckin' Buchinsky. LEMME TELL YOU. Mort fuckin' Buchinsky is fuckin' dead already. In the water. Out the water. D'you copy? D.E.A.D.! What the fuck d'you think his first name sounds like, if it isn't I-fuckin'-talian for dead? MORT. MORTO. Comprendez? Over and outsky, Mortally fucked Buchinsky. No stars are gonna turnout for some cockamamie schlockflick for fuckin' charity! Wake UP! Where'd you get this idea that anyone other than the fuckin' press could dream up such a crock of SHIT!? HIS CAREER HAS BEEN DEAD FOR YEARS. DECADES. GONE. FINITO. The cast he's got only agreed to sign up because of Jj Dagney. Don't fucking kid yourself, kid. Jj Dagney. He's the man, not old Morty. Don't insult my fuckin' taste and intelligence. NO ONE, I REPEAT, NO ONE, NOT ONE OF THE GUEST STARS IS GONNA GET PAST THEIR FRONT DOORS TO SHOW UP FOR A CHEAP REMAKE PIECE OF DINOSAUR CRAP CALLED FUCKIN' *ZEITGEIST*. HAVEN'T YOU HEARD? IT'S ALREADY OVER-BUDGET AND THEY HAVEN'T EVEN TURNED OVER A FRAME OF FILM YET. *SHITEGEIST*, THAT'S WHAT THEY'RE CALLING IT. WE ARE TALKING *WATERWORLD* MEETS *HEAVEN'S GATE* MEETS *HUDSON HAWK* MEETS *LAST ACTION HERO* MEETS *THE* FUCKING *POSTMAN*.'

Randy has so hyperventilated in the pursuit of sufficient vitriol that he has collapsed forwards and is now wheezing on all fours atop his antique Sri Lankan dining table (he had climbed onto it when he shifted up into capital-letter gear).

The dogs have romped in to add their vocals to the proceedings, and take up the decibel slack while Randy recuperates, readying himself for round two. Barely missing a beat, and without hushing the hounds, he inhales and hurtles forth with his views about the contracted cast.

'Lemme tell you something about Kyla fuckin' Bergman. The American public will never, NEVER buy that cunt as the new Sigourney Weaver. She is as cold as fuckin' ice. And the only reason she's got where she's got to is that she is married to that overpaid WASP fuck Eagles. The guy is fuckin' cross-eyed and his hair is receding. Lemme tell you something for nothing, the only decent cast they've got is Georgia Sepulveda, cos she's the only actress who everyone knows is as insane as the plot of this fucking non-movie. IT'S A NON-MOVIE. D'YOU COPY THAT? A BIG FUCKIN' NON. This will sink the fuckin' studios and I'm not gonna be around when they start yellin' BRING OUT YOUR DEAD. DO YOU HEAR ME? YOU FUCK? HUH?? YOU FUCK-FUCK! IT. IS. UN. FILMABLE! UN. D'you hear me? UN. NOW I'D LIKE TO HEAR IF YOU HAVE ANYTHING TO SAY?'

By the astonished expression that rearranges his now swollen features, the other party clearly does. And after a few seconds his post-medication-and-therapy voice returns.

'I would be honoured . . . Of course . . . It'll be a privilege. They actually requested me personally? . . . Whatever you say . . . I thank you . . . I will.'

He gently replaces the receiver, gulps and then gulps again.

'Richard Eagles and Kyla Bergman have personally requested my executive producing services on *Zeitgeist*, based upon my work on *Hectic*.'

# PART TWO

# *ZEITGEIST*

## *THE MOVIE*

# THE DIARY

# 3 April

Multiple commissions to design and decorate the Winnebagos for the core cast. Randy's word was to go the Full Monty.

'It's gonna be a tough shoot for all of us and the stars have to be deluxed out – give them everything they'll ever need and then something extra at your discretion. I mean it, when I say no expense spared. You have my authorization. By the way, thanks for the new antique kennels. I love 'em.'

Georgia's hand was still in plaster when we sat down to go through her requirements.

'I want EVERYTHING. Right? This fucking town OWES me!'

She banged her cast down on the table for emphasis. I ticked down the list of TV, video, shower, bath, bed, CD, refrigerator, phone, fax and e-mail usuals, and assured her that the sitting area would be substantial.

'I don't like the *sub*, part, Vy. *Stantial* is the word for what I have in mind. Right? Right! Are you doing anyone else's?'

'Potentially,' I said, as dismissively as I could.

'You make sure that my trailer is the EXACT same size as those other cocksuckers'. Right? I will NOT stand for my first day's shooting being ruined by finding out that I've been shunted off into some shower-stall-sized toilet. Right? And then have to walk past Ms Hall and Ms Bergman's Babylons-on-wheels. RIGHT?!'

'Whoah, Trigger. Georgia – everyone is getting the exact same size of trailer. Randy has specified equal favoured nations stipulations in your contracts to avoid any aggro.'

'Don't get vernacular with me. It doesn't suit you. Speak properly. It's one of your greatest assets.'

'Why, thank you.'

'Don't mention it. What about Scarlett?'

I assured her, 'There'll be plenty of room for her to visit.'

'Could you organize interconnecting doors?'

I was missing something here, and she answered before I could ask.

'Didn't you know? My Scarlett is going to be in the movie. She's playing Kyla's daughter. So I want to know if our trailers can be linked together.'

Java could barely talk, such was her rage when she heard this news. So she burst into tears instead, tears being to Java Hall what tea is to India – her supply is endless. Amid sobs, and much grinding of molars, she yelped, 'But where is the justice in this decision? I am the only one with my own, naturally conceived [debatable] child. Mona's the exact same age as Scarlett and is even in the same improv class. Why didn't Mort audition Mona? I suppose this was Bergman's idea, was it? Infertile witch. So just to get one over on me, Kyla La-di-dah has some ancient old has-been's adoptive child to play her daughter. She knew Mona would have been perfect, but no. It's her way of pulling status.'

I swabbed her swollen cheeks and tentatively suggested that it was unlikely Mort would ever have intentionally slighted Mona, explaining that, as Mort had directed Georgia in her first picture thirty years ago, they knew each other.

'And for the record, Georgia is not exactly ancient.'

Her muffled sobs fooled me into thinking that she was accepting this, till I realized that she was merely waterskiing up to speed when she let rip, spraying in all directions:

'She is *ancient*! And what's more, they are all star-fuckers. The only reason they're using Scarlett is that she's been on the news so many goddam times playing Little Miss Calm-and-Perfect every time her gun-toting lunatic of a so-called mother wants some publicity!'

She had a point.

'Kyla's problem is that she has never had any tits,' she spat, then sneezed.

'Java, this is not getting us anywhere. Yours aren't natural, remember?'

She fisted a bunch of fresh tissues and retorted, 'They were! Before Mona milked them down,' the memory of which unleashed a fresh cascade of water.

'This is such a great role for you. Sexy, demanding, challenging, funny. You're perfect for it.'

Ah, we were back on familiar Astroturf. She snorted to attention and snivelled, 'D'you really think so? They don't just want me to sling off my bra, one last time?'

'Of course not. From what I recall, Stella Stevens never exposed herself in the original *Poseidon*.'

The contrast between Java's public persona of supreme poise and this private mayhem recalls a Dalí portrait. All open drawers and limbs on fire. The combination of her dressing gown, worn-out slippers, unwashed hair and make-up free face as she shuffled through the tissuescape left no room to doubt her white-trash roots. This is what her mother must have looked like before she was burnt to death, having failed to switch off a deep-fat fryer.

'I still want his sperm.'

'Now whose would that be?' I asked, in the hope that Connor might have been usurped by some new obsession. Java stung me with a 'don't fuck with me' look.

'Connor Child's. And I *will* have him!'

'What do you want in terms of your trailer requirements?'

'Apart from him? Everything Kyla's getting.'

That settled that, then.

171

# 4 April

'I want a different trailer design to Richard's,' instructed Kyla, cool, clear and not a scrap of acknowledgement of the Picasso drawing or exchange of bodily fluids in this study some weeks ago. She truly is a Hitchcockian customer. Simply dressed, flat-shoed and blond-chignoned. Direct and quietly awesome. In all, everything Java Hall wants to be. I had to remind myself that this latter-day Novak was only twenty-eight.

Naturally her choice of trailer interior is minimalist with four variations of soft white. No distractions. Meditative. And yes, medical. All the usual furniture and gadgetry is to be struck, save for a sound system to provide peaceful classical background music, 'the choice of which I'll leave to you, Vyv.'

She never talks about her co-stars – not because she is too discreet to do so, but rather due to her total absence of any interest in them. Her conviction of her own talent and skill is complete. Cosmic. Which gives her this slightly remote, royal air that succeeds in impressing some, and infuriating attention freaks (Java, Georgia).

I have decided to take Java at her word and have ordered that her trailer be identical to Kyla's in every detail. What I haven't told Java, though, is that Kyla will be bringing her own gymnasium-on-wheels, which will be parked alongside her minimalist trailer. I intend to do my utmost to ensure that I am not within earshot when Java sees it.

Met Connor at his newly set-up office in Santa Monica to discuss *his* trailer.

'Isn't this neat?' he admired, pointing at the various details of the room. It was a fifties den, replete with jukebox, Coke dispenser, pool table, milkshake bar and stick furniture. Curtains featured cowboys bronco-ing up and down the fabric.

'This is what I want. Exactly! D'you think you can do it?'

'I don't see why not.'

Then, while Doug licked Connor's '14' feet, his master outlined his desire for an antechamber, or 'character decompression' room.

'I reckon I'm gonna be so damned happy all the time in the den that my acting might suffer, and I'm supposed to be playing this space captain in crisis, as they call it. I'll really need a halfway house to get myself in and out of character.'

'Gotcha! You want to be able to commute between your past and the future setting of *Zeitgeist*.'

He nodded vigorously.

'Do you want this to include an interlocking door, perhaps on a delayed timer, so that you are required to spend a minimum couple of minutes between the set and your den in the decompression chamber?'

He thought this a quite brilliant idea.

I had done such a design once before, for a now-legendary actor cast to play Luciano Rimini in a Mafia epic. We devised a replica of Luciano's grandmother's kitchen – cramped, cast-iron stove, permanently slow-cooking pot of tomato and basil sauce presided over by a non-English-speaking Italian widow (in fact a retired character actress who gave the best uncredited off-screen performance of a Mama Corleone you will sadly never see) playing his grandma. She knitted and cooked and always kissed him as he came and went between scene breaks and camera set-ups. It worked a treat and the advertising posters concurred by announcing HE *IS* LUCIANO.

Connor decided to invite only crew members in for pool, excluding other actors, for fear of character contamination.

Called Harold and Tony, who assured that all the paraphernalia for the den was a phone call away and that they had a fifties TV in perfect working order. I have decided to buy everything, rather than hire, as I suspect Connor will want to keep everything after the movie wraps.

# 5 April

For Technophobe, the novelty of having had his power supply suspended has been worn down by acute inconvenience.

'My ice cream supply kept melting in the paraffin-fuelled fridge, so I got reconnected.'

The house smelt of fresh paint and burning candles, which were in evidence everywhere, and I congratulated myself for insisting on water-based emulsions lest he incinerated himself. I looked around for signs of techno-reversion, and the only evidence was the latest miniature handycam, lying blinking on its side in the corner.

'Aren't you proud of me? Still free of any fuss.'

'Congratulations, Mobe. What's that blinking in the corner?'

He stuttered, blushed and explained that, 'I just *had* to get one. It's so neat and compact and utterly beautiful and they tell me that the picture quality is professional.'

I could not help myself asking, 'Do you know how to operate it?'

Moby skittered a bit and said, 'Working on that. Working on that one. Now!'

And he was off down the verbal highway of what he wanted in his trailer which provoked an episode of career confession time.

'You know something, Vy? I've been in this business – how many years? I've lost count of how many pictures I've been in. Never saw half of them, and the reason for that is that I never really got to play the lead roles. This role in *Zeitgeist* is the best part I've had in years. Nobody ever asked me before what kind of trailer I wanted. And to tell you the truth, it's made me feel a little embarrassed. Like I'm not worthy. I know this is gonna sound maybe insane to you, but I want my caravan to be mirrored. Top to bottom, and I'll tell you why. It seems like the more movies I make, the less visible I've become. My shrink thinks it's the reason I got so into the technical collecting. But here's my problem. He has asked me to repair a CD player for him, and I can't bring myself to tell him no, because I reckon if he finds out I'm cured and can't fix anything, he'll dump me from his client list. And his list is the one thing that still makes me feel like I'm in there. If he drops me, I'd probably never get employed again. So the reason I want mirrors is so that I will see myself at all times, from every angle, so I'll know I'm someone. I think the Native Americans were right when they claimed that the camera takes away the person's soul. I feel invisible. And I want to become visible again.'

I felt embarrassed that a man of his age and professional standing could be so crippled with such terror at being exposed.

'Ted, your shrink can't fire you. You hire him!'

'You wanna bet? I'm his least famous client. I've gotta hang in there. There is too much riding on this role to lose. At least in my role as the engineer I won't have to really know *how* to work any of the technical shit. Can you help me?'

'Teddy, you can have all the mirrors you want.'

(I hadn't the heart to tell him, after his total clear-out, that his technical expertise was the main reason for his casting. Mort had asserted, 'Here is an actor who can actually fix something other than his make-up or a drink!')

'I have this theory. I've worked out that every star has a mirror image or alternative to themselves. Except me! Take Meryl Streep – her alternative is Glenn Close. Each got about the same number of nominations . . . but Meryl got the two Oscars. They could be sisters, except one is just a bit off-looking. Same with Harrison Ford and Steve Martin. Apart from the hair colour, these guys could be brothers. Except one is in action and the other in laughs.'

He laid out stills of each actor side by side on the centre table.

'D'you see what I mean? Check out Jack Nicholson and Keith Richards . . . it's why I reckon Jack has that rock 'n' roll crossover appeal. There's more – De Niro and Keitel, Oldman and Roth, Streisand and Cher. It's like the stars have twin-like versions of themselves, doubling up and ensuring their supremacy. So you gotta be real careful in casting things, because sometimes they can cancel each other out, or cause combustion of talent that overwhelms the rest of the movie. Oh yeah, and look at these two pictures – Sharon Stone and Faye Dunaway. They're the same, I tell you. It's uncanny. Al Pacino and Joe Pesci.'

He shuffled and cross-examined his collection of stills that he had convinced himself were photographic proof of his skewed convictions.

'So you feel that you have no twin, then?' I asked, trying not to indicate that I thought the folks in the little white coats would be coming for him soon.

'I do, but only in spirit, rather than in looks, which is my problem . . .'

'Who would that be, then?'

'Travolta!' he uttered without a second's doubt.

(Ye Gods!)

He packed up all the stills and put the envelope under his arm as we walked to the front door.

'Vyv, I am trusting you with this. Please don't breathe a word of my theory to anyone. I don't want them to steal it from me.'

'You have my word.'

Confirmed by phone that Richard Eagles wanted nothing out of the ordinary, except for the retractable Slinky tunnel. Nikki coordinated with the trailer companies for construction work to begin.

Marga was contracted to be exclusively available to the cast of *Zeitgeist* with the proviso that she would never have to be on the actual set, so as to avoid any contact with Jj Dagney. The following message was SOSing on my service when I got home:

'Hi, Vyv? Randy. Emergency. Need some personalized shopping for the main cast ASAP. Want to gift them all in style, but as I have none, need your help. Shop Barney's. You choose. Have account. Go all the way.'

You might think that buying gifts for people who already have everything would be a problem, but not a bit of it. The mere gesture of being given something for nothing warms that near forgotten little part of their hearts which remembers what it was like when no one gave them anything apart from a rejection slip of the tongue. In my experience, the larger and more ostentatious the gift, the less likely it is to be appreciated, revealing more about the inflated ego of the sender than the needy recipient. 'Small is big' is my gifting policy. Made a list:

1. A prize piece of crystallized quartz for Georgia Sepulveda chosen by Randy Rottweil will be a guaranteed triumph.
2. Java Hall – (a manual on chaos control?) faith pebbles of spun glass.
3. Connor Child – baseball bat signed by Di Maggio.
4. Kyla Bergman – vial of sperm? . . . stuck on that one for now.
5. Richard Eagles – original biplane miniature from the thirties. (He flies.)
6. Technophobe – Snow White's stepmother's magic mirror?
7. Scarlett Sepulveda – growth retardant pills?
8. Me? – Mogadon.

## 10 April

MR. & MRS. MORT BUCHINSKY

&

MR. Jj DAGNEY

REQUEST THE PLEASURE OF YOUR COMPANY
AT A BLACK AND WHITE BALL
ON SUNDAY, THE TWENTY-FIFTH OF MAY
AT EIGHT O'CLOCK

THE *ZEITGEIST* BALLROOM, PARAMOUNT PICTURES

DRESS: GENTLEMEN—BLACK TIE
LADIES—BLACK OR WHITE DRESS
RSVP 0800 BALL

It was Kitty's brainwave. And the studio's nightmare. She had been to a black and white party given by Dominick Dunne in the early sixties and had been toying with the idea of mounting something extravagantly similar ever since.

It is no exaggeration to report that within forty-eight hours of the issue of gold-embossed invitations 'the community' has gone pandemonic. If anything is guaranteed to advertise your ignominy, it is exclusion from the list to end all lists.

The Samaritan helplines have reportedly received calls from people feeling seriously suicidal. One particularly distressed caller wailed, 'How famous do you have to be in this town?' but later called back, hugely relieved to have received an invitation that must have been delayed in the post. This story was relayed in a recording that went out on CNN.

I have personally been offered thinly veiled bribes from two ex-clients who have previously reneged on decorating payments, and though not inclined to revenge I couldn't help stifling a smile as each tried to worm up some renewed contact. With which I, perhaps scurrilously, played along. With the result that I have been paid, and paid them back by regretting 'that I am unable to influence the giver of invitations in their favour'.

## 14 April

Randy declared today that Mort and Kitty have turned film land into 'a kibbutz'.

'Getting all these stars to work for charity money – it's hard to believe.'

Jj and a clutch of executives have been none too quietly fuming about the fact that the venue for the ball – Paramount Picture's largest sound stage – is now known to the general public: 'Every stalker in the universe will be there.'

I was overseeing the installation of a Tundra sculpture in the

VIP section of the commissary when I overheard a high-up in a particularly distraught state bellowing down his mobile, 'Do you people have any idea what kind of security operation is going to be required to protect the talent?' His lips curled back on themselves to expel this last word. 'Think presidential times twenty. Is what I am reckoning.'

At a later meeting, Mort came up with a brilliant idea: 'Charge 'em.'

'To come and watch? Are you outta your mind?'

To which he very reasonably replied that since the fans would be coming in busloads anyway, why not provide temporary amphitheatre seating and charge them an entry fee as they walked through the metal detectors?

'That way we get to have a genuine crowd of stargazers rather than having to hire background artists. The press will go berserk. The pre-publicity will be unprecedented. It cannot fail. At the rate we're going, we could end up *making* money from something that were it to be staged conventionally would cost a fortune. Good will all the way. And the biggest concentration of star talent that's ever been. Think about it – everyone dresses themselves, makes themselves up, arrives in their own limos. (Though I'm gonna encourage people to share for a change. But I mean really share.) And they don't have to do anything other than be themselves and have a fantastic dinner with their peers with dancing afterwards. They'll get the chance to meet anyone they maybe never did yet, with the full assurance that anything compromising will be cut from the final movie. Multiple cameras. No sets. Jj says that everything can be computerized in afterwards, so instead of an anticlimactic wrap party at the end of the movie, we launch ourselves with the greatest party this town has ever given itself. On film!

'Paramount, Twentieth, Warners and Disney maybe will pay for the food and chefs and you know and I know that film stock is cheap. We'll shoot the shit out of it all night long from every angle, including the longest tracking shot known to cinema, and more importantly, it'll be in actual time. No retakes. A one-off. Like my old days in live TV. One night only.'

I've never witnessed executive-gawp before, but the collective slackening of jaws as Mort outlined his plan was something you will just have to imagine. Mort was so blithely confident in his plans that he made everything sound perfectly logical and simple. He left before collective breath could be exhaled in disagreement.

## 15 April

Meeting with Über-chef Wolfgang Puck, whom I have known on and off for years, our paths having intersected most especially at house-warming shindigs – his food, my interiors. (He owns a string of eateries, most notably Spago's.) We match each other perfectly in our mutual enthusiasm for servicing an all-star clientele.

Mort and Kitty have elected me responsible for coordinating with Herr Puck, which is always a pleasure as he knows precisely what to conjure up to satisfy the acutely varied dietary curlicues of movie actors. Due to the numbers of guests, it has been decided that a combined waiter-service and buffet is the most practical choice.

Here is the menu that Wolfgang came up with as an initial offering.

### Zeitgeist appetizers
Maine Uni' (sea urchin) peeky-toe crab ceviche with black seaweed
Warm lobster salad with mustard potatoes, Chino beets, lemon olive oil
Smoked salmon and sturgeon with dill crème fraiche and herb blini
Chesapeake Bay soft-shell crab tempura with pickled ginger vinaigrette
Pan-roasted Sonoma Liberty duck breast, with tamarind-ginger glaze
Scallion bread and Napa cabbage salad
Young green asparagus salad with watercress, leeks and truffle vinaigrette
Salad of baby greens, with crispy squash blossoms and very old balsamic
Heirloom tomatoes with Roquefort, spring onions, extra virgin olive oil
Filet mignon tartare with Dijon aïoli, young arugula, croutons, quail egg
Marinated Japanese hamachi, seaweed salad, yuzu, sticky rice

Seared scallops with sticky rice and Wasabe mayonnaise
Butterflied sesame shrimp
Plain grilled vegetables, Parmesan shavings, summer truffle vinaigrette

## Antipasti, Pastas
Steamed zucchini blossom stuffed with porcini
Spicy couscous and swordfish involtini
Cannoli with caviar and traditional condiments
Piadina of prosciutto and Provolone
Ringolotti with mascarpone, ricotta, Romano and white truffles
Risotto with Santa Barbara spot prawns, squash, caramelized onions
Tortelloni with artichokes, goat cheese, truffles and shaved Parmesan
Parsley angel-hair with Maine lobster, garlic, chilli, olives, basil tomatoes
Tagliatelle with wild mushrooms, caramelized shallots, porcini essence
French cep risotto

## Entrées
Roast Maine monkfish with lemongrass, jasmine rice, basil coconut curry
Grilled tuna with shoe-string fries, Armagnac and five peppercorns
Pan-roasted red snapper with ratatouille vegetables and basil potatoes
Sautéed Alaskan halibut with Maine crab, celery, new onions, garlic, thyme
Pan-roasted wild striped bass with toasted sesame, carrot purée mash
Sautéed Atlantic salmon with eggplant, sweet peppers, olives, rosemary
Grilled dourade with Chino vegetables, artichokes, coriander, olive oil
Sautéed Dover sole with mushrooms, flageolet, fava and lima beans
Roast Cantonese duck with wild huckleberries, star anise, ginger, bok choy
Quail stuffed with figs and foie gras, with Cippolini onions escarole
Pan-roasted poussin with mushroom risotto, leeks, spinach, garlic, thyme
Roasted chicken with asparagus, porcini, crushed fingerling potatoes
Apple-cured Sonoma veal rack with morels, leaf spinach, shank jus
Roasted Côte de Bœuf with braised celery, pommes aligot', onions
Grilled Moroccan-style rack of lamb, tagine, dried fruits, couscous, Harris
Sautéed calf's liver with sage polenta, roasted shallots, crispy onions
Wiener schnitzel with warm potato and mâche salad
Beef stew with onions, marjoram, Hungarian paprika and home-made spätzle

## Desserts
Forest berries fruit pyramid, meringue and raspberry coulis
Frozen chocolate almond bananas

181

Berry wontons in passion fruit and ginger dipping sauce
Panacotta citral in filo pastry
Chocolate pretzel bonbons
Espresso meringue
Checkerboard shortbreads
Spring brioche tart with apple, pear and plum Calvados ice cream
Imported and domestic cheeses with grilled walnut bread

The actual coordination of everything we have left in the good hands of a catering producer, who, off his own bat, has offered Moët et Chandon the 'unique opportunity' to supply the bubbly for the occasion, gratis, to which proposition they have agreed, based on the phenomenal free advertising guaranteed by their label being on view at every star-crammed table. We have delegated the table and flower design to Michael Venedicto who is in turn coordinating with the *Zeitgeist* production design team. Everyone approached so far already knows about the event and is basically choking to be involved.

## *17 April*

Avi Korein, security adviser to the stars, has come on board to mount and coordinate the massive security operation. He had done extraordinary and subtle protection work for Georgia Sepulveda post her public shootings and has the innate grace of being able to dissolve himself into the background while keeping tabs on everything. Apparently the LAPD plans to draft in a special unit to cope with the demand.

## 20 April

'What the fuck am I going to wear?' congests phone, fax and e-lines. 'Who is going and what will they be wearing?' has begun clogging up airtime on chat shows, daytime discussions, *Oprah*, *Rikki Lake*, MTV and the tail sections of evening news programmes.

A Website has been set up, along with Internet caller wishlists proposing names that fans specifically want to see together. Someone out there has taken the initiative of mapping out a Lust Tree, detailing who has had whom and calculating the number of ex-partners, wives and husbands who will be mingling.

## 21 April

The Internet Lust Tree has been published in the Calendar section of the *LA Times*, with cartoons of the various culprits drawn by Risko. A lengthy article concerned with the socio-political implications accompanies the tree, under a banner headline, HOWCHA MAGOWCHA? (attributed to Fanny Bryce).

The Business section has computed the collective worth of the guests, and it's a figure so staggering that I shan't vulgarize this sentence by revealing it. But I *can* reveal that my buttocks were gravitationally pulled south into the nearest shock-absorbing easy chair.

The free LA weekly paper headlined, somewhat unkindly I thought, 'JURASSIC PARTY – See the oldest dinosaurs in town lumber out for one last snort', then listed the possible elder statespersons who might be wheeled out for the night, concluding with an RIP hitlist. The combined producing studios took out a double-page ad in *Variety*: 'ZEITGEIST – UNFILMABLE? The Might-geist movie is unstoppable'.

The image that really caught my eye though was Alfred E. Newman's grinning face on the cover of *MAD* magazine surrounded by star caricatures. Inside was a cartoon spoof of what the film might be like, which is an honour of sorts in itself. They have retitled the movie *Fanquest*.

Kitty has confirmed that the guest list includes directors, producers and writers (space permitting), but no agents. 'You gotta draw the line somewhere!'

★

## 25 April

### KYLA BERGMAN CHOOSES GALLIANO TO DO DRESS DUTY

This news relayed from the pages of *Women's Wear Daily*.

It has been revealed that the characters in *Zeitgeist* will spend the duration of the movie in a single outfit, worn for the New Year's Eve party aboard the *Zeitgeist* spacecraft, on its inaugural flight. Sources reveal that like the *Titanic*'s maiden voyage, the mission is a disaster, and the characters face a fight for survival wearing the clothes they have chosen for the party.

They need to be adaptable, glamorous and able to withstand severe heat, cold, flooding and explosions. Speculation is rife as to which stars will wear whose designs. The dress code is black and white, which promises a visual cohesion not normally associated with the style choices of that essentially seaside resort town they call LA.

It is expected that jeweller Harry Winston will be cleaned out, or shall we say loaned out, of its entire stock come the gala ball on May 25th.

Seasoned style-watchers hope for a Cecil Beatonesque parade of My Fair Ladies, while less optimistic cynics predict a Guys 'n' Dolls fiasco.

Kyla Bergman, leading lady of *Zeitgeist*, broke her silence today and announced that John Galliano at Dior is her choice of designer. The star was seen entering his Paris atelier yesterday for consultations.

I was at Java's home to discuss projected plans to convert her interiors into a Moroccan palace when she started punching *WWD*.

'Have you seen this?'

I knew I was more than about to.

'Miss Kyla icebox Bergman was seen entering his Paris ... something French ... Who the fuck is paying for this? Nobody offered me a freebie to Paris to choose a frock! I'm calling Mort.'

The *WWD* was flung aside as her finger missiled for a phone. Mort's number was engaged, so she flung herself onto a sofa that was so riddled with cushions that she had to fight off a bunch to park herself onto it. Then she gritted her teeth and announced, 'Galliano was my first choice.' And like a child given sympathy for a sore bit, the full impact of her grievance suddenly took hold. She inhaled a gallon of air, opened her mouth and let rip a caterwaul of pain so profound that even my powers of resistance were challenged.

'But, Java, it's only a dress. It's not Bosnia, my sweetheart.'

Well, it might have been. My usual shoulder to cry on got a violent shove, followed by a volley of cushions aimed at my head. I just managed to prevent her fingers pulling off my left earlobe.

(I'll write her next sentence without the snifflings and wails, which slowed her word-flow to a snail's pace ...)

'You don't understand. It's never only *a dress*. You stupid male! That woman is determined to pull rank on me and I will not be put down.'

My attempted *You should use this for your part, don't waste these emotions on me* earned me my second slap.

She instantly regretted it and pulled my head onto her lap in order to stroke my stinging cheek.

'That infertile Swedish witch has Richard Eagles. At home. On set. In tow. Wherever you don't wanna know, they're there! Carrying on like they're on some kind of permanent honeymoon. Letting me know that I am a single mother and actress with every breath they take. It's time I had a turn at that stuff. I give, give, give and give and what do I get in return? Old guys. Divorcees. Recovering drug addicts. Alcoholics. If I'm LUCKY.'

185

I must have snored off, as I awoke alone amidst the cushioned chaos.

★

## 27 April (a month to go)

'I am stunned that any Hollywood event could be taken so seriously!' I heard a renowned figure who had obviously not been invited declare yesterday. And it was proving true; the invitation is a Richter scale reading of one's professional standing.

What I particularly approve of is the way in which Kitty insists on everyone being treated like everyone else. No preferential slithy toving. No tier system. Considering the level of sycophantic indulgence that folk take for granted, as a star-status right, her democratic attitude has been greeted with incomprehension in certain circles.

Imagine that after years of struggling anonymity you finally succeed. Overnight you are given preferential service wherever you go. You get a table at that fashionable restaurant on the day. Shop assistants get erect at the sight of your potential purchasing powers. Parking attendants call you Mr, Mrs, Mz, and whip out your vehicle so you don't have to queue on the sidewalk with ordinary mortals. Airport officials are thrusting out arms to lighten your luggage load. Cab drivers smile. Walk down the street and people say 'Hi!' with possibly more enthusiasm than they might greet a long-lost relative. Designers offer to provide clothing for that special occasion. Shops open up especially early. Or particularly late. Tickets for that show that's booked solid till next spring? No problem.

Movie-star normality is a succession of 'Yessirees', so imagine then the shock-horror when some faceless critic trashes your noble efforts mercilessly, spitting 'NOsirees' all over the place!

I walked down Fifth Avenue with Richard and Kyla a couple of years ago, and I swear to you, everyone was smiling. At them. They

186

had got so used to it that they never noticed. When I pointed it out, Richard thought it was because the country was economically up and folk were just feeling happy. Bless him.

Likewise, Java and I were in the Beverly Hills drugstore one morning – she needed some shampoo and headbands for Mona – and there was a queue of three elderly women at the till. Java looked at her watch, tut-tutted and whispered to me, 'I've never had to queue in here before. Let's go somewhere else.'

I thought for a second that she must be kidding, but no, she was already on her way back down the aisle to dump her goods.

'Java, we are on our way to have a leisurely lunch, you're between films, we are in no hurry, let's just wait and pay.'

She swung round and asked, 'What's the matter with you? I know all that. It's just weird. This store always used to be empty at this time of the morning. I never had to wait in line before.'

The gal was more mystified than annoyed.

OK, so now the star is in that restaurant, at that show, in that store, in that queue – now, everyone wants some.

*After all, who the fuck d'you think made 'em a star?*

Can I have an autograph?

Can I have a picture with you?

Can you lend me some money?

Can you just come over and say hello to our friends over there?

Can you donate something to charity?

Can you become patron—?

Can you donate a large portion of your salary to this list I have here?

Can you impregnate me?

Can I have lunch with you?

Can you give me a job?

Can you read this script I've just written?

I know we've never met, but I feel this psychic bond with you, can I come round?

Look, while we're waiting for the contractions to speed up, I'd like to pitch you this brilliant idea I have for a movie. Perfect part for you.

Sorry to bother you while you're in the middle of your dinner, but I just happened to have a copy of a script I wrote for you about an aeronautical engineer who has given up his job to become a postal delivery clerk. It also happens to be the story of my life, so I can vouch for its accuracy.

I hope you don't mind my saying this, but would you mind giving this script to Connor Child when you see him? We think his career is going to be really mega. I read that you knew him, so I thought it'd save postage and agent delaying tactics.

I know I probably shouldn't be saying this to your face, but my wife and I have never liked you, or any of your movies.

Before I remove these molars, I'm sure you won't mind it if I take this opportunity to tell you this story I have been working on, which I know will make a great movie. It's a horror story.

Rinse, please.

## *28 April*

### FLAMES OF FAME

*TIME* magazine's cover story has assembled an august body of social anthropologists, media analysts, psychiatrists and man-on-the-street opinion polls to discuss the hegemony, semantics and dialectics of celebrity, as a late twentieth-century phenomenon.

First up is a lot of gas from a particularly outraged evangelist who claims, 'Fame is the new spiritual flame, lit by Satan, to try and extinguish the light of Our Lord.'

His view is opposed by a lecturer from Harvard, holder of a master's degree in iconography studies, who points out that the outraged evangelist is the most famous face in their group, as a result of his TV satellite God station.

Followed by paragraphs of 'There is no God any more' declarations and ruminations on the basic human need to have faith in something, so why not celebrities? It concludes with a detailed analysis of how the *Zeitgeist* party is a kind of insanity. Resoundingly supported by an esteemed worthy who moots, 'There are no rational reasons for this hysteria, but many, many irrational ones. Consider all the people excluded. Not invited? At a deeper level, all of us who are not invited feel a concomitant sense of exclusion, and no one, if I may put this in layman's terms, wants to feel left out. That is the power of Faith. It is all-inclusive.'

★

## 1 May

Today, a new term entered the vernacular.

An anonymous studio honcho claimed that he thought it unlikely that there was sufficient time to prepare an event on this scale. Kitty responded:

'This is America, folks. Think how fast the British people got together to prepare for Princess Diana's funeral. Within one week, everything was arranged to perfection. We've got a month. Mort and I see it like this; remember those forties Garland–Rooney pictures? Well, I say to you all: we've found a barn, you bring along some drums, make some food, sing a song, and let's put on a show. It's as simple as that. They say that the Golden Age of Hollywood is gone. We are saying, WATCH THIS SPACE! It's going to be a ZEIST!'

And this morning, those chirpy folk on *Good Morning America* topped and tailed their celebrity news update with a new tag-line: 'It's a Zeist.'

Chuck went further and declared that he was 'feeling Zeisty all over'. Cracked them up.

# 4 May

Lawyers acting on behalf of the studios have lodged a copyright request to protect the *Zeitgeist* logo for all future merchandise.

Kitty levitated about her office, on permanent oxygen overload, singing: 'I feel Zeisty, oh so Zeisty, I'm as feisty and Zeisty can beeeeee, and I pity anyone who's not as Zeisty as me.'

Every note as flat as Nevada. Like Carol Channing at 16 r.p.m.

# 20 May

Last-gasp invitation seekers are still doing everything they can to secure entry and the Buchinskys' phone lines have been besieged night and day: couriers, messages, faxes, e's, flowers, poetry, gifts. Anything.

Mort is so wound up with the writers and pre-production demands that the Ball is essentially in Kitty's court. Everything and everyone conduited through her, helped by a posse of female – except for me – assistants. Bliss! The general filth of their candour is a privilege to be party to. Being so outnumbered, I think they forget I am there, and any notion I had about women being of a more demure demeanour has been permanently sluiced as they snicker-snack through the guest list in graphically sexual terms: who they would or wouldn't do it with, sparing not a single hairpiece, facial tuck, shoe lift, corseting or penile extension on this rich and famous list.

## 21 May

Answer machine message from Georgia—

'Does ANYONE know what the fuck is happening out there? Vyvian? Pick up! I'm talking OUT THERE, right? Right! You're not there. Just wanted to say that as sure as snakes, I would never have been on that guest list if I wasn't cast in the movie and I would never have been cast in the movie if I hadn't threatened to blow my brains out in the CBS parking lot. Right? Damned RIGHT! So what am I saying? I don't know. Jeezus. I think someone has stolen my personality . . .' Click.

No chance of that, babe. You're par for your course.

## 24 May

The hairdressing fraternity today was basically divided into three camps.

The first was the most relaxed, doing snips here and there for the 'Meg Ryan just outta bed' look.

The second, with gangs of assistants, was snapping hairpins and pieces, extensions and side-partings, in pursuit of Jennifer Aniston's quasi-sixties scoop.

The third were hairstylists from a bygone age. You know the ones – they're always called by their first names, like Kurt of Vienna, or Salvatore di Roma. They have now been exhumed and flown in to rekindle their bouffant and back-combing skills one mo' time, taking many a star by the nostrils, back to those ozone-defying days when fourteen cans of hairspray did the trick of conjuring up the Hollywood Bowl.

# 25 May

Was this the night that never was? I'll guide – you judge – let's see . . .

Perfect evening. Melrose Avenue was policed and cordoned off either side of the Paramount Pictures lot. The criss-crossing search-lights in the night sky could be seen from all four corners of the city, with an effect not unlike that of Speer's Nuremberg Rally designs. Helicopters, flying in arrivals, were picked out by the illuminations – at one point there were so many that it was like a scene from *Apocalypse Now*.

Tiers of stadium-style seating had been erected either side of the avenue and were jam-packed with fans, many of whom had been there for days, armed with blankets, food, binoculars, cameras and camaraderie. They were all dressed in black and white, as if they too were attending the ball. Fifteen seconds of fame had already been bestowed on the real diehards, when they were interviewed for various TV stations.

'We are *all* starring in this movie. This is history.'

Spontaneous applause broke out as each car and 'copter divested itself of stars. Sony had provided pop-concert-sized video screens which brought each arrival into close-up, instigating Mexican waves along the length and breadth of the avenue.

T-shirts with printed-on bow ties and ruffles were selling fast in the side streets off Melrose. Queues of fans snaked back on them-selves, waiting their turn to pass through the turnstiles and metal-detector units. The atmosphere was nothing short of a carnival.

Mort had had the brilliant idea of laying a camera track along the full length of the cordoned-off road, and Jj devised a mount for quadruple cameras, remote controlled, that could swivel and zoom independently of one another while moving up and down the track, attached to an aluminium retractable crane. This enabled the crowd to see themselves on the giant screens, alongside their arriving idols, thus essentially breaking through the barrier between the public and the celebrities. Grown men in the crowd were seen weeping in close-up when Arnold Schwarzenegger stepped out, to a cheer that was truly thunderous. Likewise for Sigourney Weaver. People shouted out favourite quotes. Sang theme songs. Celebrated. And defying the protocol of locked shaded-glass windows – metal detectors having given some sense of security – many stars took the risk of leaning out to shout back greetings to the crowd. Goldie Hawn went a step further by suddenly popping through the roof of her limousine, like a golden-haired rocket, provoking an instantaneous standing ovation from the crowd closest to her car. Always alert to pick up on a good thing, the cars behind her started sprouting stars through their sunroofs like so many Jack-in-the-boxes.

Medics were on hand to be walkie-talkied over to wherever there'd been a fainting or collapse by the ever-vigilant security and cop forces.

Oh, I forgot to mention that in order to keep everyone behind the metal barriers, they had been wired up to give a substantive electric shock if touched.

At one point, a helicopter hovered overhead in a near-stationary holding pattern, its undercarriage kitted out with its own spotlights, which were focused on a rope ladder that slithered out, swinging back and forth in the light evening breeze. All eyes looked up as a tuxedoed figure started climbing down, facing towards the body of the 'copter, so no one could tell who it actually was. Various *Harrison!*s and *Sean!*s assailed the expectant air, till Jim Carrey swung himself around and skewed his face into trademark manic mode.

The crowd went cacophonic and rhythmically clapped him down, rung by rung.

And on, and on, and on they came. Endlessly. Everyone standing. Shrieking, laughing, crying, jumping, stomping, disbelieving their unexpected proximity to so many, many idols. Stars whose twinkle had been dimmed by absence were welcomed back with the warmth accorded those first returning astronauts.

There was an appreciably restrained vocal response to mark

Christopher Reeve's arrival. Many wept. Most clapped as if their lives depended on it. A lone voice trilled out, 'You're a true Superman, we love you, Chris!'

The wheelchair-bound man smiled, his face magnified in extreme close-up on every large screen. He caused more faintings than most.

And still they came. The press corps were clearly staggered by the turnout, if their jabberings were any indication. *Miraculous, incredible* and a lot of *unbelievables* issued forth from a gang usually completely inured to fame.

Once the celebrities had alighted, they walked through a plate-glass covered tunnel, which was brilliantly lit from all sides and resembled a giant glow-worm. Warm and secure, they waved and red-carpeted their way into the converted sound stage.

I'd suggested a visitor's book for signing and Kitty had already secured offers from both the LA County and Guggenheim museums to buy and display the leather-bound volumes. In accordance with ball etiquette, there was a receiving line and a liveried announcer, who read out the names of each guest as they were presented to the Über-couple, Kitty and Mort. Jj – supposedly indifferent to stars – had argued, 'That stuff is a crock of pig shit to me, so why don't you count me out and I'll get the whole thing filmed?' Being of leprechaun dimensions, he had ensconced himself in a specially designed crane 'basket', rigged out with a camera, which was able to swoop and glide high above the proceedings.

A specially created control room, crammed with monitors and gadgetry, had been set up on the studio floor, from where the second unit camera crew were able to remote control yet another camera, attached to the end of an Akela crane, which was capable of extending and retracting to wherever they chose to go, enabling smooth and continuous tracking shots along the lengths of tables. At the perimeter of the room the two cranes resembled giant spindly necked metal giraffes, bobbing and lifting, swooping and lowering over the crowds.

'If this is what going to heaven will be like, include me in!'

quipped Lauren Bacall, giving Mort and Kitty a combined hug, throwing her head back and laughing her throaty laugh, which had the effect of making time stand momentarily still. Down the line, air and flesh were kissed. Reputations stroked reputations. Up-and-comers genuflected before over-and-outers. Exes avoided exes, collided or confided.

'D'you know something, this is the only time like this I can think of where no one is being officially honoured, roasted, toasted or Oscared. Hell, isn't that some relief?' smiled Jack Lemmon, shaking his head.

At the far end of the room, Quincy Jones, Courtney Pine, Paul Simon and Stevie Wonder were pumping out some smooth variations.

Kitty and Mort welcomed everyone as though they were just having a few close friends round for a pre-dinner cocktail. The only giveaway was the miniature flesh-coloured earpiece and lapel microphone attached to Mort, who would whisper directions between greetings to the various technicians monitoring and filming proceedings.

'Some turnout, huh?' Mort was visibly bucked.

As the room filled up, the pop of a thousand magnums of champagne being topped punctuated the babble. People cheered. And toasted a night of political incorrectitude. Most surprising was the absence of any dress-code-breaker. Everyone was in black and white. If not a tux, then something equivalently distinct. Even Tom Waits had relented, and arrived in dishevelled Victorian top hat and tails, like the Artful Dodger.

Perspex tables were laid end to end diagonally across the expanse, in two endless rows, covered in glassware, including transparent plates lit from below with the most flattering salmon-coloured gels to illuminate every face and dewlap, like candle-glow. Before the guests took their seats, the two lengths of tables looked like a crystal runway, magicked up from fairy-tale glass. They had been designed to fit within the confines of the spacecraft, which was to be computer-generated in later.

Mort made his way to the band podium, tapped the microphone on its squiggly Philippe Starck stand and said:

'I'm just sorry to see so few of you folks could make it here tonight! However . . .' he paused for the laughter and applause to subside, 'you know the deal. We are all aboard this cockamamie spacecraft, bound for I know not yet where. Kitty'll know, and Wolfgang has prepared us a little something to eat. Some of you guys tell me you can sing, and some of you claim to be able to dance a little. So, let battle commence. Oh yes, I almost forgot, my partner in crime Jj Dagney is going to be shooting a little tracking shot overhead, but you won't even know it's happening and ladies, I give you my word of honour, your cleavages are safe.

'At midnight, we'll have the traditional countdown to our own special *Zeitgeist* New Year's, and I believe we have a couple of surprise musical treats in store for you.

'Lastly, I'd like to pledge a toast to my darling wife, Kitty, who has put up with me, and let's face it, most of you, for the last century, and though it costs me some to say it, I still love the ol' broad as much as I do a good game of poker.'

Applause was tumultuous.

Dagney tracked the entire table-lengths in a single smooth ride, and reversed all the way back again, to ensure maximum coverage.

The actual cast were unscripted and mixed with their peers, seemingly oblivious to the fact that this was the actual first day of filming. Every table was wired for sound. Every star had been assured that nothing would make the final movie without his or her consent.

After dinner, tables were removed and the chairs set to the sides, clearing the centre for dancing. John Travolta sashayed out with Uma Thurman on his arm, and the band obliged with an instant segue into *that tune* from *Pulp Fiction*. People formed a huge hand-clapping circle. No sooner was Uma twirling than he slinked back into the crowd and greased out again with Olivia Newton-John at the end of his arm.

Patrick Swayze followed suit with Jennifer Grey, and then

Gregory Hines started tap dancing, joined by Christopher Walken. Shirley MacLaine shimmied forwards, followed by Rupert Everett, who started a conga behind her, gathering a trail of stars in his wake – Madonna, Billy Crystal, Sharon Stone, Woody Harrelson . . . you get the idea. Tony Curtis and Jack Lemmon did a rumba.

No matter how famous, rich, sophisticated or legendary, everyone was watching everyone else.

'There's more rubbernecking in here than Jabba the Hutt,' pithied Sandra Bernhard.

The musical jamming ranged from riffs by Bruce Willis, guitar solo from Keanu Reeves, blues notes from Sally Kellerman, slide guitar courtesy of Lyle Lovett, concluding with Whitney Houston lullabying 'I will always love you' to Dolly Parton, who mugged and pouted like Betty Boop.

Robin Williams took over for the final countdown, doing a different character accent per descending number.

The lights were dimmed way down, and silhouetted on the bandstand were seven diminutive figures.

At the stroke of twelve, streamers and lasers criss-crossed in a strobed frenzy, suddenly cut off by the sound of female voices swelling out 'Auld Lang Syne'. The line-up was Whitney, Dolly, Bette Midler, Madonna, Diana Ross, Celine Dion and Barbra Streisand. As the lights came up on them, the approbation of their peers was little short of deafening; it sounded enough to raise the roof. And lo and behold, that's exactly what it did. The roof of the set opened like an observatory, revealing state-of-the-scenic-art space, the Earth moving slowly across the lower half, giving the impression that we were revolving around it! Mort and Jj had pulled off a brilliant coup. But this wasn't all.

Their masterstroke was the silkily staged arrival of Tibet, God only knows from where, but a narrow metal crane arm swung into view, as though transporting a being from 'out there'. Standing statue still, aloft in the air, this eighteen-year-old girl's entry stopped your breath with her beauty, grace and Dolce e Gabanna Versace-tribute dress consisting of cream shredded silk-chiffon held together by a multitude of small safety pins, making her look like an ethereal post-midnight Cinderella. Her blonde hair hung like flax, framing her cut-glass profile and amnesia-white complexion. Her feet were bare.

Connor Child had been cued to take her hand as she stepped down in an entrance as effortlessly natural as it was fantastically calculated. Nobody had a clue who she was. Which was the whole point of her: as if immaculately conceived for stardom. In the silence of her landing the crowd was stunned to a hush, then applauded and applauded.

Without an apparent scrap of make-up or guile, Tibet made everyone else's dress and flesh look positively Tyrannosaurian. She was a revelation, a child of the new millennium. She and Connor walked through the parting crowd, reached the middle of the room, turned to one another and began a slow dance.

The hypnotic quiet of this annunciation was broken by what sounded like a billion tons of shattering glass.

People scrammed. In all directions. Screaming!

'CUT!'

In the chaotic circumstances, Mort sounded like God.

It took several minutes for the chaos to subside and for people to readjust. There was undisguised 'I could've had a heart attack!' rage in certain quarters, but for the most part Mort's chutzpah was cheered to the rafters.

He said through an old-fashioned De Mille loudhailer: 'What can I say? You're all fabulous. Talented. Gorgeous. And anyone who wants to kill me better move fast, cos I think I've only got about four seconds left on my old ticker.'

He fake-staggered backwards into the arms of Kitty.

The band obliged them with a medley of all the theme tunes from his most famous pictures. And that was it.

At 1 a.m., a breakfast of smoked salmon and scrambled eggs, hash browns, kedgeree, bagels and Danish pastries was served. Quincy and Co. played till four. The last twinklers left at dawn.

Media coverage has been a maelstrom. Editorials full of outrage at such extravagance in the light of the economically challenged and homeless – 'No amount of charity ball philanthropy can disguise the venal self-aggrandizement of the self-congratulatory community called Hollywood.'

Estimated costs of the evening run from extravagant to apocalyptic, depending on which publication you read. The supposed number of guests ranges from five hundred to five thousand. Best- and worst-dressed lists are trumpeted from every fashion page, accompanied by lavish photo spreads. And to what will be the undying delight of the studios co-financing this whole shebang, the word *Zeitgeist* is everywhere.

★

## 26 May

Jay Leno's show this evening featured an insert monologue, in which he was padded up and bald-pated to resemble Brando in Captain Kurtz mode. In lieu of 'The horror. The horror,' Mr Leno gasped, 'The Talent. The Talent', with a mock-up background display of famous faces cut off at the neck, impaled on sticks.

Dave Letterman arrived on the set of his show wearing a blond wig and a safety-pinned suit, as did his entire band, who struck up a version of the Eurythmics' 'Who's That Girl?'.

Tibet has become infamous overnight by *not* appearing on any chat show, and there has been saturation coverage of her heavenly arrival at the party.

'A Star is Torn' is the favoured headline as details of her dress are columned, inch by inch.

Word of the longest tracking shot in cinema history has been leaked, provoking Camille Paglia to froth onto her soapbox and denounce the Hollywood male obsession with the longest tracking shot: 'Mine has got to be the longest, the biggest and better than anyone else's. It's pathetic. Mort Buchinsky is a typically menopausal male, boasting about his tracking prowess at an age when it is patently obvious he couldn't get his own shriveller to stretch more than a couple of millimetres. The Tibet syndrome is yet another excuse for Hollywood to feast like Dracula on the blood of a young virgin. It is paedophilic.'

'Virgin? My ass! Who the fuck does she think she's kidding?' spat Sepulveda in response.

In a town where history is generally given a backseat ride, the Guggenheim, at the behest of that great diplomat, Shirley Temple, announced that it has established an archive of memorabilia – stars have already pledged their dresses, invitations, napkins, glasses, anything. There will be video installations of the parade of star arrivals and the public Mardi Gras that ensued outside.

Mort has been surprise-gifted by Kitty with a total blood transfusion: 'Going to get you pumped full of some fresh young stuff to get you through this shoot, honey.'

Marga is on masseuse-rotating duties between Georgia, Java, Kyla, Richard and Randy.

I spent too much of the day inspecting and flowering trailers for the start of shooting tomorrow. Have decided to install an aquarium in Technophobe's trailer, as a gift from Randy.

## 27 May

The make-up and wardrobe call was 5.30 a.m. I never visit sets if I can help it, but as so many of my clients are all in the same picture, and I am responsible for the design of their mobile homes, Mort asked if I'd be around.

A corner section of the ballroom set had been recreated upside down for the first scene. The ceiling–floor was heaped high with fake broken glass. This scene was Connor's biggie. As the young captain of the spacecraft, he had a two-page monologue, detailing the remaining survivors' chance of escape.

The special effects of the craft splitting in two, crashing through the atmosphere and plunging into the ocean were being filmed with models on separate sound stages.

Connor arrived an hour earlier than his official call, and snugged himself away in his character chamber. The scene required suppressed hysterics, and there were strict instructions not to disturb Mr Child other than his actual call to the set.

I was in the make-up trailer with Java and Kyla. New Age music floated through the aroma of cappuccinos and the whirr of hairdryers. The gradual breakdown of the costumes according to each character's escape struggle has been carefully plotted, and there were a dozen replicas of each outfit in descending order of distress. Today was the first scene post-crash, so the clothes were at their best, likewise the hair and make-up.

Java, facing the mirror, had her eyes transfixed on Kyla's face, reflected next to her. Kyla had her head back, two cucumber slices covering her eyelids, listening to music on her earphones as her hair was prepped.

Java whispered to her hairdresser, 'Do mine exactly like hers.'

'But it's going to be a continuity problem – her hair is in a different style . . .'

He realized his mistake midway through his reply. You could tell by the deflation of breath. By the end of his sentence he was barely audible. Java was transmitting an ice pick look via the mirror. Not wanting to rock the boat this early in proceedings, he obliged. Oh, boy.

I went outside for some pre-dawn air and was perplexed by the bobbing about of a small light in the distance. Upon closer inspection, this glow-worm proved to be a flashlight in the hands of Georgia Sepulveda, who was using it to light her tape measure, which was stretched from one end of Kyla Bergman's trailer to the other.

'Just measuring to make sure I'm not getting fucked over.'

I assured her that all the vehicles were of an identical size.

'When are those two bitches going to be finished in hair and make-up?'

'Georgia, I have no idea. You know far better than I do how long these things take.'

'I should have been in first,' she declared as she began remeasuring.

'I heard that your call was later, to give you longer in bed.'

Uh oh.

'Who told you that?'

'Can't remember. Some assistant or runner.'

'What, they think I'm too old, do they, and that I need more sleep? Am I right or am I RIGHT!? Let me tell you something – they've got them in first because they've got higher billing than me.'

'Georgia! The billing is alphabetical. Sepulveda comes after Bergman and Hall.'

She mumbled her disagreement and said, 'You gotta plan me a new route to the studio. On my way here this morning, I passed three fucking billboards with either Bergman's or Streep's names forty feet high. I can't take that kind of visual harassment every day.'

'But I gave your driver the specific route instructions a month ago so that you wouldn't see any billboards whatsoever. What happened?'

'I told him to fuck the route and to get to the studios via Sunset.'

'You know that you are guaranteed to be wall-to-walled with posters on that stretch. That's where you had your accident.'

'I know that, Vyvian! I just thought at this ungodly hour of the morning the lights would be off and I wouldn't be able to see any of the names. It was also a superstition thing. I crashed on Sunset and it led to my career revival and getting this role.'

'Well, don't go that route again during the shoot. You know what it does to you. It's very bad for your blood pressure.'

A runner came up saying, 'Sorry to interrupt, but you're needed in make-up.'

I thought I could escape, but Georgia had other plans. She gripped my wrist and frogmarched me over to the hothouse.

Technophobe was seated closest to the door, having a head-wound prosthetically applied and painted.

Java was in tears. Awash. Brenda, her Irish earth-mother assist-ant, was massaging her shoulders, which heaved up and down with each gulp of air.

The hair and make-up team were all revolving eyeballs, silently advising, 'Don't ask.'

Kyla stood up, checked her reflection, pouted her lips and said thanks on her way out to her trailer. No sooner was the door shut than Java erupted. Tear-ductress supreme. Her make-up ran down her face in rivulets. It was impossible to fathom what she was warbling about, but 'hair' was the most consistent word that corked to the surface.

Apparently Jj had steamed into the fray with all the tact and charm of a retreating water buffalo, accusing Java of changing her hairstyle completely, thereby making a nonsense of the continuity.

Precisely Java's mission, but she was in denial about her cloning contest with Bergman. All hands rallied on deck to repair her swollen-eyed mess.

Mort came motoring in, full of new blood, and tried to diplome his way through her problem. But as is so often the way with sympaticos in such situations, instead of quelling her tears he unwittingly unleashed a fresh flow. An assistant proffered two bottles of Evian in case of dehydration.

'She . . . hates . . . me!' came yelping out of her lipstick-smeared mouth.

Mort decided that as the scene of the day focused on a confrontation between Connor and Richard Eagles he could shoot around Java if she was not visually ready.

'I will be ready, Morty, I will be. It's just hard for me, you know.'

His 'I know, honey' prompted a fresh cascade. Mort winked at Brenda, who dipped her chin discreetly, and he left.

'He . . . is . . . so . . . kind.'

However, her howl upon seeing the gymnasium trailer attached to Kyla's Winnebago finished her off. My explanation that it was brought in at Kyla's personal behest and expense cut no mustard.

'She is determined to outdo me, no matter what! She knows I have big thighs and having her personal trainer and gym here is designed to underline my saddlebags.'

Her freshly applied make-up was sobbed south.

Kitty and I made our way through the snake of cables all over the studio floor to the set. The actors were rehearsing the dialogue. Or to be more accurate, Connor Child was going through his lines and camera positions opposite Richard Eagles' stand-in.

Java, Georgia and Kyla took up their positions lying among the glass debris, having their make-up and hair checked.

When everything was ready to shoot, an assistant faxed through a request for Mr Eagles to come to the set, please.

This was a new one on me. And everyone else. Usually, someone goes over to the actor's trailer, knocks and says, 'Ready in five,' or 'We need you now.' Not Richard Eagles. He was not even to be phoned. But faxed.

A side door has been assigned exclusively for his entrance and exit, attached to which is the customized retractable caterpillar. Eagles entered, and was given his position by his stand-in.

Mort waited a couple of beats for everyone to settle down, then the first assistant director called, 'Action.'

Connor gave his all on the first take, flexing every facial muscle for maximum expression, vocally somersaulting his way through his emotional range and conveying the depths of his commitment to save the remaining surviving passengers 'on my craft'.

It impressed everyone. Almost. After Mort had said, 'Cut,' Richard Eagles put his hand up, took a minute, looked around the cast and crew, then turned back to Connor and in ringing tones asked: 'What the fuck do you think you were doing?'

In the stunned silence that ensued, we all experienced the heat of cremation by humiliation. This was going to be the wingspan test between the threatened megastar and his up-and-coming rival. Richard had clearly heard too much talk of Connor Child being the new Eagles. His claws were out, and on the evidence of this shaming he was going to be taking no prisoners.

Connor so admired and looked up to Eagles that he was unable to fully comprehend the ferocity of his idol's attack.

'I'm sorry,' came his halting, confused response.

Georgia Sepulveda was having none of it. Before Mort could utter a word, she weighed in with: 'Connor? Your work is totally honest and uncompromising and I for one want you to know that I thought your take was brilliant. Am I right? Or am I RIGHT?'

Although addressing Connor, she was looking Richard Eagles baldly in the eye; then she flicked focus to Mort and said: 'Sorry, Morty, to interrupt, but I for one am not going to stand for any of this kinda shit, from anyone. The kid's got it.'

Mort smiled his avuncular smile, nodded to the first assistant director and said, 'Let's do another one.'

He knew that if he allowed himself to be thrown from the saddle at this stage he would never get back in it.

It is difficult to describe the spectrum of emotions playing across Richard Eagles' beaky phizog. Incredulity was the dominant contestant. I doubt he had been challenged or spoken to like this for many a year, certainly never by a supporting artist, and even more certainly by a supporting artist who had been in the career-wastelands of oblivion for so long. And absolutely never in front of an entire crew. Having played his highest-status card, Sepulveda's intervention had challenged his authority in such a damaging way that he was in a quandary whether to stomp out or stay. Battle lines were drawn.

Curiously, Kyla, whom you might have expected to be partner and wife in this situation, was apparently heedless of her husband's predicament. In the gluey silence she asked for a make-up touch-up as though nothing had happened. Java was so stupefied by

Kyla's cool that it took her a full minute to get back into her tear-filled state befitting someone suffering post-flight crash trauma.

It was only 9.30 a.m. on the first day of filming. The logistical nightmare of shooting the New Year's Eve party live, unrehearsed and unrepeatably less than forty-eight hours before paled beside this complication. No matter how Mort steers things along, there is no escaping the fact that everything from now on will be governed by this incident.

Mort called an impromptu meeting with the writers during the relighting break. He has decided to make this contretemps the basis for a developing dramatic rivalry in the actual story, so that Art will imitate Life. He was fired up by the possibilities, where lesser directors might have felt their project under serious threat given the budget, the length of the shoot and the status of Richard Box-Office Eagles.

Lunchtime, and I did not quite know where to go without stepping on someone's fragile toes. So I opted for Connor Child, assuming he would be respectfully left alone. I knocked quietly on his door and went in. He was mid-conversation with his acting coach on a mobile. I picked up a magazine and pretended to read.

'No, no, carry on . . . well, my instinct was to tear my fucking trailer to pieces, and then go and torch *his* trailer, but I just put myself in my decompression chamber, and I'm already feeling a whole lot better . . . No you're right, I've gotta use this rage. And I did in the second and third take. Listen, thanks a lot for taking my call at such short notice.'

Connor slung the phone into his kitbag, stretched out and said: 'Sorry about that, man, but I needed professional advice. What d'you wanna eat? You know what I feel like right now? A proper hamburger from Hamburger Hamlet. C'mon.'

He put on a biker's helmet, found another and gave it to me.

'Are you allowed to leave the lot like this during shooting hours?'

'Hell, no, but see if they can stop me.'

Before Security had time to register, we were on the back of his perfectly restored Triumph motorbike, heading for the studio gates.

Midway through our burgers, Connor said, 'I don't get that guy. He is the biggest star in the world. He's got a beautiful wife. Rich as royalty. Why'd he have to lay into *me*?'

That afternoon, Richard Eagles made a great public display of camaraderie, claiming that he had been so caught up in the moment during Connor's big scene that he had lost himself. He went up to Connor and gave him a hug, teetering on his tiptoes, for despite his built-in shoe lifts he was markedly shorter. The younger man gracefully accepted this gesture, while Eagles eyed the cast and crew for their reaction. No one wanted a War of Words on day one, and Eagles notched up some good-guy points for this gesture, despite the fact that he had been the perpetrator in the first place. Just as he had hijacked Harrison Ford's Oscar win by being the first up on his feet, so he managed to fool the crew that Connor was actually to blame.

But he didn't fool Georgia Sepulveda. And she knew that Eagles would never forgive her insurrection.

At the end of this very long first day, Georgia hauled herself up from her suffering supine position in the debris, yanked at her padded waist and bust (for the Shelley Winters *Poseidon* profile), to the amusement of the crew, and declared: 'Morty! You and I have been in this business one helluva long time, and it's been a helluva long time since I've been so close to this much talent, but you have found yourself a Cracker Jack in young Mr Connor Child. It's a privilege.'

Georgia's padding and make-up has given her the dimensions and size of personality of a much older woman, conferring on her the look and status of an old broad, able to say and do whatever she wants. She applauded Connor, looking about for support, and got it. The crew joined in.

I saw Richard Eagles' neck colour up fast as he deliberated what he should do next.

207

Georgia beat him to it by slinging a padded arm around his neck and walking with him towards his special exit door, saying: 'Well, kid, one thing we all gotta get used to is the comers coming up behind us. All the time. Embrace 'em, is what I say.'

She topped it off by kissing his cheek, then turned and swanked off to her trailer.

I just caught sight of Eagles standing momentarily frozen before he wiped his hand slowly across the cheek that had been kissed, turned and disappeared into the Slinky.

## 28 May

Randy emerged from the Eagles trailer shaking his head from side to side. This I saw through Georgia's window. He stood in the middle of the parking lot awhile, heaved his shoulders up and down, then turned towards the caravan I was in. Uh oh.

Georgia was midway through being padded up and blowing gaskets. It took more than a few knocks on the door for Randy to get the courage to bang loudly enough to be heard.

'Come in!' she commanded.

He did not know where to put himself, so kept his eyes fixed to the floor. Georgia looked like a German hausfrau dominatrix. By the look on her face, she knew all too well what Randy was here for, but was determined not to help him out in any way.

He cleared his throat and ventured, 'Georgia, I need to talk with you privately. When you have a moment.'

She turned and slapped the air with a smile. 'Randy, my old darling! How long have we two known each other? For ever, right? RIGHT! You can say whatever you have to say to me right here and now. I have no need to be private about a thing. Fire away!'

He wasn't convinced. Shook his head and riddled up more frowns.

'It's a very delicate matter, Georgia. I'd really appreciate it if . . .'

208

'If ol' Georgia could lay off young Eagles, right? Am I right or am I RIGHT?! Now, you listen up, Randy my darling. And listen good.'

She was kneeling in front of him, thrusting her enhanced mammalia towards him. 'I don't care who the fuck Richard Eagles thinks he is, BUT! I will not stand around and allow that kind of public humiliation shit to be pulled on anyone, especially not on a younger, more vulnerable talent like Connor Child. Do you hear me, Randy? Mmhhhm?'

Randy was caught between this mentally unstable devil and the deep blue sea of Richard Eagles' furious eyes.

'I need you to let Richard know that you are not going to demonize him. I need your personal guarantee on this, Georgia. He is in a very strong position in the industry just now and without wanting to insult you, your position is somewhat more tenuous, if you see what I mean?'

'Are you threatening me, Randolf Rottweil? Because if you are, I think you know that this is not the best route for you boys to be tracking along!'

Eyes to the floor all round. Georgia, now fully packed into her padding, which was a dirty white, trundled up to her mirror to check out her artfully dishevelled make-up and hair.

'Let me put it this way; if Mort Buchinsky is unhappy with my performance, he will be the first to let me know. He directed me in my first ever picture. Now! If that little jerk has something to say, I suggest he say it straight to my face and not get you, OR his agent, OR his manager, OR any of his endless entourage of geeks to come and do his kvetching for him. Do you hear me, Randolf?'

'I hear you, Georgia. We just need to keep things kosher on this, OK? There's too much money at stake and too many reputations, including your own, to risk letting anything like this get outta hand. OK? OK?'

'Relax! – My daughter is playing his wife's screen child. Everything is gonna be just fine. Right? RIGHT! Now I need to get myself ready.'

Georgia held on to her upholstered sides until he had left and then let rip a screech of triumph. She turned to me and, thrusting her hand at my unsuspecting crotch, stage-whispered, 'I've got 'em right there. Right? Damned right!'

I graciously escaped, scrotus intactus, on the pretext of getting some breakfast, only to be surprised from behind by a familiar voice.

'You've been avoiding me.'

It was Kyla. But by the time I had turned, she had already stridden past, towards the sound stage.

I could feel an attack of anticipatory anxiety approaching, so opted to U-turn and head for the car park. I had just about made it when I heard horribly urgent footsteps running up behind me.

'Sir? Mr Buchinsky wants to see you in the make-up trailer immediately.'

'Oh, fuck.'

Mort and Jj were standing either side of Java, who was seated in the make-up chair. No New Age music this morning. In fact, no one was speaking. Yet. The make-up and hair team were combing out hairpieces, washing brushes, keeping busy. Jj looked up at Mort, then back at Java's reflection and declared, 'She looks like a *Cosmo* cover girl, not a victim of a major spacecraft crash. And her hairstyle looks like the salon version of Kyla Bergman's.'

The disdain in his voice was matched by the dejection in Java's eyes, which were *La Bohème*ing water at full throttle down her face. She sniffled up a squelch of protest.

'I am not "she". I am a person. An artist. I have a name.'

'You are a pain in the ass,' declared Jj, who was steaming for the door.

Mort gripped her shoulders and shook his head.

'He doesn't understand, honey. He's a technical mind. But you have to face the fact that we cannot shoot you with your hair looking like this. It does look uncannily like Kyla's and we'll have continuity problems. Look, Vyv is here, and he'll oversee your haircut. I'm needed on the set.'

He leant over and kissed her, shook my hand and winked on his way out.

Java's pupils were pulsating with shock. Nostrils flaring. Lips quivering. She looked at me with the silent accusation of a lamb prior to slaughter. Her hair was wetted down, scissors at the ready, and she clamped her eyes tight shut, which were still leaking like faulty fire hydrants.

'My hair is my life,' squeaked out.

'We'll only cut a couple of inches, Java,' consoled her hairdresser. She might just as well have said Java was about to be beheaded.

'Two INCHES?' She threw her head forward so violently that she banged her forehead on the counter.

The scissors snuck in and cropped off a wedge. Java jerked up, put her hand to her mouth and went running out of the bus.

'It's always like this with her. Done her last three movies and it's always the same,' was the resigned response from the hair person.

'But this is insane,' I said.

'No, this is normal.'

'What now?'

'She'll try to throw up and come back in here and say, "I couldn't even throw up." '

Ten minutes later she stomped back in; 'I tried to throw up but I couldn't. I've got to eat something.'

A runner was dispatched to get her double BLT toasted sandwiches 'with extra mayo'.

Tibet bounced in, wearing a micro-mini, bare midriff and a Barbie-doll sized bra that just about covered her cupcakes. She spoke as if her tongue was highly sprung.

'Hi!'

She squirreled about in her bag, retrieved a CD and was midway through replacing the New Age disc, when she laughingly said, 'You gotta hear this.' Turned up the volume and plonked herself into the make-up chair, jerking to the sounds of Prodigy.

'Have you had breakfast?' someone asked.

'Yeah. Two fruit smoothies. I feel great.'

When the platter of toasted BLT heart attacks arrived, Tibet asked, 'Who are those for?'

No one answered, and the runner placed the plate tentatively in front of Java. Smiling, she picked them up and passed them over to me.

Tibet said: 'Your make-up looks great, Java. You really do look like you've just survived a major crash. You know something, Vy, that food is really bad for you. I've just read this amazing book about food combining which I'm going to give you.'

'Thanks, Tibet. I can't wait.'

Over and out. I need to get back to fabrics, plaster, plumbing, plans and peace.

## 31 May

Kitty called, worried that Mort was going to have a heart attack at this rate. She's asked me to go on the payroll as an ambassador–peacekeeper sort of thing. Apparently I'm the perfect man for the job because I know everyone, but I'm no threat to any of them professionally.

I've agreed, but, looking at my hairline in the mirror, wonder if I'll lose the lot with this decision, like Robert Duvall did playing the Consigliori in *The Godfather* – a role not unlike the one that Kitty has just outlined for me. I ponder to my reflection out loud:

'Professional friend, auxiliary to the director, right hand to the Powercell, but powerless. The keeper of secrets. Buon giorno, Consigliori Vyvian.'

How could I resist? It is the apotheosis of my personality.

Mort called an emergency press conference. Key members from each department had been summoned to the studio boardroom to be briefed. Including me.

The studio heads were huddling when we all trouped in, and the meeting began on a sustained note of barely contained rage that informed every detailed sentence.

'Someone, somewhere, somehow, has made video recordings of on-set activities. Specifically, the misunderstanding between Connor Child and Richard Eagles on the first day of shooting. Specifically, the little upset concerning Java Hall's haircut in the make-up trailer the following day. Security on this production is at an all-time premium. Someone, and we are not saying who we think it might be, but someone on this crew has landed this production in deep, deep shit. There is no polite way of saying this. The damage is this: someone has sold the tape to a cable station which aired the first episode at two a.m. last night. As of now, there is video footage at large of what can only be described as a declaration of war between our two male leads. The press is assembling in the parking lot as we speak.'

This truly was deep.

'Not only was it broadcast, but they promise to have another exciting instalment for the nation at the same time tonight. And some smart-ass at a terrestrial network has offered big bucks to run it on prime time ASAP. We have served an injunction. Our lawyers are on to it, but what we can't do anything about is the fact that it's out there. You will appreciate that the press frenzy is growing by the minute. We propose that the actors be informed and persuaded to give a brief press call to try and quell this furore. However, more importantly, we have to trace the source. We have seen the tape, and the mystifying part of this whole mess is the totally amateur quality of the shooting. Everything has been shot from a sideways angle, no doubt to maximize its anonymity.'

Accusing eyes paraded up and down.

'Do you have any idea what make of camera was used?' I asked.

All these strangers' eyes turned to meet mine.

'Not yet.'

Mort decided that this was to be our first official joint mission – to cajole the three protagonists to act friendly for the press.

Jj opined that if we hadn't cast stars in the first place, 'None of this kinda shit would ever have come down.'

We three-pronged our way towards the trailers. Morty to Georgia. Me to Technophobe. Jj to the upside-down set.

'Come in, Vy. What's all this shit about delayed shooting?'

Ted Moby was busy feeding his tropical fish. I told him what I'd just heard. He choked, lurched back and slumped into a Shaker rocking chair. He sat there, stunned, head in hands, rocking back and forth. Groaning rhythmically.

'Oh, Jesus. Oh, Jesus. Oh, Jesus. Vy, you gotta save me. Oh, Jesus. Oh, Jesus. Oh, Jesus.'

'Explain?'

His terror was appalling as he gabbled his way through what must have happened. He had obviously left his new camcorder switched on, lying near the set and on the make-up counter, and run the battery flat in the process. He had then taken the machine into a Korean repair shop for fixing.

'I didn't know what was on the tape, and I couldn't get it out of the machine because the battery was fucked.'

'Where is the camera right now?'

'Still at the repair shop.'

'Who saw you with it?'

'No one saw anything. I always keep the camera wrapped up in a hand towel, so it doesn't intrude. Oh, Jesus, God Almighty, save me O heavenly Lord.'

'Too late for prayers, Teddy. I'd advise you to stay schtum. What I need from you is the repair ticket, so that we can decoy any trace-back to you.'

He fumbled about in his Prada holdall, found the crumpled ticket and examined it as if he'd drawn the winning number for a five-year stay in a Spanish Inquisition cell.

Mercifully, he had not given his address or phone number, and was soon on his knees praying that the Korean man 'will just remember me as another Caucasian gook'.

'Let's hope it never gets to a police line-up situation.'

Technophobe got condom-close and breathed, 'Vyv, promise me, PROMISE ME, you will never, ever tell a soul! And I swear, I will NEVER buy another gadget again. Ever.'

I nodded assurance and left him to jelly about.

During the lunch break, the infantry of press were given an impromptu display of motorcycle antics, courtesy of those alleged enemies, Connor Child and Richard Eagles.

They rode together back and forth, helmetless and laughing, in and out of the throng, answering any question that could be heard above the din of the motor and Doug's barking. The sight of Richard Eagles holding tightly on to Connor while looking nonchalant was Golden Globe Award winning stuff.

Connor decided when enough was enough and, revving the engine hard, yelled, 'Thanks for comin', guys, but some folks have got a movie to make. See ya!'

Connor's Steve McQueen act won him the total approbation of the press, the crew and the studio honchos. As well as seriously upping Java Hall's oestrogen levels.

I had to warn Georgia to restrain herself from cooing too heartily over Connor's triumph in front of Eagles. But to his credit, and perhaps because of his business sense, Richard made a great and continuous show of camaraderie towards Connor.

Technophobe was complimented by Mort and Jj for his 'incredibly believable act of sustained and continuous shock'.

## 5 June

Scarlett knows all her lines and shows an uncanny knack of hitting her appointed camera marks with the precision of a seasoned professional. Hard to reconcile with the, let's say, 'fluid' style employed by her mother, who drives the focus puller crazy – she is incapable of repeating her actions in the same way ever. 'I am an artist,' is her withering response to such pedantic requests.

Kyla and Scarlett bonded instantly, instinctively recognizing one another's utterly ruthless hearts (beating at athletically low speeds).

Georgia was invited into Kyla's trailer for lunch today, so that real mother and screen mother could get to know each other. I was the gooseberry, at Georgia's insistence, who said, 'No way am I going into that iceberg's igloo without your support.'

'But you'll be with Scarlett, and I think this is an exclusively female thing,' I challenged.

'That's exactly what worries me.'

Georgia linked arms and frogmarched me to Kyla's Winnebago, banged and entered, but stopped in her tracks when she found herself in the all-white interior.

Kyla and Scarlett hadn't arrived yet.

'This is fucking spooky. It's like an asylum!' she said, looking around.

'I designed it, Georgia, thank you very much.'

'No offence, honey, but this is like Eskimo land.'

Kyla and Scarlett arrived. Kyla looked behind my eyes and said, 'This is a surprise honour, Vyvian?'

I stammered out something about being a friend of the Sepulveda family.

'No need to explain. Welcome. Sit down.'

We sat on cream cushions around a low Japanese table.

'D'you eat sushi, Scarlett?' asked Kyla.

Scarlett nodded and sat with a perfectly straight back. Georgia inclined her head to one side and inspected her offspring as if for the first time.

Kyla handed me the teapot and asked if I'd be so kind as to do the honours. I dutifully poured out four small thimblefuls and caught Georgia's eyes, which were silently asking, 'Is this happening to me or is it the hash?' There was no denying that the atmosphere was severely formal and made us all terribly self-conscious. Nobody spoke for what seemed to stretch out for a couple of years. Oriental music plinked out from a hidden speaker, and Georgia almost lost it. She suddenly looked up and said, 'I knew Yul Brynner, you know. Way back.'

Kyla smiled and nodded, and Scarlett gave her mother a look which said, *Don't be a retard.*

We were saved by the arrival of the chef, who placed platters of sushi before each of us, then left without a word. Chopsticks up and we were off and eating, except for Georgia, who just sipped tea.

'Would you prefer something else, Georgia?' enquired Kyla.

'No, honey, I never really eat lunch. I'm so padded up, it'd just make me all uncomfortable.'

We ate in silence, till Georgia broke it by saying, 'Maybe I'll just have a little something.'

Instead of picking up something from her own plate, she reached over to Scarlett's and picked up a tuna morsel. Her years of dieting have turned her into a habitual thief of other people's food; she is forever denying herself, and then leaning over for 'a little something' from someone else's plate. Years of correctional transference therapy have clearly been to little avail. The tuna and rice combo was almost in Georgia's mouth, when Scarlett's fist beat it. She took a bull's-eye punch at her mother's mouth and said, 'I've told you a thousand times, Mother, leave my food alone.'

I had counted to five before Georgia was able to summon breath to gasp, and then bellow. The blow was so potent, there was blood streaming from her mouth down her chin, onto her padded front.

Kyla didn't flinch.

Scarlett carried on eating and leant over to retrieve the lump of sushi that had dropped from her mother's grasp.

Georgia burst into tears and put both hands to her bleeding maw. I handed her a napkin. She stuffed it to her face and then pointed towards her bag, mumbling and gesticulating.

I reached over and handed the bag to her. She frantically scrabbled for a phone and punched out some numbers.

Kyla watched with the gleaming dead-eye of a Great White.

The phone conversation that followed between Georgia and her child's therapist (who was having breakfast in New York) is something I'd rather not repeat. It was bad enough hearing her pathetic pleas while the little perpetrator sat calmly eating as if nothing had happened.

When Georgia clicked off, she apologized profusely to Scarlett, saying, 'Mommy's been a very naughty girl. I promise I will *never* steal your food ever again, sweetheart.'

Scarlett looked up and said, 'I accept. But promises are like piecrusts. Easily made and easily broken. Says Mary Poppins.'

Her self-possession left a taste of aspirin in my mouth. Georgia was so grateful for this chink of acceptance that despite her obvious pain and the profuse bleeding she leant over to hug Scarlett. But was stopped: 'Don't. You'll get blood on my costume. It's continuity.'

That finished me off. She *was* Damien.

Kyla stood up and went to get some more tissues and ice from the kitchen.

'You'll need that attended to, Georgia. I'll look after Scarlett for you.'

★

Georgia called me this evening and whispered, 'I think my daughter is possessed. There's something not normal about her.'

Java was next in line on the blower, and I belatedly realized that, as I was officially on the payroll, I had no way of ever being off duty.

I was spared not a single detail of her growing obsession.

Ever since she saw Connor and Doug on *Letterman* all those months ago, she had decided he was the man for her and plagued him with the 'I want your sperm' missives. Now that she is working with him, she feels there is no need to send messages, when she can wield her magic at first hand. What is so frightening is how

Connor's genuinely good-natured 'Hi y'all' warmth is so wilfully misinterpreted as a full frontal flirt-alert. She has decided that the scripted love scene between her character and his is the perfect moment to move into the courtship, capitulation and commitment phase. None of which Connor has any idea about, though he has taken to gibing her in the make-up trailer about their approaching screen sex scenes, joshing that he will have to wear metal underwear to keep himself in control – which Java has misread as a declaration of his burning desire.

I suggested that he might have been joking, especially as he announced this to one and all at 6.30 a.m.

'No, uh uh,' she assured me. 'I know men. He's probably just shy, and that's his way of letting me know that he feels the same about me. I've seen how he looks at me when he doesn't think I'm aware. I'm sure of it.'

'But, Java, a man who jokes about metal underwear in front of everyone including Kyla, Georgia and Tibet doesn't sound the shy type.'

'That's where you're so wrong, Vyv. I know men. And he wants me. Just you watch and see.'

## 11 June

Georgia requested that her make-up be done in her trailer, 'So that I can be with Scarlett.'

This way, her facial damage could be explained away as a brilliant make-up job.

Unfortunately, the scenes she is scheduled to shoot this week are with Jj. Her character has to crawl through a corridor over dead bodies in search of her husband, surviving an explosion along the way.

Jj is in his element dealing with the inanimate, but this was his

219

first shot at directing a star actress. Without a smidgen of tact, he scrutinized Georgia's swollen mouth and said, 'This make-up is way over the top. It looks fucking ridiculous.'

He attempted to wipe some of it off, but Georgia's hand intercepted his with a Stallone grip, as she said, 'Don't you DARE touch an actor's face, young man. What you are looking at is the work of a highly professional Oscar-winning team of make-up artists. As NONE of us have ever been in a crash like this story, I think you might just give my make-up the benefit of your doubt.'

Being the seasoned survivor that she is, Georgia presented him with three photographs of facial wounds from a medical book, as backup.

Jj had lost interest in her by then, and decided to increase the size of the explosion to justify her injuries.

'He is a sadist,' said Sepulveda.

## 12 June

Mort invited Java, Connor and me over for dinner, to prepare for the shooting of the love scene. Ice-breaking, jaw-relaxing stuff. No sooner was dessert done than Java suggested they mark through the kind of sex she had in mind.

Kitty discreetly dimmed the lights and flung some scatter cushions on the floor. I don't think Connor had any notion about how things would evolve, and he looked about with all the confusion of a Labrador puppy.

Java talked her way through the dialogue, while getting her hands all over him.

Mort asked, 'Do you think it's appropriate for you to be undressing him?' But Java didn't flinch and carried on pulling off Connor's shirt. Mort piped up, 'Honey, I think we get the idea, you don't have to do it for real just now.'

'Oh, but I do, Morty. Just give me some space to show you.'

Connor was not consulted in the matter, but gamely fumbled at her, bemused more than anything else. Java was now kissing him passionately, while undoing his belt and trousers.

Kitty's eyes were saucering. Doug had started barking. We watched. Java suddenly leapt onto Connor, straddling her legs round his waist, causing him to stagger back against the wall. Knocking a painting askew. Mid-grope, she turned and gasped, 'This is when I think I should get hold of some overhead fixture, so that I can haul myself up and get my legs round his neck so he can eat my pussy.'

Connor started to laugh, but was gagged by her tongue plunging south down his throat. Doug's excited barking covered up the giggles that assailed the audience.

When Java had gorged herself sufficiently, she slithered down the front of him, and for a moment we all thought she was about to pry into his pants. Thankfully she didn't pause, and prostrated herself at his feet. Heaving.

Connor gingerly pulled his clothes back on, tried to get Doug to quieten down and asked Kitty to point him in the direction of the nearest bathroom.

Java tilted her head to one side and asked, 'So what do you think? Do you think it'll work for my character?'

Mort poured himself a mahogany whiskey and replied, 'Perhaps in the light of your terribly shocked state and your injuries, that kind of athleticism might be inappropriate. Possibly. I'm also not sure that there is anything overhead that you could feasibly grip on to.'

Java turned over onto her stomach and lay looking up at him like a dishevelled Sandra Dee about to break into song, her hands cupped beneath her chin and her legs crossed and swaying in the air.

'Don't worry about that, I've already had a word with the designer and props department and they said the upside-down ceiling is easily fitted up with a secure holding.'

Poor Mort. He diplomatically waded in deeper. 'Watching how

221

you did that, Java, I have to say that for most of the action, your clothing masked Connor completely, and from a technical point of view, it's going to be a problem to get his face in shot with your legs and dress wrapped around his head.'

'So what are you suggesting, that I take off *all* my clothes? Is that what you're saying? That is so *yesterday*, Morty.'

'Java, this picture is aiming for a PG rating. I don't think the studio is going to buy *Last Tango in Space*, that's all.'

This was definitely not what Java was wanting to hear back. She rolled over, wiped her smudged mouth and straightened her clothes.

'So how are we meant to convey our passion for each other, then? Just stand around and smooch?'

Connor returned wearing a somewhat sheepish grin.

'Mort is cutting our love scene, Connor!'

Poor, poor Mort. He shook his head and put his hands up in the *whoah* position.

'Java, sweetheart, honeypie, nothing has been cut. This is a creative collaboration.'

'Don't infantilize me, Mort. I'm an adult woman. I will not be hoochy-coochy talked to by you or anybody. If you want to treat someone like a sex-object puppet, why not set your sights on Tibet. She *is* a child! Connor, I'd be grateful if you could give me a ride home now, if that's not asking too much?'

Connor acquiesced, shrugging, 'I gotta be up early for shooting, Mort, get myself prepared and all. Thanks so much for a wonderful dinner, Kitty.'

We uneasily took our cue from his charm and tact and were bidding goodnights at the front door before any further damage was done.

Mort was on the mobile before I was down the drive.

'What am I supposed to do? She has it in her contract that she will not do any nudity, despite nineteen of her pictures featuring her tits, and now she wants to be Mrs Tarzan of the Thighs? Am I missing something here?'

I implied that she might just have the tiniest, weeniest crush on her co-star and that this might have coloured her judgement.

'But, Vyvian, you've read the script. These two characters have an impromptu kiss and fondle in the midst of their panicked situation, more to comfort each other than anything else. Not the fucking *Kama Sutra*.'

'If it gets ugly, why not just shoot the first part of her plan and cut when she goes Olympic?'

'There just isn't time for that kinda shit.'

If Java calls within the hour, it will be to report that nothing developed. If not, she will be Cheshire-cat purring all over the set tomorrow, to let everyone know she got him. Either option is a bad one.

No call has come.

## 13 June

Today, a closed set. Notices were plastered all over the studio, and walkie-talkies crackled with the no-go situation. A skeleton crew of absolute essentials was permitted to light and measure camera tracks and focus points with Java and Connor's stand-ins. A debris-disguised metal rung had been bolted into the ceiling for her coital gymnastics.

When everything was ready, Java arrived with two assistants, a hairdresser, a make-up artist and Brenda, leading without looking left or right. She was swathed in an oversized Ralph Lauren white towelling robe with her hair done up in pre-crash mode. I looked around for Jj but was told that he was still shooting Georgia's explosions next door. Ahhh.

The nonsense of Java looking pristine after the catastrophics she is supposed to have survived was prompting whispered asides. She was having a fresh coat of lipgloss applied when Mort meandered over and said to Connor, 'I need you to get your hands into her hair ASAP and muss it up good and proper. Hopefully she'll be so carried away, she won't notice. Then I'll be able to cut in and get round the bouffant.'

'The what?' asked Connor.

'Her wig.'

Connor looked none the wiser, but understood that her hair was his priority.

'I'd like to do this wide shot in one take, Mort,' she demanded. Mort nodded. To whatever she requested, really.

None of us was prepared for her attack on Connor. No sooner had she started to kiss him than she ripped his shirt off, struggled with his trousers, and then, before pouncing, pulled her dress over her head. Groaning and sucking and licking and thrusting, she was making all manner of animal grunts by way of accompaniment, then reached up and gripped the cross-bar. Unlocking her lips from his, she hoisted herself upwards, then clamped her thighs around his head, concealing most of it, save for a shock of blond hair protruding like startled grass.

Every human present was agape or grinning. Mort, to his credit, let her carry on till she had orgasmed – the signal for which she gave by ululating like a grief-stricken African.

'Cut! Perfect, Java. Perfect, Connor.'

Java was euphoric, swaddled up in her robe, and she said, 'God, that felt so real.'

Connor's legs were very shaky. I still couldn't work out whether they had or hadn't done it the night before.

'Do you wanna go again on that, Mort?' Java enquired enthusiastically.

'Java, it was so committed and passionate that I think it'd be a shame not to come in close for some detail on your faces, if that's all right with you? I specifically mean the kissing section up front.

Gives us a chance to get really intimate and involved, before the actual act. Which is perfectly covered by the wide tracking shot already.'

Connor looked stricken for a second, till he realized that he didn't have to shoulder Java's Krakatoa all over again. At that moment, I knew that he was not remotely interested in her.

Poor Java. Poor me – who will have to hear the sorry saga played out in five symphonic movements in the coming months. Oy!

Mort seamlessly shot all the pre-*Tango* close-up footage he needed, with clothes mostly on and hair completely dishevelled. The crew was astute enough to cotton on to what Mort had done, and what had been expected to take all day to shoot was completed by lunch time.

Java insisted I eat with her. The state of her trailer about matched her hair. She was a gal who could infuse an empty room with chaos. Every surface was crammed with discarded clothes, toys, bits of sandwiches, make-up, half-full cups of cold coffee, magazines, loose CDs and stockings. The TV and radio were competing with one another at a low volume. Joss sticks smoked away in a clutch in the corner.

She pulled the door closed and said, 'Vy, he is IT. We had such a good talk last night on the way home, and he was just incredible today, don't you think? He did everything I wanted him to. I just know that he is going to be a perfect father for Mona.'

'You got *really* close, then?'

'Uh! Close? Like this!' and she crossed her fingers.

'So you're in love?'

She nodded and hugged herself at the same time.

'I don't want to do a dampener, but is this reciprocated?'

Java shot me a look of rat poison.

'He doesn't realize it himself yet, but he will. I just know it. Haven't you seen the way he keeps looking at me and making jokes? It's sublimated lovemaking, Vyvian, I know. That scene we just did is the scene of this movie. You watch. No one gives a shit about the special effects. Seen too many already. But *real* on-screen passion requires chemistry, and if there's one thing we've got together, it's that chemistry, Connor and me. I'm going on a mega diet from this moment.'

## 24 June

Randy, Mort, Brenda, Security, two lawyers, Java's agent, manager, and publicist – and I – gathered in her trailer for a pre-shoot meeting at 7 a.m.

Java was informed that any further harassment of Mr Connor Child, by anonymous letter or any other means, would lead to a court order. She, Ms Java Hall, was to maintain a discreet distance from Mr Child at all times, unless required when 'in character' to be in close proximity to him. Furthermore, Mr Child's girl-friend, Tibet, was not to be approached by Ms Hall under any circumstances. Tibet and Connor had become an on-screen/off-screen item since the ball, providing gossip fodder for the global 'feeders'.

'Finally, the script is being rewritten to avoid any future confrontations between yourself and Mr Child. In order to maintain professional relations and avoid any delays to the production of the feature film *Zeitgeist*, we would appreciate your full cooperation in this delicate matter.'

Java's tear ducts were opened to maximum. It was hard not to feel desperately sorry for her.

When the stern-faced delegation made its exit, Brenda supplied Java with a whole bottle of Evian, lest she dehydrate completely. The poor creature was incapable of speech, such was the depth of her shame and sense of injustice. I wrapped my arms around her as she shuddered continuously.

Mort, fearful that he would fall further behind schedule, was adamant that Java shoot her scenes with Richard Eagles today.

'We'll have the writers incorporate some back-story stuff for you about ... about a lost child or parent or something, so that it's appropriate for you to be in an emotional state.'

Java couldn't believe what she was hearing and spluttered, 'If you treat me like a fucking puppet, I'll *act* like a fucking puppet.'

But there was little conviction in her protest, and she crumpled into Brenda's arms for a comforting dose of the *there, there, my dears*.

She was taken to the set aboard a golf buggy, as her legs were so wobbly.

Jj, whom it was deemed best not to inform about the sperm brouhaha, blundered in with even less tact than usual: 'Why does her character have to cry all the time?'

Java replied with a Mississippian torrent.

'My character is in a state of shock and crisis. I cry. All right?'

Richard, unaware of what had just gone down in her trailer, came to her defence: 'Why do I get the impression from the way you speak to actors that you believe they have purposely set out to annoy you?'

Jj, a man for whom smiling was an unnatural act, blinked twice, then spread his mouth into a grimace, causing his nostrils to flare back, and his miniature teeth to be exposed in a way that, frankly, we could have lived without. He turned and went back to the camera to do some fiddling about.

Java snorted up and stemmed the seepage long enough to articulate a 'thank you'. Richard obliged by giving her a big hug.

Between Java's water-sodden cheeks and Georgia's still purple lips, it looked like the make-up department was heading for an Oscar nomination for sustained realism.

# 7 July

We have embarked upon the water-flooding sequences. Everyone has been warned that they will be wet from dawn to dusk for the best part of a month. The script writers have established that the spacecraft wreck will be floating upside down, at an increasingly perilous angle, somewhere in the Indian Ocean, in order to justify the water being warm. The craft had lost all communications contact after the collision and explosion, and when part of it plummeted back to Earth, the assumption on the ground was that all the passengers were lost.

A vast water tank has been built inside a sound stage, and the hydraulic engineering perfected for *Titanic* will be used to lift or lower whole sections of the spacecraft into or out of the water. Expert crew, veterans of watery epics ranging as far back as *Jaws*, are on hand to speed the shooting process along. But water is water, and it is never as controllable as you hope it might be.

Technophobe's shock had eased off considerably until he was given two pages of technical gobbledegook to learn, describing the escape route options and mechanical impediments facing the survivors. Try as he might, he could not learn the wretched words. Made all the worse by Mort's very public announcement:

'If ever there was a guy born to convince and charm an audience with his techno-jargon skills, it's our man Ted Moby. The only actor I know who can fix anything. We asked the writers to create a truly complex techno-soliloquy especially for you. It's all yours, Teddy.'

I sat up with him most of the night as he trawled his way through the califragilistics of each section, trying to set a pattern in his head, but to no avail. He awoke like an amnesiac.

Imagine then his relief when Mort took him aside midway through the endless technical setting-up this morning, and cravenly apologized for the fact that his two pages were having to be cut down – 'The water level rises much quicker than expected in this section, and there just wouldn't be time to accommodate the whole speech.' Mort mistook the catatonic smile of relief on Techno-

phobe's face for the brave smile of a defeated thesp, and promised
to make it up to him. Technophobe realized that by giving off little
dejected looks he got a load of conciliatory attention from crew
and cast, who needed to feel sorry for someone else other than
themselves, drenched as they were. Even Java's much flaunted bra-
less wet top half was waning as a topic of conversation. She has
forsaken her Connor diet and is now eating for three. The costume
department has asked me to have a word. But I called her agent
instead, who in turn called her shrink to see what could be done.

★

## 28 July

Still in the water. The studio has an all-pervading smell of damp.
Morale low. Major fatigue and exhaustion in all quarters. The star
party seems a lifetime ago.

Tibet has taken to making mobile phone calls between takes to
anyone who will talk to her. At one stage, Mort was about to give
her some detailed direction about a scene when she put her hand
up and said, 'I'm talking Mort, just wait till I'm finished, OK?'

Mort uncharacteristically grabbed the phone out of her hand
and threw it as high as he could into the air. It clunked on a
lighting bar, then plopped back down into the water. 'You are the
most unprofessional, unprepared, arrogant young person I have
ever had the displeasure of having to deal with. As from now, you
are banned from bringing a mobile phone anywhere near my set.
Is that understood?'

She stretched her arms above her head, yawning, and replied,
'And you are an old man, Mort. Give me a call when you've
calmed down.'

Georgia started laughing first. 'Look at us! Rich and famous,
wet and miserable. Am I right, or am I RIGHT?! Anyway, don't
worry, boys, I'm going for my big Shelley Winters swim-to-the
death tomorrow, and then I'm outta here.'

Scarlett looked at her mother as if she was an alien's afterbirth.

Connor was caught between comforting Tibet and apologizing to Mort, but as Java was still hugging him close, he kept his distance and threw his umpteenth stick of the day for Doug to swim after. Only the dog seems happy to be splashing about incessantly, week after week.

Press interest has begun to focus on the spiralling production costs, and all the usual 'Sinkgeist' headlines accompany every new setback.

An indication of how interest has waned is the absence of any competition between Java and Kyla. Java has long given up trying to compete with Kyla on the stomach-crunch-exercise scale of things, having sacked her shrink and resolved to eat her way out of her unhappiness as inflicted by Connor's rejection.

## 31 July

Georgia's farewell dying swim was delayed by two days due to technical difficulties. This phrase was given the full-throttle choir treatment every time the first assistant director began making an excuse.

Today, Georgia, more energized than anyone had ever seen her before, shouted out: 'DUE TO TECHNICAL EXPERTISE, I SHALL BE UNLOCKING MY PADDED BODYSUIT AND RELEASING MYSELF BEFORE YOU LOVELY PEOPLE THE MOMENT MORT BUCHINSKY YELLS CUT ON MY DEATH SCENE. HOLD YOUR BREATH, BOYS!'

However, the jamming of one of the underwater cameras meant that shooting was brought to a standstill for a few hours. Georgia, to the acute embarrassment of Scarlett, threw herself into a cabaret act of jokes and songs, delivered with such bravado that she was forgiven for flat notes and limp punchlines.

Mort's interest in the project has been diminishing by the day, as the technical demands predominate. 'This stuff is not what I know about. It's dead.'

When the cameras were ready to roll, Georgia warned that she would only be able to do a couple of good takes due to the heaviness of the padding and the distance she had to swim underwater. Paramedics were on standby, and Georgia's refusal to let a stuntwoman do the difficult part had upped the interest in her scene, which involved her diving off an upside-down platform, holding onto a rope and swimming till she found an escape route on the other side of a collapsed shaft.

Mort's affection for her attitude was undisguised. 'Say a prayer for yourself, ya old broad! Now get in that water and go drown! And ... ACTION!'

And Georgia ploughed into the water, took a massive breath and swam. And swam. And swam. Followed by three cameras and their attendant crews in diving suits.

They filmed continuously. It was Jj's idea to do it without any cuts. The paramedics were not convinced that this was safe or wise. Neither was Randy, who kept yakkering on about the insurance risks. Crew members crammed along the overhead lighting walk-way, following her underwater path below.

Georgia was shattered as she emerged gasping and flailing at the other end of the underwater tunnel. Her breath came in short convulsive inhalations and expulsions, so much so that Jj had to physically restrain the medics from breaking through and giving her mouth to mouth. Flailing like a beached and dying whale, cradled in Richard Eagles' arms, emitting whinnies of pain, she segued into her scripted dialogue:

'I did it, I did it. I told you I could and no one believed me. I don't think I'm gonna make it, but I want you to give this locket to my darling husban—' and she was gone.

Richard bent over her sodden hulk and hugged her tight, enabling him to get his eyes in close proximity to his hands which were larded with menthol, as he cannot cry on cue. That did the trick. His instant flow was worthy of Java Hall herself.

Mort held off shouting cut until Georgia suddenly arose from her death by lifting her arms in mock slow motion and wrapping them around Richard's back. She squeezed him for all she was worth and then kissed him full on the smacker. Rolled over, still holding onto him, so that she was now on top of Mr Box Office, who was pinioned to the deck. To Richard's horror and the crew's delight, Georgia wheezed, 'You ain't seen NOTHING yet, baby!'

And proceeded slowly to undo her top, while singing 'The Stripper' in All-flat minor. Off came the blouse. Off came the hairpiece. Each flung into the water. Then she teased each ribbon-tie of her padding loose with her teeth. One by one. Still singing. The crew gave a slow hand-clap and wolf-whistle back-up.

Mort signalled to keep rolling, and Jj, for once, was smiling his vampiric best. Off came the upper half, a soaked set of falsies and fat arms, revealing her real flesh underneath, rash-red from being encased for so long.

'Open your eyes, Richy!' she cooed. 'Here they come!'

And true to her word, she unclasped her bra and let lose her lalas. Leant forwards and shimmied her shoulders at him. Then stood up, pulled off her skirt and with molto bump and grind ra-rah-rah undid her lower padding, gripped the chunky thing once it was loose and swinging it around her head three times before letting it fly across the water.

She looked in astonishingly good shape and suddenly young again, having been trussed up into old gal mode for so long.

Richard Eagles was still prostrate beneath her, held in position by her feet, either side of his waist. Georgia was seconds away from performing her own one-woman *Full Monty* and Richard Eagles had the best seat in the house.

She obliged by changing tunes just prior to the actual divestment of knickers, blasting out, 'I BELIEVE IN MIRACLES.'

With which she ripped off her underwear, specially Velcro'd for the occasion, flung her arms in the air and yelled, 'CATCH 'EM IF YOU CAN, GUYS!' slinging her pants up, leaving her standing stark naked.

Mr Eagles closed his eyes. The rest of us cheered and stomped and shouted. Georgia had stage-managed her final day on the movie with the seasoned skill of Gypsy Rose Lee.

She swanned back into the water, turned to Mort and Jj, and in the sweetest Betty Boop squeak asked, 'Are you satisfied, boys?'

Mort walked forward and held out his hand. Someone was ready with her towelling robe. The crew were still clapping. Mort put up a hand for silence and announced, 'Due to technical difficulties, we are going to have to reshoot this whole sequence all over again. Ms Sepulveda, please get padded up again.'

Three hundred people held their breath and all that could be heard was the lapping of the water and buzz of lighting equipment.

'Only kidding.'

Mort's timing was as sound as ever. It was the catharsis everyone had been longing for. There are weeks if not months still to go, but Georgia's departure felt like it could be the end.

Scarlett was scarlet with embarrassment. Technophobe was hoping against hope that he'd be able to keep a straight and distraught face when he had to act sad over the dead body of his screen partner. For which Georgia very gamely got back into her padding and costume.

At lunch, she asked me, too casually for comfort, 'Just what is that Slinky corridor contraption of Mr Eagles made of?'

I heard 'parachute silk and aluminium spines' come automatically from my mouth, during which my brain tried to scramble and decipher her intent.

I didn't have long to wait.

At five o'clock, when her death scene was completed, the cast and crew assembled outside the vast studio door to wave and wish her goodbye, despite the fact that she'd be back to visit Scarlett who was scheduled to work till the end.

I knew the moment she got into the driver's seat what she had planned. Her chauffeur was plonked beside her on the passenger side. Georgia waved and kissed the air in one big mwaah, revved the engine hot-rod style, then flattened the accelerator and tyre-screeched off, heading straight for the Slinky. She ploughed through it and careened round a sharp bend, billowing fabric in every direction.

We almost expected to hear an off-screen crash-bang-walloping explosion, but none came. To his credit, Mr Eagles hasn't said a word about his ruptured Slinky, and I will make it my first call tomorrow to get another one delivered pronto.

## 2 August

National Enquirer this morning: KYLA BERGMAN – 5 MONTHS PREGNANT!!!

I almost crashed my car.

The magazine store on Fairfax had an entire shelf displaying and repeating this revelation. I bought every copy they had, in a demented attempt to delay my demise. Started shaking all over as I read the copy.

> Kyla Bergman, currently working on the ill-fated *Zeitgeist*, mega-million disaster epic dubbed *Dollarheist* by industry insiders, is PREGNANT. The twenty-nine-year-old star was unavailable for comment, but a close friend confirmed yesterday that Kyla was WITH CHILD. She was photographed leaving a well-known Hollywood gynecologist's with a great big smile on her face. Despite her attempted disguise of cap and sunglasses, there is no mistaking who the happy mother to be is. You can see in the photos that she is sporting a bump approximate to FIVE MONTHS already. It is well known that she and her husband RICHARD EAGLES have been trying for a child for some years without success. Close sources confirmed that he is the baby's NATURAL FATHER. Rumours of FERTILITY TREATMENT and ADOPTION have dogged them wherever they go.
>
> This should satisfy all those sceptics. She is being written

out of *Zeitgeist* so that she can devote all her time to preparing herself for the miracle of MOTHERHOOD. Her screen daughter, played by four-year-old SCARLETT SEPULVEDA, that cutie-pie STARLET, will take over Kyla's scenes. RICHARD EAGLES is reported to have said: 'THIS IS THE GREATEST CHRISTMAS GIFT WE COULD EVER HAVE PRAYED FOR. WE HAVE BEEN BLESSED.'

I read, and reread, looked and relooked, pinched flesh, punched leg, slapped cheek and stared. Took stock.

1) Georgia – over and out.
2) Java – banned from interaction with Connor and Tibet.
3) Richard Eagles – diplomatically distant.
4) Jj – almost on no-speaks with cast.
5) Mort – holding on. Just.
6) Technophobe – in gadget remission remorse.
7) Randy – dyspeptic.
8) Doug – barking.
9) Kyla – pregnant.
10) Me – jinxed.

I sat paralysed. Looked up at the lights changing from green to orange to red to orange to green and back again. Heard a quote from *Hamlet* come eddying down my stream of consciousness, and bob to a halt. I wrote it down – 'When sorrows come, they come not single spies, But in battalions!'

Called Marga. 'Have you heard the news? WHY didn't you tell me?'

She said, 'Why would I?'

Oooooooo, boy!

The press had already staked out their territory either side of the studio gates. They had long lenses, short lenses, large cameras, small ladders. The lot. If they only knew.

Act nonchalant. Isn't that what you're supposed to do? So I nonchalanted my way over to the make-up trailer as per. But I can't act. What to do? What to do?

My vision was impaired by a hovering Picasso drawing that seemed to dangle and accuse wherever I looked. Went inside. All was preternaturally calm: Java midway through make-up, triple-decker club sandwich, headphones on ears.

Tibet on her mobile, seated at the opposite end of the bus.

Technophobe in between, fiddling with a CD portable. Smell of coffee. Sleepiness at the start of another watery day.

No Kyla. No Richard. No Connor. No Doug.

Didn't anyone else know?

'When are the others due in?' I asked.

'Not in today. Got to complete the tunnel swim with Tibet, Ted and Java.'

I U-turned before Java had a chance to harpoon me over for some TLC. If ever anyone was in need of some Tender Loving Care, it was my shock-absorption system. How could I have been so stupid?

Drove down to the ocean and parked. Watched the waves and schemed a scheme to stow away on the next vessel bound for Vladivostok.

I asked myself: What if Richard never finds out? Why would I be a possible suspect sperm donor? No way will his finger be pointing in my direction. Of course it won't.

Halfway convinced, I sped home. Resolved never to part with sperm unless officially contracted. Resolved to refuse to be Consigliori on a movie ever again. Resolved to stick to soft furnishings. Got in and slumped. Eye caught by insistent red light flashing.

Seven phone messages, four from Kyla. 'Come over.'

This was not what I had in mind. Called first. All she said was, 'I can't talk. Get here. Fast.' I did. Drove at kamikaze speed, recklessly hoping I might get impaled prior to the sure-fire horror that lay ahead in the Pacific Palisades.

'Grow up! What's a little sperm shared between friends, hmm?' I said to myself as I struck up a smile and swung the car as close

236

to the front door as I dared, figuring that if I needed to I could leap in and skid off in homage to Starsky and Hutch.

Flo and Devonia were waiting to usher me in. Smiling. As was I. Hard. The scent of fresh freesias was all-pervasive and served merely to torture me further. How could anything smell this good when things were so bad?

We three walked briskly towards Kyla's study, the very room where the deed was done. I couldn't quite muster any pleasantries. Flo opened the door and let me pass through. Devonia asked if I wanted anything to drink. Then they left. Me alone.

Waiting. Checked the glass door into the garden. Locked. Shit! As I turned around, Kyla entered, raised her arms in the air and padded towards me. Without saying a word, she wrapped herself around me and hugged as if her life depended on it, her five-month bump all too prominent.

Why hadn't any of us noticed before? She drew back and grasped my face in both hands.

'You wonderful, wonderful, wonderful, generous, gorgeous man, you! Look!' She ran her hands over her belly. 'We are going to have your baby.'

'But how do you know it's mine?' came quavering out.

'You are the only person it could be.'

'But we only did it once!'

'Precisely!'

'What about, what about Richard?'

'He is ecstatic!'

'So he has no idea that it was me, then?'

'How do you mean?'

'Richard – your husband, my employer – he thinks it's his?'

'Of course he does.'

'How'd you convince him?' I was edging my way towards the door.

'I didn't have to.' Her look of triumph paralleled my unvarnished fear.

'I haven't a clue what you're talking about. Where is Richard?'

'Right behind you.'

My knees went first. Buckling forwards. Followed by the rest of me. Richard and Kyla helped me up. Then hugged me!

'It was my idea,' said Richard. 'We can never thank you enough.' I could feel my eyes dilate and swivel about the room.

'Your idea? What, to let me have sex with your wife on the off chance that she might fall pregnant?'

'Let's sit down and I'll explain. Do you want something to drink?'

'Yes. A triple tequila and vodka bomb, please.'

Richard and Kyla were knee to knee on the opposite sofa. Richard began:

'Vyvian, of all the people we considered approaching, you were the only real contender. Everyone else was too much of a liability. We trust you implicitly. We weren't sure whether you were AC/DC, no offence, but in all our dealings, we could find nothing to confirm either way. We also knew that you were totally discreet, and as far as we knew have not exactly bed-hopped your way through this town. Which you will appreciate was important for us, from a disease point of view.'

Kyla took over.

'We also had no idea whether you would be willing. So rather than sitting round and discussing it with you, or asking if we could get you to donate by test tube, we decided to opt for the pounce. Which was taking liberties, no question, but we had been advised that the chances of instant impregnation were likely to be that much higher than intravenously, if actual entry occurred. Something to do with the hormonal adrenalin activity that is naturally triggered in the act of copulation. Can you forgive us for being so presumptuous?'

They looked imploringly at me like two repentant tots.

'Do you intend to pretend it's Richard's?'

They looked at each other, looked at me and nodded. 'That is, if you wouldn't mind?'

'But what if the child looks like me? I'm somewhat taller than Richard!'

Kyla smiled reassuringly and said, 'I'm tall, and so is everyone else in my family, so that really won't be a problem.'

'How will you explain this sudden fertility?'

'Remember that Indian trip we went on? Well, when we came back, we leaked to the press that we had been to see a healer. The timing all fits perfectly. There is nothing to worry about.'

Richard's business brain spoke next. 'We are assuming that you have no desire for any children yourself.'

'Uh uh.'

'So you wouldn't have any problem signing a confidentiality statement, ensuring that you will never sue for paternity rights or attempt to blackmail us? I'm sorry to have to mention this, but it's a penalty for being who we are. We're sure you understand.'

My head was nodding in a variety of directions all at once. I realized this when I saw the look of panic attack their faces.

'I mean, yes. Of course yes. Anything you want. I'll sign.'

He went to the roll-top French writing desk and returned with a page of legalese and pen. I didn't read any of it, just signed on the dotted. Kyla burst into tears and came over to embrace me. Followed by Richard, in much the same state. Felt embarrassed.

'Do you know whether it's a boy or a girl yet?' I queried.

'Doesn't matter. We are just ecstatic to have one.'

This set both of them off again, then Richard sniffled into control, looked me in the eye, with that selfsame burning intensity which had garnered him an Oscar nomination for *War!* and said, 'Vyvian. You will never have to work again for the rest of your life. I have set up a trust guaranteeing you a substantial salary in perpetuity.'

'You only needed to ask, you know. None of this is necessary,' I lied.

'It's the very least we could do. I know you find money talk vulgar, so I won't mention the exact figure, but when you get the first instalment, let us know if it seems inadequate.'

'This is very flattering and very embarrassing. I really don't know what to say.'

Kyla leant forward and put her long pale finger to my lips.

'All we ask for is total secrecy.'

'Just in case at some point in the future, God forbid, something should go awry in our relationship, I should let you know that I have a video-recording of your antics, should we be forced to go to court. I'd hate to have to accuse you of philandering with my wife.'

Richard Eagles laughed his way through these last two sentences, making light of what was an undisguised threat. I choked.

'Are you going to abandon *Zeitgeist*?'

'Not at all,' said Kyla. 'We've spoken with Mort and Jj and the writers are going to incorporate my pregnancy into the script. They think it'll add a real dimension to my character and up audience sympathy. Now, we know it's your day off, but we'd love to take you out for a celebratory lunch, if that's all right with you?'

'Sounds good to me. Where?'

'Chez Panisse.'

'But that's in San Francisco!'

'Berkeley. Richard'll fly us up in the Lear jet from Burbank. Land in Oakland an hour later. Thirty minutes by car and we're lunching upstairs. OK?'

'OK.'

Is this the true meaning of a starfucker?

Indeed, in what seemed like a trice, we were eating Alice Waters' fêted Panisse cuisine. Topped off by a massage and spa at the Claremont Hotel nearby. No press. No fuss. Just the 'four' of us. Perfect!

★

# 10 August

Java Hall has taken the news of Kyla's pregnancy really badly. Her lexicon of 'infertile witch' abuse required a reshuffle, rethink and update. She was feeling acutely isolated. When I casually asked her how she was today, she looked up and replied, 'How am I? How are the Indians in Idaho? Who cares how I am? Those disenfranchised, dispossessed and abandoned souls have been betrayed by us all.'

This was not a good sign. Her trilling notes of anthropological despair sounded like an overture for a fresh dose of her own troubles. And sure enough, the curtain went up on them, then and there.

Brenda, her stalwart sidekick, had finally had enough and resigned, though Java said she had merely got homesick for Ireland. 'Here's the letter she left for me – read it.' I moved to the other end of her trailer, as her incessant chewing and crunching was shredding my nerves. She had started broadening out at an alarming rate. However, no signs of tearflow. Yet.

Dear Java –
Forgive me. I'm off. Back home. It's been grand. It's been great. But it's been too long. I long for ugliness. Imperfection. Bad teeth. Untended hair. Unmanicured hands. Lined faces. Saggy breasts. Uncoordinated clothes and publicity-free talk. The world beyond 90210. A world without Agent. I feel that my life here has become like a familiar fart. You never notice your own stench until you look to the skies and breathe. It's visible fart-fog up there. Bad.
I owe you everything. But I'm gone. Your loving and devoted friend. Brenda.
P.S. All love to Mona. X X

As I looked up, she said, 'Can you believe that? After everything I have done for that woman? Abandons me just when I needed her most. Just wanted out. It's beyond the beyond. People are so selfish! Can you believe it?'

241

Sure can, sugar.

'I've had a change of heart about the house. I think Moroccan is going to be too ethnic for me. Is it too late to change?'

Oh, fuck.

She had moved into a hotel during the conversion of her house into a Moroccan palace, and fobbed Mona off with that relative in Pasadena. Brenda had abandoned ship, and now Java was going to be truly High Maintenance.

'Java, about the Moroccan game plan. Your house is halfway through a total conversion right now. It is going to mean a huge delay, and you won't able to move back in as planned when *Zeitgeist* wraps. Are you sure you want to do this right now?'

'Maybe what I should do is go find *my* roots. My mother told me we had some Scottish blood way back. Who knows, there might be a whole clan of Halls waiting to embrace me into their fold?'

'But if it's your mother's side, surely her maiden name wasn't Hall?'

This flummoxed her for a moment.

'Yeah, right. I can't quite remember what her unmarried name was. But you're right, maybe I should just wait till the Moroccan is completed before I change my mind.'

The knock at the door was my excuse to vamoose. But it wasn't a runner coming to get Java to the set, it was Mort. He looked as if he'd been caught out. Fumbling words about and talking in gibber.

Java gave him a welcoming hug and said, 'If you weren't married, Morty, I'd be having an affair with you!'

He blushed all over, and instead of laughing it off looked like a kid caught with his paw inside the cookie jar.

Oh, no. Not Mort. Not Mr Married-forever-to-Kitty Mort. Not with Java!

I excused myself and wandered off, wondering when this dangerous liaison had begun. Maybe this was why Brenda had departed?

Surely Mort wasn't taking the risk of lunchtime assignations? It was only when Kitty called to confirm that our supper date would be at 9 p.m. because Morty had a script conference again with the writers at the Mondrian that I worked it out: Java was staying there; the writers, having long since left due to spiralling budgetary costs, were now holed up in a bungalow in Los Feliz – 'Someone's gotta take the squeeze.'

Poor Kitty. I resolved that she was never to find out.

So Java had progressed from thwarted courtship phase through a brief neglected malaise and was now firing on philandering cylinders, headed most certainly for desertion-and-heartbreak burn-out ...

## 18 August

Jj convinced the money men and Mort that in order to keep the tension rising the characters needed to be in jeopardy almost constantly, i.e. – more detonations and debris. 'We've spent so much money already, why not go the whole fucking way?' he reasoned, all too persuasively. Instigating a week of extra explosions, freak floodings and detonating egos.

## 27 August

Scripted confrontation scene between Connor and Richard, arguing about which direction the survivors should head in. (The scene takes place in the power plant, which is the biggest set constructed so far, featuring vast fuel tanks, turbines and piping.) Unscripted scene between the directors:

Jj had vociferously argued that the whole set was an unnecessary and old-fashioned indulgence that could have been done using

243

miniatures, combined with live foreground elements which could be composited together in post-production.

'Live foreground elements?' retorted Mort. 'I call these elements *actors*, Jj. What's more, no matter how effective the compositing, my eye has never been fooled yet. It's not something I can put my finger on so much as the feeling. The eye senses the lie of it and as this is the climax of the story, the last big dramatic human blow-out before they escape, it's essential that it looks real!'

This argy-bargy shunted back and forth endlessly.

Mort, with the full support of his cast, declared that the sense of danger and peril so crucial at this point of the story depended on them being very high up above the fuel-lit burning water rising far below them.

'But they're actors, Mort. For fuck's sake, they're paid to *pretend* they're frightened.'

'Jj, no actor, no matter how gifted, is going to act as shit-scared standing two inches off the ground, backed by a fucking blue screen, as they are if they are negotiating their lives way up there.'

Kyla's pregnancy put all these negotiations into a new perspective. It was decided that both she and her screen daughter Scarlett would work with Jj on the blue-screen miniature version, while Mort directed the others on the real thing.

Connor, as leader, had to cajole and convince the exhausted survivors that it was worth going on, despite the death of Georgia's character and of Technophobe's. (He had been thrown off balance by an unexpected explosion onto a mass of buckled metal, and been impaled.)

Java was required to cling onto her lover's legs (Richard's), as she was suffering vertigo. Crying hysterically every time she looked below. The wardrobe department were having to constantly monitor both Tibet and Java's costumes, as they had got into an unofficial competition to see who could expose the most flesh. So far, Java had managed to expose a breast, but fortunately Richard's arm prevented full exposure, so they didn't have to reshoot.

Just prior to a take, Tibet countered by 'accidentally' snagging her dress which miraculously ripped, exposing her legs all the way up to her cheeks.

Java yelled down to wardrobe: 'Tibet's torn her dress, we can't shoot.'

However, Tibet knew they were way too far away and what with the fire and steam effects and multiple cameras about to roll, she wasn't about to be fiddled with.

'We gotta shoot NOW!' bellowed Mort.

Java let out an allegro of wails.

'CUT! CUT! CUT! WHAT THE FUCK DO YOU THINK YOU'RE DOING?' (Mort was stationed beside a video monitor half a mile down below at floor level.)

'I'm acting!' she quavered.

'I CAN'T HEAR CONNOR'S DIALOGUE OVER THE STEAM, FIRE AND YOUR YOWLING. I'VE GOT A HEADPHONE HEADACHE. CAN YOU CONTROL YOURSELF!'

Java had never heard Mort speak to an actor like this before. She let go of Richard's legs, prostrated herself on the grid and got $H_2O$ing. I could see Tibet smiling even from this distance.

Mort responded by announcing: 'GOING FOR A TAKE. STAND BY. AND ACTION!'

Java's screen survival instincts prevailed and her hands shot up and onto Richard's calves.

'CUT!'

During the reset Java insisted on being craned to ground level. She stormed up to Mort and demanded an apology. Tibet lit a cigarette up above and gloated.

'I am not an "element", Mort. I have feelings. Lots of them. I am an artist. I need nurturing. I need care.'

Mort listened and then tried to put his arm around her.

'Don't touch me!'

He did anyway and they rumpled off pushing and pulling in the direction of a side door.

Sixteen minutes later, Mort returned, looking unmistakably zomboid. His post-coital stare was that obvious. Java stepped back into the hoisting crane, this time showing no signs of fear whatsoever.

Tibet said, 'It's a miracle. You've been cured! How'd you do it?'

The scene took a week to complete.

Connor plunged to his 'death', having heroically sacrificed himself by leaping onto the lever in order to open the escape hatch for the remaining survivors.

## 4 September

It is getting Agatha Christie-ish, with more and more characters dying daily. And still the shooting goes on. It has been decided that Kyla, Scarlett, Java, Richard and Tibet are to endure one last tunnelling sequence, during which the latter three will be killed, leaving the pregnant Kyla and Scarlett to be saved.

In order to dampen down the speculation regarding the budgetary bloat (rumoured at a quarter-billion and counting), a public relations gesture was deemed politic. After incessant executive vacillations, it was decided that Scarlett and Doug would guest on the *Leno* chat show, the wisdom being that they'd be a) adorable, and b) unassailable – what would a four-and-a-half-year-old and a dog have to say about budgets?

The corporate hovercraft of nervous egos in suits inflated themselves with the positive benefits of this publicity stunt. 'We can't lose.'

And thus it came to pass.

Scarlett was escorted by a circle of unctuous adults reassuring her, 'No need to be nervous, sweetheart.'

'But I never am.'

Randy confirmed, 'It's true!' And with a drum roll she toddled onto the stage, Doug in tow. No sooner had the audience *aaah*d their approval, than Mr Leno asked, 'What is it like being directed by two different grown-ups?' Doug barked his reply and got a round of applause.

Scarlett told him to shush. She was sitting bolt upright on a specially made miniature chair that allowed her feet to touch the floor.

'Well, Morty is a very ol' guy. And Jj is a very short guy. He promised to show me his special little j soon. But don't tell anybody. It's our secret.'

Leno looked quizzical. 'Where does this special little j live, Scarlett?'

'In his pants, of course, you silly!'

Leno announced an abrupt commercial break.

The executive entourage stormed on stage, removed Scarlett, chair and all, the band covered up with music and Doug went doolalley, pursued in all directions by three security hulks.

Randy lost it. *This cannot go on air* picked up molecular speed and he could be heard screaming: 'THIS CANNOT GO ON AIR!'

A rumble of panic quaked every clipboard and headphone up and down the corridors. Randy bolted for the control room to secure the tapes. The press gang from both parties put their heads together in a scrum of hysterics: 'What. Are. We. Gonna. Do?'

Randy was approaching combustion point.

'Why did those men pick me up off the stage?' asked an indignant Scarlett. Adult faces turned as one and looked down at her, not knowing what to say. Just then, a buffalo stampede of security pounded past in pursuit of Doug. I had a split-second brainwave and asked Scarlett if she could call Doug to heel.

'Sure. *Doug! Doug!*'

There was an about turn of scuffling, squeaky boots around the corner, as Doug responded, and he came pelting towards her, with his front legs set into stiffened brake mode. I picked Scarlett up, Randy got hold of Doug's lead and we and ran for the exit. Into a car and drove at speed to Sepulveda Central.

'What are we gonna say?' Randy was losing weight, by the word.

'Why was everyone shouting?' enquired Scarlett.

'They were trying to catch Doug,' I feebled forth.

Randy was on the mobile to every lawyer and honcho he knew.

Georgia was waiting for us at the gates. She got into the car with frightening calm, cuddled Scarlett and said that Maria had made some home-made cookies for her and was waiting in the kitchen. Scarlett ran off, calling 'Maria, Maria!'

The second she was out of sight, Georgia thrust her hands around Randy's short neck and tried to strangle him for all she was worth. 'YOU. FUCK. PIG!! DIE!!!!!'

I did my best to get between them, but her rage was so volcanic that I ended up getting punched as well.

Just before Randy lost consciousness, she let him loose, bundled out of his car, into hers and accelerated off into history.

She returned half an hour later and announced that she had just shot Jj Dagney.

'Mortally?'

'I hope so!'

'What are you going to do now?'

'Don't ask,' she said, unnervingly glittery-eyed, then went upstairs, grabbed Scarlett, an overnight bag and declared: 'We're going on a little trip.'

## 5 September

Jj isn't dead. He was shot in both knees, arrested and indicted for suspected child abuse. Marga promptly made a written statement accusing him of rape.

Georgia and Scarlett are on the run.

Agents, managers and lawyers are threatening to sue the studios if their star clients are not cut out of the picture.

## 6 September

Shooting has come to a standstill. It's mayhem, and everyone wants a piece.

The fugitives were spotted in Bakersfield, out in the Mojave desert, and escorted by a crowd of vociferous supporters to the local police station, where the competition between getting statements and getting autographs was intense. Warning shots were fired to quell the chaos. Attempts to clap Georgia behind bars were thwarted, and a handcuffed compromise was reached, until lawyers and higher-ups arrived to deal with the situation. Georgia's raised cuffed hands provided the perfect photo opportunity for 'Mother as Martyr' headlines.

Jj has been assigned round-the-clock security surveillance in the hospital. Female nurses have come out in support of the Sepulvedas, by refusing to administer to the kneecapped Jiminy Cricket. (Their moral objections break the code of conduct stipulated for nurses, and the refuseniks face possible disciplinary action from the Medical Board. However, it has been deemed prudent to assign male nurses to deal with Jj's knee surgery aftercare.)

The studio has forked out for Georgia's bail, so that Scarlett can complete her part in the film, with her mother at home, rather than in jail on an attempted murder charge.

## 8 September

Filming has resumed. There is pressure to complete Kyla's scenes as she is worried about her pregnancy being at risk.

Marga has been subpoenaed to give written evidence against Jj in court, which means being facially exposed – in public, prompting her to seek a surgeon. Java suggested carbon dioxide laser resurfacing and gave me the number of her specialist.

Transpired that I decorated his home five years ago, and he is more than willing to fit Marga in at short notice.

It will take five weeks to heal and repair completely, which times perfectly with her scheduled court appearance, set for the 12th of November.

## 15 September

Four months of filming have taken their toll and Mort is looking cement-coloured.

Tibet and Java competed for the 'most picturesque death' prize. In the spirit of which, Java incongruously asked Tibet what her favourite childhood restaurant was. The ingenue was so taken aback by this personal interest that she blurted out Hooter's before she'd had time to plot anything.

Java smiled and said, 'Just what I thought, steakhouse people. Figures.'

The effect was lethal. And Tibet knew it.

Scarlett has returned to work with a social worker, Georgia, her nanny and a behavioural monitorist. All of whom seem redundant, as the little mite picked up where she had left off as though nothing had happened.

'She's in denial' is the whispered wisdom.

In order to downplay the national outrage levelled at Dagney, Mort has granted the *LA Times* an exclusive interview, in which he details how *Zeitgeist* is 'in essence a post-feminist morality fable, featuring a cross-section of strong-willed female characters ranging in age from four to fifty-something, who outlive the menfolk. As in life. I can't give away the ending exactly, but affirmative action is in the hands of the ladies.'

Java's last day. Unfortunately, I was the one she called on the mobile during the lunch break. 'Come quickly. Please.'

I excused myself, trying not to alarm Randy away from his veal chop, and strode over to her trailer. Knocked. The door was locked. So announced, 'It's me.'

'I can't move. Get a Teamster over, but don't let him in,' came the plaintive instruction from within.

I obeyed and approached the Goliath guarding the skeleton keys and explained my predicament. He set aside his styrofoam lunch-box, burped and said, 'No problem.' I thanked him and entered.

Mort was stark naked and lying on top of Java in the middle of the floor, her limbs flailing underneath him.

'Is he dead?'

'Oh, please God, I hope not,' she gasped.

He didn't seem to be moving of his own accord, but was rather jerked by Java's attempts to free herself. I knelt down beside him and felt his pulse.

'I don't dare move him. I'll get a medic. Keep talking to him.' I realized I hadn't a clue what to do and snatched this instruction from a vague collection of clichés accumulated from old TV shows. Then ran, shouting, 'DOCTOR. EMERGENCY. PARAMEDIC. EMERGENCY,' in all directions. My call was answered by someone who came running up behind me.

'Maybe I can help?' We ran back to the trailer and he confessed that he was an actor who had recently dropped out of medical school after two years, having decided to try his luck at landing a role in *ER* in order to combine his twin passions for dramatic and medical theatre. 'So I'm not fully qualified, but—'

Java screeched, 'SHADDUP. A man might be dead on top of me!'

The young intern was so stunned to recognize the famous face shouting at him he was almost too flustered to attend to Mort, but pulled himself together in time to diagnose, 'Yes, he has had a heart attack, and we gotta get him onto his back immediately.'

I helped him heave Mort off Java, and he thwlopped onto the floor like a vast jelly.

'His heart is dysrhythmic – it's beating irregularly. I need to do CPR.'

'What's that?' demanded Java, scrabbling for her dressing gown.

'Cardiopulmonary resuscitation.'

He ordered me to apply pressure to Mort's chest while he breathed into his mouth.

Just then, there was a banging on the door and the resident nurse from the *Zeitgeist* unit burst in. A Teamster must have alerted her to Mort's condition, because she arrived equipped with a set of chest compressors and ventilation tubes to reinflate his lungs.

While the two medics plied their trade, the nurse asked Java to describe the sequence of events.

Mort's body lay inert, grey and covered in sweat. Java draped an Hèrmes scarf over his shrivelled genitals, then stuttered out her answer . . .

'He orgasmed and made a tremendous groaning sound. I thought it was animal pleasure at first, as he tends to be noisy, but then he just collapsed. That's when I panicked and called Vyvian. The mobile was the only thing I could reach. He was too heavy to move.'

'How long ago was this?'

'Maybe ten minutes.'

'Shit. He might make it if this works. Was he conscious at all?'

'I don't know.'

They had inserted tubes down his throat and were pumping in air.

'Is this who I think it is?' asked the medic-thesp.

'Mort Buchinsky.'

'Wow. I really admire his work. D'you think he might give me an audition?'

Even Java recognized his importunity and shrilled, 'Pump, you bastard!'

Other faces appeared at the door asking if they could assist. Java grabbed a Balinese sarong and wrapped it around her head in a misguided attempt to hide her identity.

'He's unconscious – let's go!'

Mort was heaved onto a gurney that the props department happened to have handy, and wheeled it towards a Cherokee jeep. Loaded up and left.

Randy kept wringing his hands more fervently than Lady Macbeth, muttering, 'No one must ever know. No one must ever know. No one must ever know. No. No. No.'

I ended up having to make the grisly call to Kitty, after advising Java to relinquish her position once Mort was in the hospital.

'But I can't abandon him now!'

'What about his wife of a zillion years? You want *her* to know about this?'

'Maybe you're right.'

'Java – you're potentially culpable for killing the old guy!'

This notion *uh-huh*d her backwards, into the jeep and back to the studio. The medic-thesp appeared just as she left and said, 'Damn. I really wanted to get her autograph.'

'What's your name?'

'Chris Fingal, but I'm thinking of changing it.'

'Listen, Chris, I can get you that autograph, but I need a favour from you.'

He was puppy-eyed at the prospect of proximity. 'Whatever you want.'

'This is a very delicate situation we're in here. Mort Buchinsky is a happily married man of many, many years, and it would kill his wife if she found out. Do you understand what I'm saying?'

'Yeah, yeah. So you think that maybe in return for my silence Mr Buchinsky might give me an audition?'

Why did his reply still surprise me?

'Let's just hope that he makes it through the next twenty-four hours. Why don't you give me your number and I'll make sure that you get seen by him when he is up and running again. Or better still write down your address, so I can send you Java Hall's autograph.'

'You got it. I can't thank you enough. This has been a really momentous day for me. Thanks a lot.'

'Don't mention it.'

Kitty pitched up twenty minutes later: 'Is he alive?'

'Just.'

'I told him this picture would kill him.'

We walked quickly and in silence to his bedside, where he was wired up, tubed, dripped, monitored and bleeping. Still unconscious. Kitty greeted the medics and squirrelled her way between them to his bedside, touched his hand and announced, in her deep gravel tones, 'You are not going to die on me, you old bastard. We're gonna go on that diet. We're gonna have a holiday. Do you hear me? You better wake up, Morty, I've got a lot to do today, honey. I can't be sitting around here while you have a seizure for the rest of my life. Now can I? We've been married how many years now? I lost count. But it's somewhere around For Ever. So don't leave me just yet. I've got plans for us.'

She looked up at this audience of strangers and winked.

## 27 September

Condition stabilizing. Mort is conscious. An insurance claim is lodged for the lost day of shooting. Java has been prescribed sedatives and restrained from paying a hospital visit. Kitty is on a round-the-clock vigil (as are the press), having slept beside Mort in a child's cot.

Stars express their support for Mort and one by one withdraw their demands to be cut from the movie while agreeing not to pay bedside visits due to the press gang posted outside the hospital.

Emergency studio meeting in the wake of the respective imprisonment and hospitalization of both directors. Concluded that the first assistant director be assigned the task of completing the last week of principal photography.

## 29 September

The rescue of Kyla and Scarlett is completed.

The last remaining sequence to be shot involves the electrocution of Java's character. Something which the crew are particularly looking forward to.

Due to the technical complications of setting it all up, the actual fizz, crackle and pop moment is delayed and rescheduled for tomorrow. Prompting the departing Georgia, with Scarlett in tow, to demand of an understandably distraught Java, 'Aren't you dead yet?'

## 30 September

What began with an all-star cast of thousands plus two directors is ending with the demise of a single scantily dressed Java Hall, taking instructions from an assistant director, surrounded by an exhausted crew of mostly men in shorts.

There were no suits on show, as they were too busy dealing with lawyers, budgetary overload, insurance claims and getting the movie ready in time for a summer blockbuster release date.

This isolation and sense of abandonment were perfect fuel for Java's finale. She gave her all – rattling and rolling her eyes, writhing and convulsing as the volts stuttered through her body. The moment she had jerked her last jerk and lay dead, the three-hundred-strong crew applauded. Deeply. Vociferously.

'CUT!'

No one could quite believe it was all over.

Such was Java's overwhelm at what she interpreted as the depth of the crew's appreciation that she felt compelled to haul herself up from the grid, grip the railings with all the tremulousness of Eva Peron and launch into her 'Don't Cry for Me' schtick.

'I had no idea you all cared so much. Thank you! I'd just like to say, this hasn't been an easy shoot for me. For any of us. As you all know, I have a terrible fear of heights; our beloved Captain Mort lies on life support as I speak; Jj is incarcerated downtown; but you, the crew, have been like a family to me . . .'

Someone mimed vomiting.

'. . . Making it all the harder for me to leave and say goodbye to you all, knowing how intense this whole experience has been. I find myself suddenly alone, so alone. I shall miss each and every one of you and I'd like to take this opportunity to wish you all joy in the onward journey we call Life. I'm sorry, I'd like to say more, but it's just too much—'

She broke off. An assistant guided her into the crane compartment, which was then lowered down to ground level, whereupon she Niagara'd her way out to her trailer.

## 3 October

Jj has been bailed by the studios prior to his court hearing and hidden away in order to allow him to oversee the complicated post-production and special effects work. The budget is rumoured to have edged towards the $300 million mark, but nobody will confirm or deny.

Scarlett revealed that Jj hadn't actually *done* anything, thus providing his defence team with ammunition to have the case dismissed. Upon hearing this, Marga was all the more determined to face the ordeal of a court appearance to have him put away, and booked in for her dermabrasion immediately.

Randy has scarpered to China to do the merchandising deal for the *Zeitgeist* launch, which will include everything from T-shirts, plastic miniatures, model spacecraft, pens, buttons, pencil-tops, 'Doug' soft toys, board games, cards, flags and 'Scarletts' in three sizes to CD-ROMs. He has sent me an e-mail requesting that I remove everything from his home and put it into storage as he wants to go Oriental on his return, adhering strictly to Feng Shui guidelines.

## 10 October

Java called.

'I think I've met *the* one. He is younger than me. He listens. He thinks I'm a great actress. He loves Mona. He understands the acting business, as well as medicine. I'm gonna be set up for life. My psychic confirmed.'

'What's his name?'

'Actually, you've met him. Chris Fingal.'

## 25 October

Card from Bora-Bora:

Dear Vy,

Tibet and I got married on the beach here last night. Wanted you to know before the world finds out. See you when we get back. Can't wait to test the glass fireplace.

'Gotcha!'

Best, Connor

## 14 November

Jj Dagney has been sentenced to seven years.

## 28 December

Mr Richard Eagles and Ms Kyla Bergman welcome the miraculous arrival of their son, Kennedy Jurgen Tryon Vyvian Fitzgerald Bergman Eagles, born at four minutes to three on Christmas morning in the Cedars Sinai Hospital.

I am both father *and* godfather. Chokes me up.

The *Zeitgeist* summer release date will not be met 'due to unprecedented post-production requirements'. It has been postponed until next Christmas – fifteen months after Java's last stand.

## 15 February

Went downtown to Tundra's studio to oversee the installation of ten tons of white sand, sufficient to cover the floor and create low dunes. Six Arabian tents were erected, replete with Persian rugs and Moroccan candle lanterns arranged around a central gas fire that seemingly flamed from nowhere. A Pacific Rim banquet was being laid out on the perimeter.

The dress code was 'Barefoot'. The guest list: four hundred intimate friends of Richard Eagles and Kyla Bergman. The party was to celebrate the christening of 'our' son. And, rather more unexpectedly, the wedding of Tundra and Marga.

Marga stipulated that there be no cutlery or crockery: 'Let the rich eat with their hands.'

The novelty of celebrities being able to enter and leave by the same door, without having to scuttle through the kitchens and out the back with the trash, was a conversation starter.

Tibet and Connor's marriage had lasted only four months, but they graciously attended with new partners and kept discreetly apart. As did Georgia and Java – relations are now at an all-time low since Scarlett was signed up to a three-picture deal at Disney, while Mona is still tapping and pirouetting in vain. Java arrived arm-in-arm with her fiancé, Chris Warner, formerly Fingal.

Mort and Kitty Buchinsky arrived fresh from a trip to Vegas in their '62 Chevy, where they had repledged their marriage vows – 'For the next fifty years,' growled Kitty.

The talk of the evening was Jj Dagney's recent appearance in *Premiere*'s 'Where are they now?' page, photographed wearing a bright orange jumpsuit in a prison work gang collecting litter along the Pacific Coast Freeway.

The celebrations lasted until dawn, and the absence of shoes prompted Richard Eagles to declare the event 'truly democratic'.

Particularly touching was overhearing Jodie Foster sharing child-star chat with Scarlett. Seeing Lourdes Ciccone free-form dancing in the dunes. And witnessing Randy Rottweil, released of the tyranny of shoe lifts, looking like a little boy again – five foot tall and trotting!

Technophobe's 'computers for beginners' course, recently completed out in Glendale, has transformed his features; for the first time since I met him, he has lost his permanently perplexed look.

▶▶ FAST FORWARD TWELVE MONTHS ▶▶

# 29 MARCH – OSCAR NIGHT

*Zeitgeist*: nominated for a record-breaking sixteen Academy Awards. Georgia Sepulveda was awarded Best Supporting Actress (making the cover of both *Time* magazine and *Gun Monthly* – a record in itself).

The movie won in every technical achievement category, as well as Best Musical Score, topped off with the Oscar for Best Picture.

It was Mort Buchinsky's night. He went home clutching three statuettes, not only for Best Picture and Best Director, but also the Irving Thalberg Lifetime Achievement Award, which he claimed wasn't his at all, but his wife's. He summoned Kitty to come up on stage and accept it from him. They got a prolonged standing ovation, and the last I saw of them that night was at the *Vanity Fair* party at Morton's. Kitty was performing a perfect headstand in the middle of the floor.

## 7 April

Phone call.

'It's me – I've gotta talk. My billboard billing and photo likeness are not the same size as those of the other actors.'

'Java, it's two a.m. Where is this billboard?'

'On Sunset.'

'What are you doing in front of a billboard at this time of night?'

'I'm not actually *in front* of it, you dummy. I can see it through the new high-powered telescope I've had installed in my bedroom.'

Click.

The sequel is in pre-production. I'm holding my breath.